D1593588

TEACHING INTRODUCTION
TO WOMEN'S STUDIES

TEACHING INTRODUCTION TO WOMEN'S STUDIES

Expectations and Strategies

BARBARA SCOTT WINKLER AND
CAROLYN DiPALMA, CO-EDITORS

Foreword by Frances Maher

BERGIN & GARVEY
Westport, Connecticut
London

Library of Congress Cataloging-in-Publication Data

Teaching introduction to women's studies : expectations and strategies /
  Barbara Scott Winkler and Carolyn DiPalma, co-editors ; foreword by
  Frances Maher.
     p.   cm.
  Includes bibliographical references and index.
  ISBN 0–89789–590–8 (alk. paper)
    1. Women's studies—United States. 2. Women's studies—Study and
  teaching—United States. I. Winkler, Barbara Scott. II. DiPalma,
  Carolyn.
  HQ1181.U5T43   1999
  305.4'07—dc21   99–14379

British Library Cataloguing in Publication Data is available.

Library of Congress Catalog Card Number: 99–14379
ISBN: 0–89789–590–8

First published in 1999

Bergin & Garvey, 88 Post Road West, Westport, CT 06881
An imprint of Greenwood Publishing Group, Inc.
www.greenwood.com

Printed in the United States of America

The paper used in this book complies with the
Permanent Paper Standard issued by the National
Information Standards Organization (Z39.48–1984).

10 9 8 7 6 5 4 3 2 1

Contents

Part III   Theorizing Expectations

Part IV   Applying Strategies

Part V   Conclusion: Undoing Our Habits

Foreword: Knowledge and Resistance

Frances Maher

The major feeling I have after reading through the diverse and stimulating essays in this collection is one of the infinite difficulty and complexity of teaching "Introduction to Women's Studies," and the absolute impossibility of designing a course to fit everyone. For the authors here and for many of us, Women's Studies, and especially the introductory course, represents a primary challenge of our teaching careers—namely how to engage students, often young and privileged women, with the issues of societal power, domination, and resistance that come from studying women's lives. It sometimes seems as if the rest of the curriculum can proceed along the smooth and well-marked paths of celebrating and enacting the points of view of the dominant culture, leaving Women's Studies, like women themselves in most cultures, with the responsibility for all the people at the bottom and the margins, whose lives and truths the dominant curriculum can cheerfully avoid.

Before they turn to their specific approaches, most of the authors in this collection grapple with the paradoxes and complexities of this position. Vivian May describes its incompatible dualisms:

Women's Studies is simultaneously thought to be safe and risky, soft and hard; a place for dialogue and disagreement, a space exemplifying harmony and oneness as well as discord and difference, a biased, subjective area of study as well as an open-minded, analytical discourse; it is both like home and hostile territory. Framed by classic, subject/object dualisms, women's studies is simultaneously beyond the pale and acceptable: it is both like the witch/bitch of the academy and the fair maiden/fairy godmother.

Furthermore, many echo Karen Bojar's wish: "We hoped the course would change our students' lives and the lives of their children. This is quite a burden for a three credit course, but for many of us women's studies is a *cause*, not simply an academic career."

Added to this complexity and urgency is a third theme which recurs again and again throughout the book, which is the difficulty and necessity of getting our students, who are mainly white, female and middle class, to grapple with the societal difference and with their own positions of privilege. As Lisa Bowleg puts it, rather than exploring the lives of women of color, "students wanted to learn about women who were like themselves." Student resistance to Women's Studies takes many forms, and is exacerbated in introductory courses by the presence of people who are just there to fulfill a "diversity requirement," by the fact that many classes have enrollments of over 50, and by the sheer intellectual immaturity of many undergraduates, who have yet to learn about the existence of alternative ways of seeing the world.

The authors here who write most poignantly about student resistance are not surprisingly the professors of color and one white woman who is an "out" lesbian. Bowleg, herself "black, middle-class, openly lesbian," reports that her predominantly white students did not want to do an assignment about a woman who was "different" from them: "we are all just people, aren't we?" Audre Brooks and France Winddance Twine had to deal with student complaints to the administration, as some could not handle a course centering on the experiences of women of color, taught by a black–white team. Margaret Duncombe, in confronting her students' fear of lesbianism, asks what are they *really* afraid of? She concludes that it is feminism, not lesbianism, which is the real threat to the gender system. "Feminism decenters men and as such is a violation of deeply held gender norms, which exposes young women to risk." She has learned to confront the power of the lesbian label and to work for a classroom which is not conventionally "safe"; rather she seeks to guarantee students that "their ideas will be listened to attentively, taken seriously, and responded to civilly."

Each of the essays in this book deals with problems like these, and each offers, if not solutions, then approaches which have confronted the problems and yielded success with students, at least some students, at least in some of the contexts in which they were tried. No one claims universal applicability here. Because Women's Studies, particularly "Intro," is about all the women in the world, or rather about gender relations, which include race and class relations, all over the world, and because our teachers and our students are so various, and because we all, teachers and students, want the course to speak to our lives and our commitments and not just our academic knowledge, there can be no general "Intro" course, in the way that there can perhaps be a generally accepted body of knowledge for, say, "Introductory Psych."

But does that mean that none of these essays can speak beyond its own context? On the contrary. The probelms described above are shared by many of the authors here. And the approaches are detailed, imaginative, and varied enough so that we all can find here some ways to proceed: there are essays on teaching specific texts, teaching interactively with new technologies, even on committing "outrageous acts" to challenge the gender system. One of the key points to be gained from putting all these essays together is the importance of knowing who your students are and listening to them. Some of the most useful exercises discussed help them to learn about themselves, by positioning them within the larger social structures we want to make them aware of, whether it is white privilege or compulsory heterosexuality, ableism or class superiority. Glyn Hughes, for example, writes cogently about the role of men in the Women's Studies classroom, whose presence may act to disrupt easy male/ female dichotomies in favor of a more analytical look at the categories of gender relations. "Calls for women's space, when they occur in denial of the differences among women, also obscure connections between men and women at the register of privilege." He has students locate themselves with a "boxes of privilege" exercise, much like Helen Bannan's list of catagories in "My Father's WASP."

All in all, this volume, like the dualisms of Women's Studies itself, is both eye-opening and familiar, depressing and energizing, sobering and exciting. Above all, the book is an illuminating look at a terrain which will always be rocky and risky as long as we are in charge of *all* the knowledge about and for the rest of us—that is, all the peoples ignored or distorted by the traditional academic curriculum. This knowledge is deeply susceptible to student resistance because it challenges the securities of their hold on the world. Yet it is a knowledge also continually forged in resistance to the patterns of domination in our society. This collection offers a myriad of ways to fashion those multiple knowledges and to build that resistance.

Acknowledgments

We would like to acknowledge the efforts of those who made this work possible. We wish to give special recognition and appreciation to Serina Beauparlant, who, early in the process, gave a serious hearing to Barbara Scott Winkler's initial idea for the book. We both found her questions and support to be tremendously helpful. We would also like to send a special thank you to Lynn Taylor for her immediate recognition of our project as valuable, for her energetic continued support, and for her extra assistance with the various teams at Greenwood Publishing Group when we were confronted with unforeseen difficulties. Thanks also to all the "Teaching Introduction to Women's Studies" panel members at the 1997 National Women's Studies Association annual conference for making clear how vital it is to learn classroom expectations and strategies from each other. We also thank Marianne Bell and her staff at the University of South Florida Information Processing Center for their flexibility, accessibility, and careful preparation of the manuscript.

We are grateful to the West Virginia University (WVU) Eberly College of Arts and Sciences Office of the Dean and the WVU Center for Women's Studies, especially interim director Barbara Howe, for their generous financial support and encouragement. We are also indebted to the University of South Florida (USF) Research Council's Research and Creative Scholarship Award for financial support, to the USF Department of Women's Studies, and especially to Elithea Whittaker for extra assistance.

Working on a book is never an easy task, and the process of working on this one became increasingly difficult as both of us discovered and faced a significant health problem while the work was in progress. For this reason, we are especially thankful for the support of our friends and families.

Barbara Scott Winkler would like to thank her mother, Elaine Zara, for her loving and sensible advice in facing breast surgery for what turned out to be a benign mass. Barbara also wishes to thank Gregory N. Scott for his love, support, and dedication to co-parenting our amazing and adorable three-year-old daughter, Anya Qingxin Scott, who brought joy, curiosity, and humor to our busy days, making our lives truly a "new beginning," as her name suggests. Gregory also used his skills as an editor to provide another fresh eye to the manuscript in its final stages. Barbara would also like especially to thank the graduate teaching assistants who have worked with her at WVU on the introductory course for their diligence, creativity, and willingness to confront the challenges that such a course presents.

Carolyn DiPalma would especially like to thank her parents, Michael and Frances DiPalma, her sister and her family, Patricia DiPalma, Morgan Packer, and Allan Packer, and her friends and colleagues Nancy Riley, Dorrie Mazzone, Ingrid Bartsch, and Cheryl Hall for their loving, tireless, and innovative efforts on her behalf. Carolyn would also like to thank the "Carolyn and Paul Support Team" and many other friends too numerous to mention for their continued caring, attention, and assistance, and Paul Larned for his years of love, humor, strength, and unfailing support through thick and thin.

Lastly, we extend our appreciation to our contributors and to the many students and teachers from whom we have learned. Also, we are grateful to each other for picking up where the other has left off, allowing both of us to renew our energies and enthusiasm for the project.

Part I

INTRODUCTION

1

The Introductory Course: A Voice from the Broader Field of Women's Studies

*Barbara Scott Winkler, West Virginia University
and Carolyn DiPalma, University of South Florida*

This book grew out of our concerns and interests as teachers of the introductory course in women's studies. We felt the need for a text that would stand somewhere between the theoretical explorations of authority, power, and classroom dynamics provided by writers on feminist pedagogy and practical exercises provided by women's studies instructors at National Women's Studies Association (NWSA) conferences, through e-mail groups such as Women's Studies Listserv (WMST-L) and Feminist Pedagogy Listserv (FEMPED-L) and in workbooks accompanying individual introductory texts.[1] Both formats, the more theoretically focused discussions on feminist pedagogy and the hands-on exchange of classroom strategies and exercises, have been useful for instructor preparation and development. However, we believe there is a place for a book that would combine the two and their connection to the content of the introductory course. We hope this volume will help prepare the new instructor of the women's studies introductory class while also providing more experienced teachers with opportunities to reflect on the problematic and positive assumptions and techniques we all bring into our introductory classrooms.

Introduction to Women's Studies classrooms are filled with a wide variety of students: those who have taken the course to meet their women's studies requirements and arrive very interested in the material; those who are tentatively interested but hesitant about what they might find; and those who have taken the course to meet some more general institutional requirement but who may have no actual interest in women's studies. While some students arrive with nuanced understandings, experiences upon which they have been reflecting and about which they would like to be more thoughtful, many arrive informed only by mass media presentations of women and women's issues and guided by talk show formats or attack interviews as standards for behavior in classroom debates.

In the Introduction to Women's Studies classroom, then, awareness, outreach, and participatory feminist pedagogical practices meet a variety of student needs and expectations. Those who face the challenges and rewards of teaching the introductory course do so from a broad range of background preparations including the humanities, the social sciences, and the natural sciences. Some are graduate students in these areas. Introduction to Women's Studies is taught in departments of women's studies, women's studies programs, and centers for women's studies. It is taught under areas such as liberal studies and gender studies and in a wide range of public and private universities, colleges, and community colleges. Therefore, in an effort to situate specific locations in a context, each of the contributors to this volume have included selected information on their type of school, composition of their student population, their current institutional setting and issues, the impact of fulfilling requirements where relevant, their departmental or program status, class size, and any pertinent local issues. In an effort to direct the focus of readers interested in particular topics, each contributor has provided a short list of suggested readings at the conclusion of each chapter. Readers will find essays which speak to large lecture and small seminar classes in diverse settings including universities, colleges, and community colleges. Specific locations in the northwest, midwest, east, south, southwest, west, and the Pacific are represented.

Given this mix of students, teachers, and institutional locations and the overall interdisciplinary nature of women's studies, no collection could be completely comprehensive. However, it is our hope that this collection will serve as a starting point for addressing the unique issues of teaching Introduction to Women's Studies.

Articles on the introductory class have been part of the literature of women's studies since the 1970s.[2] However, we believe that a book which combines strategies for teaching and learning with explorations of why we each teach as we do is especially needed now, since the success of the introductory course in terms of institutionalization and broadened student enrollment has resulted in new challenges. These challenges come from a variety of sources. One source originates with administration pressures to increase enrollments for a given course. This results in large classes that diminish students' opportunities to process concepts that may challenge their sense of what is "normal" and right, because instructors are less able to provide the personal contact that helps initiate and sustain the kind of in-depth discussion from which students dealing with such "controversial" material can benefit.[3] A second source is a concerted backlash, both within the academy and in the larger political environment, that affects students' knowledge of what feminism is, the history of the women's movement, and the ability of women and men to contribute to effective social change. The third source emerges with the "mainstreaming" of women's studies courses, especially Introduction to Women's Studies, through campus-wide requirements and enrollment of students not formerly interested in feminist analyses, where teachers of the introductory women's studies course face the need for new, as well as continuing, tasks and strategies.

While the introductory class has developed along with scholarly research in women's studies at large, students continue rightly to expect that it will deal with their common-sense concerns about work and family, relationships and sexuality, bodily appearance, the influence of the media, violence, and even (sometimes reluctant) awareness of gender inequality and oppression, to name just a few of the issues introductory courses raise up for examination, investigation, and re-envisioning.[4] Some students are surprised by the scope of our classes and especially by introductory teachers' increasing emphasis on the interrelationship of gender to other social categories; others are hopeful; and still others are initially ambivalent, even fearful, about what they will face (Zúñiga and Myers 1993: 316–318).[5]

In many ways the introductory class "speaks" for the broader field of women's studies even when it is not the first women's studies class students take. In the late 1960s and early 1970s introductory courses often embodied attempts by students and faculty to establish a specific women's studies presence on campus. While other departmentally-based courses might include sections or even entire course content rooted in the new, emerging feminist scholarship, establishing an introductory course was often seen as a strategic move toward the creation of a program and a core curriculum (Winkler 1992: 127). Introductory courses were at this time a bid for legitimization, since they were seen by university administrators and founding faculty and students as focusing on more "academic" as "opposed" to "activist" concerns, despite the attempt by many instructors and students to recreate the atmosphere of the larger women's movement.[6]

The present image of women's studies students in this period is that they were mostly women and, furthermore, were self-identified feminists even before they walked into the introductory class. Faculty and students who have provided glimpses of those early years emphasize the excitement that co-investigation brought while critics have argued that these courses were ideologically homogenous environments.[7] Introductory faculty communicated shared assumptions that feminist investigation was valuable and exciting. Teachers like Sally Gearhart and Mina Caulfield, who taught the introductory class at San Francisco State in the mid-seventies, modeled for their students respectful, even exhilarating, disagreement and debate, through their differing feminist frameworks.[8]

While many of the first students who enrolled in early introductory courses saw themselves as feminist-identified, this was not always the case. At the University of Missouri-Columbia, for example, the "founding" students who lobbied for the first course did not enroll in the class because they assumed they were already familiar with the issues; they hoped the course would provide for others the information and insight they had obtained in their self and group study as part of the women's movement (Winkler, 1992: 64). According to Lillian Robinson (1970: 42) who taught a class at the Massachusetts Institute of Technology (MIT) equally divided along gender lines in 1970, her students were not veterans of the women's movement and were uncomfortable with making the connection between social and personal experience that has been assumed to be part of even the introductory students' expectations of women's studies education in this early period. Robinson's experience reminds us that students' educational presuppositions have been and continue to be diverse and shaped by social, political and cultural institutions other than the women's movement.

By the mid-1980s students in the introductory course who were feminist-identified were, as Barbara Hillyer Davis (1985: 248, 251–252) argues, more likely to be in the numerical minority. In her article, "Teaching the Feminist Minority," Davis noted that many of her students were what one might call "traditional" or transitional.[9] Such students, as Davis suggests, were unfamiliar with feminist pedagogy and analysis but seemed to have a "sort of instinct for sisterhood." Traditional students experienced joy in discovering mutual support and "rejoice[d] in the recovery of women's past and women's culture." This pleasure in discovery, however, did not always seem as available to the self-identified feminist minority, whose "consciousness ha[d] already been raised" and who had expectations of challenges based on their previous feminist experience and knowledge. According to Davis, this minority also "often lacked empathy with or respect for" the struggles of the traditional women (248). Davis found herself "translating" between those who were feminists and those who did not identify themselves as such.

While Davis noted that men were present in her classroom, she concentrated in her essay on the dynamics between the two groups of women students (246). Even when women's studies classes were not literally gender-homogenous, many theorists of feminist pedagogy described them as if they were, portraying women's studies classes, including the introductory class, as places of "safety" where students and faculty could talk about and examine painful subjects such as eating disorders or rape and other forms of violence against women, without fear of (male) criticism and harassment. The all-female classroom was valued as a place where differences and disagreements among women could be explored in greater depth (Winkler 1992: 341–346). It was, therefore, seen as many would like to see all classrooms: as "the most radical space of possibility in the academy" (hooks 1994a: 12). However, feminist (as well as anti-feminist) writers criticized how this image of the women's studies class as "haven" presumed sameness among women as well as stereotyped male students' attitudes.[10]

Indeed, the demographic as well as political homogeneity of the student population in the women's studies introductory course was fast disappearing in the

1980s, if it had ever existed as thoroughly as imagined. This was due, in large part, to the success of women's studies generally and the introductory course in particular. As more and more programs and even departments were established as permanent features of college and university academic and institutional life, students were increasingly likely to take the introductory course, even if it was their "one and only" class in women's studies. The inclusion of women's studies introductory courses in General Education (GED) or "core" and "diversity" requirements contributed to this trend.[11] It has brought several changes in the student population, including greater enrollment by male students.[12] As sections are added, more students are able to take the course in their first and second years, especially in those schools where the introductory course is listed with a lower division number. For these classes, the addition of more first and second-year students has made it more truly introductory because of the level of student preparation.[13] Other schools, however, encourage generalization in lower division courses, providing other windows into women's studies for first and second-year students, and see the introductory course in women's studies as more of a specialization, giving it an upper division number and hoping to draw from a pool of students more prepared to grapple with the controversies it raises.[14]

The mix of students is now more diverse in terms of openness to feminist inquiry: the feminist-identified and traditional or transitional students have been joined by students who are less engaged by the subject matter. At the same time faculty members have begun to interrogate long-held beliefs about the introductory course. This is reflected in our book. For example, Glyn Hughes questions the assumption that male students are inevitably hostile intruders in an otherwise female sanctuary while Audre Brokes and France Winddance Twine contest the notion of automatic sisterhood, not only by challenging students to address racial and class divisions but by more radically decentering the stubborn and problematic traditional emphasis on white women's experiences and concerns. While most women's studies teachers (including those who teach the introductory course) continue to value students' increased willingness to embrace feminist analyses, if not "feminist identity" itself, as the semester goes on, other teachers have also questioned the emphasis on "conversion," especially if such intellectual "proselytizing" precludes, as Kathleen Kane notes, providing space for students' explorations in possibly finding their own feminist identities.

In a conservative critique of women's studies, Daphne Patai and Noretta Koertge (1994: 81) conclude that women's studies teachers "are deliberately using their classrooms as sites for the recruiting and training of students to be feminist activists."[15] Patai and Koertge's broad conclusions that women's studies is a "closed world view" and therefore "turns into dogma that suppresses criticism of itself and blocks alternative paths to discovery" (183) are based on data which are often unattributed and relatively slim. If anything, women's studies teachers have noted how resistant students can be to an instructor's attempts to democratize the classroom (Boxer 1998: 82). Patai and Koertge (1994: 107) do not allow that women's studies "introduces students to new ideas and methods ... expand[s] their horizons ... or move[s] beyond what they already know and believe," activities they (rightfully) see as a significant goal of education. While Patai and Koertge's criticisms have had little credibility with women's studies faculty, other critiques, such as those made by often younger participants in Third Wave feminism, have resulted in self-questioning by faculty members, many of whom were first influenced by Second Wave or "movement" feminism.[16]

In the report on students' experiences of women's studies, *The Courage to Question*, Caryn McTigue Musil and others noted that as important as concerns about teaching practices were to women's studies faculty, course content was seen as the single most important contributor to change of consciousness. According to a joint National Women's Studies Association–American Association of Colleges report on an assessment study of seven programs funded by the Fund for the Improvement of Postsecondary Education (FIPSE), "content was more important to fostering personalized learning than pedagogy alone." A follow-up study of teaching methods at several other schools confirmed that "course content rather than pedagogy ... was the most influential factor" in students' ability to make connections between course themes and their own lives.[17] According to the reports of the contributors to this volume, we would argue that it is the synergy of student and teacher expectations, course content, and experience of feminist teaching/learning practices that makes such outcomes possible.[18]

Being introduced to the ways in which course material "matters" is often life-changing for students in the introductory course. Reports from the contributors of this volume suggest this is all the more reason for the introductory course to be taught in ways that are both rigorously academic and responsibly caring. This requires that teachers be prepared to recognize and respect what understandings students bring to the material and to listen to any resistance— recognizing the real distance that some students will need to travel before they feel they can "hear" and interpret what is being said by others, including the instructor, texts, and other students. Such respect for students' abilities to make meaning in collaboration with teachers and text, while providing attention to forms of resistance that block comprehension and understanding, illustrates a vision of pedagogy as far more than "entertaining" students. Instead this vision of pedagogy is about developing and appreciating the skill necessary to create an educational enterprise with contents and application that can be read and interpreted by students in ways that provide opportunities for and encourage personal discovery.

While women's studies introductory classes follow no fixed rules determining course content, a paradigm has emerged in the past decade in many introductory classes. Not only is the social construction of gender a key theme, but, as importantly, what some have called an "intersectionist" or a multiple and interlocking model of oppression has become significant in the continuing development of the introductory class. While some women's studies faculty have criticized simplistic uses of "race/class/gender" as a superficial invocation of "political correctness," introductory teachers and others have used this approach rigorously in the classroom to introduce students to new ways of conceptualizing social relations of power.[19]

The recognition of multiple and simultaneous oppressions which, working together, transform one another, was partly a response to concerns about "diversity" and division along racial, class-based and sexual identity lines that began to preoccupy women's studies practitioners in the 1980s.[20] The focus on diversity emerged largely in reaction to criticisms by women of color that their histories and perspectives had been submerged by an emphasis on gender which was unsituated and thereby emphasized white women's analyses and projections of their own experiences. Similar declarations of invisibility within women's studies by lesbians (both white and women of color) reinforced the recognition that feminism in the academy was not as inclusive nor as transformational as it could be. In response, widely used texts, including those geared toward the introductory class and feminist classroom pedagogy, increased their references to racial and sexual diversity.[21]

Both the intersectionist model and its cousin, "positionality," went further than simple inclusion of more materials on previously excluded or underrepresented groups. Articulated early on by the Combahee River Collective (1983), the action of interlocking systems of oppression is described by sociologists Margaret Andersen and Patricia Hill Collins in the Preface to their reader *Race, Class, and Gender: An Anthology*. As described by Collins and Andersen (1995: xi–xiv), the intersectionist model (or "matrix of domination" as they name it), focuses on institutions and structures of power, which they see as dynamic. Positionality further emphasizes this dynamism in power relations by focusing on their situated and relational nature. As described by Frances Maher and Mary Kay Thompson Tetreault (1994) in their book *The Feminist Classroom, An Inside Look at How Professors and Students are Transforming Higher Education for a Diverse Society*, positionality is a form of social analysis "in which people are defined not in terms of fixed identities, but by their location within shifting networks of relationships, which can be analyzed and changed" (164). The classroom, in this view, can provide what Linda Alcoff refers to as " 'a constantly shifting context' in which critique of 'woman's place' in this network of relations becomes the basis for a 'feminist argument for women' " (Maher and Tetreault 1994: 164). Both the intersectionist model and positionality enable teachers and students to get well beyond static and binary descriptions of oppressors/oppressed. In classes like Introduction to Women's Studies the focus on fluid and complex power relations have not only made visible the realities of non-dominant groups, but have also helped defuse the defensiveness of students in positions of privilege who may be seriously confronting the presence and effect of the "isms" in their lives for the first time.[22]

This collection on the introductory course reflects these and other changes in women's studies students, content, and pedagogy. The essays in this book are divided into five parts. Following the introduction, Part II, "Overviews/ Resources" features examples of course overviews in two different but comparable environments. Vivian May describes student perceptions and faculty responses to the introductory course at a four-year public university attended by mostly female students who are often first generation college-goers seeking opportunities to develop their skills and leadership capabilities in a single-sex environment. These include working single parents concerned with housing and daycare. Karen Bojar describes the course content of and student response to teaching Introduction to Women's Studies at an urban community college where students are also usually older, but are more likely to be women of color who have limited financial resources and few opportunities to develop their academic skills. While May focuses on conveying to her students the idea that women's studies is an academic discipline, Bojar concentrates on connecting classroom learning with feminist activism. Both faculty, however, disclaim "conversions" or "party lines" and explore with their students the ways in which feminism might become meaningful to them and what new meanings students can bring to definitions of "feminisms."

Vivian May also calls attention to the importance of providing "a strong theoretical framework" that "teases out students' *a priori* assumptions about gender, race, sexuality, disability, the nature of knowledge, and the structures of power." Such a framework, she contends along with Patti Lather (1991), helps us and our students to find the blindspots in the interpretative schemas and systems of meaning which we use to understand the world.

This section closes with Mary Margaret Fonow and Lucy Bailey's description of a new database resource. This resource, which teachers can use to develop a customized textbook, enables students to recognize difference and oppression while embracing personal empowerment and learning about activism.

We hope these materials will help provide both faculty new to teaching the introductory course and more experienced instructors with opportunities to reflect on their own goals and the resources to achieve them.

In Part III, "Theorizing Expectations," our contributors discuss their broad approaches to teaching the introductory course. They especially address issues concerning differences in power, privilege, history and culture, which are reflected in course content and classroom dynamics as the understanding in women's studies moves from an emphasis on a sisterhood based on mistaken assumptions of commonality and unity to a recognition and rich appreciation of differences and fragmentation.

Several contributors to our collection discuss diversity and multiple perspectives and/or explore power relations and interlocking social realities. At the same time they teach about oppression and relations of power, they also encourage students to look for evidence of empowerment and social change in their lives, and they examine and question previously held assumptions about student acceptance of and resistance to these concepts. These are also major themes in essays from Part II and IV, especially Vivian May's overview and Helen Bannan's exercise on multiple, intersecting, and contextual forms of difference and imbalances of power.

Encountering material which addresses power relations is not always easy for students, as Katherine Rhoades maintains in her study of student journals from the introductory class. According to Rhoades, students in the "border zone" of the introductory course engage in the uncomfortable process of renegotiating their previously held individualist perspective in favor of recognizing socially constructed relations that "are enacted in specific fields of power, culture, and history." The resulting experience is not one of "progress toward enlightenment" or "conversion." Instead, introductory students both identify with and resist course material. Rhoades concludes that teachers of the introductory course can help students by acknowledging students' discomfort with unfamiliar concepts while conveying excitement for the knowledge that introductory students gain during the class.

While Rhoades questions teachers' expectations of unproblematic acceptance on the part of all students, male and female, Glyn Hughes challenges the assumption that male students' presence in the introductory course creates only problems. He argues that rather than assuming that men can only be obstacles to women's learning, teachers of the introductory course can reinforce men's capacity to be potential allies. Basing his analysis on critiques made by U.S. third world feminists of white feminists' failure to recognize differences among women, Hughes argues for a more engaged and de-essentialized approach to men while affirming the ways in which "social power works through gender relations."

Working from their own experiences of oppression, Toni King, Margaret Duncombe, and Lisa Bowleg explore how best to introduce students to social relations of difference, power, and privilege. These authors explore their own and their students' social locations and the resulting relationship to classroom dynamics and course content. Examining these connections helps them define more finely tuned pedagogical strategies in response to student expectations and resistances.

King draws on her African-American womanist identity and perspective to avoid polarization between herself and her students as well as among students. She asks them to use their experiences to create a "holistic story" or collective tapestry that encourages a "loose consensus" about sexism in different social locations. King sees herself as a facilitator of "border crossings," using Gloria Anzaldua's terminology, and of "playful world-travelling," drawing on Maria Lugones's work about loving perception of and respectful learning about others' realities.[23]

Similarly, Margaret Duncombe calls on her knowledge and position as a public lesbian and teacher of the introductory course to help her students confront homophobia and heterosexual privilege. Duncombe explores the tensions inherent in respecting her students' need to affirm their perceptions and her own wish to avoid creating an uncritically "safe" classroom that makes no room for new if potentially uncomfortable knowledge. She distinguishes between her own personal and pedagogical reactions to her students' fears about lesbianism generally and her own sexual orientation in specific. In so doing, she shares with us her uncertainties as well as her expertise.

Lisa Bowleg describes how her position in relation to her students contributed to the issues facing them in learning about and appreciating diversity in the introductory class. She challenged her students' expectation that they would learn only about women like themselves and used a variety of topics and activities to examine privilege and to value the experience of historically marginalized groups. Encountering students' silences about her mostly differing social location as Caribbean-born and lesbian, Bowleg reflects on the emotional toll experienced by teachers whose identity and course content make them the prominent "other" in the introductory classroom.

Audre Brokes and France Winddance Twine, an interracial teaching team of the introductory course, tell us that both women of color and white women must prepare for the resistances of white students to course material that shifts the central focus from their experiences to that of women of color in the United States and internationally. As a Black/American Indian faculty member of working-class background, Twine anticipated that an anti-racist approach focusing on the intersections of nationality, race, class, sexual orientation, and physical ability would encounter initial resistance. However, neither she nor Brokes were prepared for how extensive or ongoing it was, especially from U.S. white women students. Student attacks focused on course difficulty and claimed bias. In response to these resistances by students who assumed that women's studies should be narrowly and exclusively defined as about themselves, Brokes and Twine developed materials introduced early in the course that spelled out expectations and increased student awareness of their own responsibilities. These helped diminish student resistance while Twine was teaching the class. However, what further surprised her and Brokes was the depth of dissatisfaction (including personal and public attacks) when Brokes, as a graduate student, continued to teach the class alone, with the same course content and anti-racist and international approach. They conclude that while factors such as Brokes's junior status contributed to student resistance, the major obstacle involved white women students' perceptions that Brokes, as a white woman too, had "betrayed" them by failing to affirm their preconceptions. Such narratives of student resistance can help us recognize the significance of course content and impact on classroom dynamics for teachers and students of all social locations.

Some feminists have grown concerned that the emphasis on difference and diversity, which is the legacy of the 1980s, has been at the expense of looking for commonalities and invoking sisterhood. The appreciation of difference, even "practicing conflict" need not preclude developing community (Hirsch and Keller 1990: 370–385). However, others, like Kathleen Kane, as a white, or *haole*, teacher in a post-colonial setting instructing students who are of diverse Asian and Pacific ethnic backgrounds, caution feminists from the dominant culture not to mistake a search for commonality with the desire "to reinvoke our own transformational experiences." As teachers, to replicate ourselves mistakes the work that is before us, especially in regard to students from whom we are different in geographical, social, and racial location. Acknowledging and prizing these differences, Kane argues that the task of de-colonizing pedagogy is both spatial and compatible with newly discovered moments of teacher and student mutual self-transformation and struggles for solidarity. Kane reminds us that the need to be vigilant while appreciating difference and working for solidarity is something for which feminist teachers must struggle along with their students. It is not something that should simply be assumed or expected.[24]

In Part IV, "Applying Strategies," contributors' essays provide examples of assignments and activities that reflect changes as well as continuities in classroom instruction. Essays by Martha McCaughey and Carol Burger and Maria Pramaggiore and Beth Hardin examine the opportunities for independent and collective student learning provided by such new resources and opportunities for communication as listservs and access to the Internet including web sites. Both sets of contributors argue that cyber education helps female students confront their fears and breaks down stereotypes about women and technology while enhancing rather than replacing the traditional feminist classroom.

Using more traditional materials, Stacy Wolf and Lisa Logan explore how popular culture texts such as advertisements and articles from *Glamour* magazine and a novel by Margaret Atwood can provide students with opportunities to develop their own relationships to the dominant culture and feminist critique.

Helen Bannan describes how her in-class exercise "MY FATHER'S WASP" encourages students to explore how their complex social identities combine privilege and disadvantage. MY FATHER'S WASP "spells out" the simultaneity of oppressions, helping students to see that we are all enmeshed in relations of power and privilege, even as we also recognize that these relations have differential and unequal impact on us, depending on our social locations.

Sandra Shattuck, Judith McDaniel, and Judy Temple encourage their students to engage in "outrageous acts" that problematize gender while Ann Mussey and Amy Kesselman promote acts that encourage personal activism.

Our last section, Part V, provides one faculty member's personal narrative of risk and grace, a teacher's and her students' story of struggle, survival, and even empowerment in a time when "things" are more likely "to fall apart." We believe that Jane Rinehart's essay can help us and our readers embrace the personal, intellectual, and political difficulties of confronting the disorientation that, as Rinehart notes, "thinking about gender produces" for teachers and students alike.

As the essays in this volume demonstrate, the real work of developing feminism and women's studies is less about safety, sisterhood, and commonalities and much more about grappling with the discomfort found in the necessary process of developing coalitions in order to engage productively in a historical moment when differences of gender, race/ethnicity, class, sexual orientation, and so on, result in imbalances of power both within and outside of the classroom.[25] This was a major part of the message women of color clearly brought to feminism in the 1970s and early 1980s. "If you're really doing coalition work," Berenice Johnson Reagon (1983: 356) said, "most of the time you feel threatened to the core."

A coalition, by definition, is a temporary alliance. Coalitions are formed in response to particular issues with an agreement to work toward the resolution of those particular issues. Coalitions are risky and uncomfortable. To succeed, a coalition must act in a way that is more acceptable to its members than the cost of their own withdrawal. The minute, careful, and unrelenting attention to process and positioning is vital in coalition work since an imbalance in any particular detail may result in the departure of some members and the collapse of the coalition. As a result of these requirements, coalitions are filled with the ironic and painful tensions of working together across differences to meet a particular need while constantly weighing the cost of non-participation and withdrawal. In other words, coalitions are not about meeting extremely long-term objectives; they are tense, temporary, and task oriented. They are active and essential tools—not calm states of equilibrium.

In a setting such as the academy, the costs—to both faculty and students (although not equally)—of non-participation or withdrawal in a classroom are embedded in a power web of institutional, professional, social, and cultural demands and sanctions. We need to be careful about what we expect of our tools. Building or improving community is not the primary work of coalitions or classrooms, but may be a goal of women's studies and feminism more generally. Building community is a complex and long-term objective, the progress of which is measured in more humble expectations and in much smaller increments than is the progress of coalition or classroom work. Long-term objectives often require a different kind of process and a more personal kind of work—and risk.

Writers on feminist and anti-racist pedagogies, many of them coming from a postmodernist or poststructuralist feminist orientation, have addressed the issue of building (or observing emerging) coalitions among students and with teachers of differing positions and subjectivities.[26] Such political work is embedded in all institutions of education, including higher education, in and out of the classroom, and reflects the contextual nature of knowledge. Courses like Introduction to Women's Studies and women's studies generally are more likely to "call attention" to and critique or deconstruct this fact. Coalition-building cannot be the only task of the feminist classroom, including the introductory women's studies classroom. However, metaphorically and actually, it can move students from assumptions of unexamined uniformity to awareness of the implications of difference and power while challenging teachers to reflect on their own internalized silences about power and privilege. As we have noted, coalitions are not about equilibrium; they are all too often about "things falling apart" since teachers and students are embedded in "multiple and contradictory subject positions" with various and competing needs (Ellsworth 1992: 106). Yet it is only by working with and through such contradictions that we can create the possibility of coming to any sense of (limited) "community" in the classroom.

Both coalition work and building communities are necessary. One type of work does not prohibit and may even encourage a desire for the other. Neither one will be comfortable or consistent, but they are not the same, and feminist teachers need to be very aware and cautious of how the need for such work makes its way into the introductory classroom. The struggle of working in a coalition is not necessarily about sharing, appreciation, or even respect (although it may include these and be bolstered by them); it is about agreeing to take a risk, negotiating the pain, and attending to the detail necessary to maintain the coalition to gain a particular benefit. Faculty, in particular because of their institutional position, may make a long-term commitment to "teaching as an ally," especially to students who are socially and institutionally marginalized. However, any one member's ability to deal with the weighty requirements of coalition-building is likely to ebb and flow for any number of reasons, either internal or external to the coalition itself. When working in an institutional setting such as the classroom, the power dynamics present even more confounding reasons. While feminists cannot (and should not) necessarily expect the "feel good" attributes of sharing, appreciation, or respect as rewards from coalition work, the benefits may be no small accomplishment and they may provide a firm yet flexible foundation for women's studies, feminist pedagogy, and the introductory classroom.

As we can see from the descriptions of the essays included here, the contributors to this volume are not afraid to articulate the struggles, uncertainties, and fractures that take place in the introductory classroom in the eighties and nineties. Several argue that the assumption of "safety," once a mainstay of descriptions of the women's studies classroom, can be misleading or dangerous. One might argue that they—and we—are in the midst of defining a "pedagogy of coalition," as well as positionality, in which students and teachers recognize that a "multiplicity of knowledges" are present in the classroom and work together in a variety of ways to explore these through sometimes shifting, sometimes intersecting, sometimes contradictory, groups and identities. Through such a pedagogy students and teachers can recognize that we belong to groups that have "unequal weights of legitimacy within the culture and the classroom," and can only develop a sense of relative safety by making space for such awareness and acting on it.[27]

Working with the assumption that safety in the classroom is not something we can—or should—ensure, Jane Rinehart in her concluding essay reinforces the recognition that faculty cannot and should not assume themselves to be "in control." Rinehart, instead, recommends that we open ourselves to the chaos and uncertainty that collective inquiry and reflection can bring to all women's studies classes, but especially to the introductory classroom.

We believe that this collection on teaching the introductory course expresses the vitality and creativity of women's studies teachers. We hope that our readers will recognize the diversity of approaches our contributors offer. As editors, we were surprised and pleased at how well the essays we had chosen seemed to provide commentary and reflection on each other. This implicitly dialogical approach, we believe, reflects the best of women's studies, as we speak *with* one another and turn away from the need to define ourselves through opposition while prizing difference.[28] If the introductory class has reflected and embodied the concerns of women's studies participants since the creation of courses and programs in the late 1960s and 1970s, then what we see here is the desire of teachers to assert the continuing validity of the enterprise, to struggle against reductiveness and to emphasize inclusion, to bring new scholarship, perspectives, and techniques into the classroom, and to patiently explore both the painful and joyful paradoxes and contradictions with which we and our students learn and live.

NOTES

1. See Lather (1991a), Luke and Gore (1992), and Maher and Tetreault (1994) for relatively recent texts on feminist pedagogy, and Fonow (1996) for an example of a workbook.

2. Examples of early discussions of the introductory course and other pioneering women's studies classes can be found in the "teaching essays," personal anecdotal accounts of individual classes, in journals such as *Female Studies* and *Radical Teacher*.

3. A recent article by Schneider (1998) in the *Chronicle of Higher Education* provides evidence that large lectures, especially, encourage disruptive behavior by students and unwillingness to seriously engage with difficult material, particularly when taught by faculty whose race and gender may still be seen as marginal by students.

4. Initially skeptical students often express their surprise that the class was "nothing like what they expected." This is a tribute to the pervasiveness of the stereotype of women's studies as "male-bashing." However, it also suggests that students are aware and already critical of at least some aspects of oppression and discrimination that introductory classes address. The basis for this "awareness" and therefore importance of incorporating students' narratives of their lived experiences as classroom text, however problematic they may be, has been addressed by writers on critical and feminist pedagogy. See, for example, Giroux (1988: chapters 8 and 15); hooks (1994a: chapter 6), Maher and Tetreault (1994) and Winkler (1997).

5. Students will sometimes state on the first day that they are afraid that "their opinions will not be respected" because they believe they are more politically conservative than other class members or than the teacher will "allow." See X. Zúñiga and P. Myers (1993).

6. For example, Winkler (1992: 52–55) found this movement orientation among the founding students at the University of Minnesota, where some located their political roots

in the New Left, others identified with radical feminism, and still others were members of the Young Socialist Alliance.

7. On critics' argument of ideological homogeneity, see Patai and Koertge (1994).

8. For counter-examples of disagreement and ideological plurality see Winkler (1992). Caulfield and Gearhart believed their ideological differences modeled diversity of opinion for their students (Winkler 1992: 359).

9. Although Davis (1985: 251–252) does not identify these traditional students as also "transitional" she identifies the process which they are undergoing as such.

10. See Geiger and Zita (1985) on sameness, assumption of "haven," and racism. Also, see G. Hughes, this volume.

11. While GED, or "core," and "diversity" requirements are not the only reason for good enrollments in women's studies courses in general and the introductory class in particular, they are a significant factor. Many students at West Virginia University and University of South Florida, the schools where we teach, when asked on their student information forms as to why they are taking the class, inevitably mention fulfilling the requirement. Some hasten to add that the class seems like one of the more interesting classes that fulfill the requirement.

12. This seems especially true at larger state schools. At West Virginia University, male student enrollment in the introductory class has been as high as one-third of the total student population.

13. Barbara Scott Winkler has found this to be the case at West Virginia University, the flagship school for the state.

14. Carolyn DiPalma has found this to be the case at the University of South Florida. At USF the lower division course Human Sexual Behavior, offered through women's studies, can be taken to fulfill a gender core requirement. This course has five or six sections a semester, sometimes enrolling five hundred students, including a large percentage of male students. It is often this course that encourages students to pursue further course work in women's studies at the upper division level. It is, therefore, an "introduction" for many to women's studies, gender issues, and feminist analyses; however, it is not the introductory course in women's studies.

15. See Patai and Koertge (1994: 81). For a similar argument about women's studies as "indoctrination" see Sommers (1994).

16. See, for example, Walker (1995). However, another collection of articles by Third Wave younger generation feminists, Findlen (1995), stresses continuity between the generations and conceptualizations of feminism. Also, Carlip (1995) provides a forum for the voices of young women ages nine to seventeen as they express their diverse concerns and hopes for themselves and for whatever relationships they have to feminism.

17. Marcia Weskott and Gay Victoria, "University of Colorado: Personalized Learning," in Caryn McTigue Musil, ed. (1992: 29); Musil, "Conclusion," (200). This report is cited in Boxer (1998: 93).

18. For other examples see Maher and Tetreault (1994). This point was underscored by the remarks of an eleven-person panel on "Teaching Introduction to Women's Studies" at the 1997 Annual NWSA Conference, where it was repeatedly mentioned that the material in the introductory course needed to "start where the students are at."

19. See remarks by Carol Sternhall and Catherine Stimpson on the problematic uses of the "iron·triangle of race/class/gender" summarized in Boxer (1998: 219–220). See also Gayatri Spivak's interview with Ellen Rooney (1989) for a discussion of the strategic use of essences and identities in pedagogical situations and Fuss (1989) for a discussion

of the circulation of essence, identity, and experience as a potentially privileged signifier in the classroom.

20. For a theory-based discussion of diversity concerns within feminism, see Carolyn DiPalma (1990–1991).

21. See Boxer (1998: 110–111) for a summary.

22. See McIntosh (1998: 94–105). See also Helen Bannan, ''MY FATHER'S WASP,'' this volume. On the uses of positionality in the classroom, see Maher and Tetreault (1994: chapter 6) and Winkler (1997).

23. Toni C. King, this volume. See also Lugones (1990) and Anzaldua (1990).

24. Martin and Mohanty (1986) make a similar point.

25. For a discussion of this issue in regard to feminist anti-racist teaching, see Ellsworth (1992).

26. See, for example, Ellsworth (1992), Orner (1992) and Winkler (1996).

27. See Ellsworth (1992: 112, 115). On positionality, see Maher and Tetreault (1994: chapter 6) and Winkler (1996).

28. On speaking ''with'' instead of ''past'' those we disagree with, see Boxer (1998: 222). On replacing previous oppositional viewpoints with new questions see Hirsch and Keller (1990: 370–385).

Part II

OVERVIEWS/RESOURCES

2

The Ideologue, the Pervert, and the Nurturer, or, Negotiating Student Perceptions in Teaching Introductory Women's Studies Courses

Vivian M. May, Texas Woman's University

I open this chapter by describing the contextual framework that shapes and influences my teaching of the introductory women's studies course at Texas Woman's University (TWU). After offering brief regional, institutional, and programmatic vignettes, I also include a fictional scenario about the first day of class in Introduction to Women's Studies to illustrate many of the stereotypes, fears, expectations, and perceptions that frame women's studies teaching. Throughout the Chapter, I include student ''voice'' whenever possible through excerpts taken from my individually designed narrative course evaluations.[1]

REGIONAL CONTEXT

North Texas is full of contradictions and is a region in transition. It has both a sprawling metropolitan area (the Dallas–Fort Worth metroplex) as well as farms and ranches. It is a region known for glitz and glamour, the cowboy mystique, racial conflict, poverty, economic expansion, violent crime, a ''country'' way of life, migrant and itinerant work, conservative politics, native Texans and an influx of ''foreigners'' and its position well within the Bible Belt.

INSTITUTIONAL CONTEXT

Founded in 1901 as the Girls Industrial College of Texas, TWU is a public university primarily for women. It was racially integrated in the fall of 1961, and all degree programs were opened to male students in the fall of 1995. Currently, about 9,500 students are enrolled, 90% of whom are women. Undergraduates constitute 56% of the student population, with an average age of twenty-seven. Graduate students constitute the remainder of the student population, with an average age of thirty-two. TWU's student body is racially diverse: 12% are African American, 8% are Hispanic, 5% are Asian/Pacific Islander, American Indian, or Alaskan Native, and 2% are international.

Most of our students are from the metroplex. Many are the first in their families to attend college; attend after participating in the paid workforce and/or raising a family; continue to work full- or part-time, and/or have young children. TWU therefore offers commuter-focused programs, single-parent housing, and day-care facilities to accommodate its range of students. Discussions with TWU students reveal that they actively choose (primarily) single-sex education because they want a participatory education and an opportunity to develop personal and intellectual leadership.

WOMEN'S STUDIES AT TWU

Women's studies at TWU started as a program housed within sociology but has recently gained independent program status within the College of Arts and Sciences. It offers an undergraduate minor and a master of arts in women's studies (the first freestanding women's studies graduate degree in the state of Texas). TWU requires three hours of women's studies as part of the undergraduate core curriculum.

Thus, our introductory course, WS 2013: Images and Perspectives, is in high demand: we offer approximately twelve sections of the course annually—about five in the fall and spring semesters and two in the summer. Enrollments vary from smaller sections of 50 to larger sections up to and even over 100 students. The course is an interdisciplinary survey, but its structure varies according to instructor. This chapter addresses how I design and teach the course for 50. Specializing in theory and contemporary literature, I emphasize philosophy, symbolic representation (in art, film, and the media), and literature. Thus, topics such as work, violence, the body (including scientific research and health care), and sexuality are explored through a humanities framework.

SCENARIO

Setting: day 1 of the semester in a classroom filled with students required to take women's studies as part of their core curriculum.

Center stage: the women's studies professor, variously perceived to be about to perform the following range of roles simultaneously:

- "Angry Ideologue," aka "Subjective Polemicist";
- "Amoral Feminist" or, more simply and succinctly, "Pervert";
- and, last but not least, the "Penultimate Nurturer," that teacher who will offer a safe learning environment without judgment, critique, or discomfort of any kind.

In the students' minds, the following ruminations:

- Student 1: "I've been told this is an easy 'A,' as it should be since it's an extra burden in my degree plan";
- Student 2: "I've heard this professor is demanding and hard—who does she think she is, anyway? This is going to be useless. Why do we have to take it?";
- Student 3: "Finally, a course where I can really sink my teeth into some political issues that have been burning within me! I can't wait to have a teacher and classmates who are in tune with my radical outlook!";
- Student 4: "I've heard that all we will study in women's studies is sex, the body, nudity in art, and other disgusting things. This is immoral and against my beliefs";
- Student 5: "As everyone knows, women's studies is all about man-hating and lesbianism: you can tell just by looking at that professor! What if people think I'm one of *them*?";
- Student 6: "I can't wait to talk about how women and men are completely equal now that sex discrimination is dead";
- Student 7: "This class will be just like sitting around the kitchen table with my girlfriends, talking over coffee about our feelings and personal experiences! I can't wait to share!"

STEREOTYPES OF WOMEN'S STUDIES: PARADOXES AND CONTRADICTIONS

The preceding scenario outlines some key issues to consider when teaching introductory women's studies. First are the fears and stereotypes of women's studies, which, in this particular instance, must be placed in the context of stereotypes about TWU as an institution. The letters "TWU" are rumored to stand for two rather different phrases or slogans: "Two Women United" (a term of affection and/or homophobia) and "Timid Women United" (an acronym critiquing and/or continuing stereotypes about women students' supposedly inherent passivity). Thus, TWU itself symbolizes a place of both convention and subversiveness, propriety and risk taking, domestic femininity and public leadership.

Although such rumors and stereotypes may seem particular to TWU, women's studies is likewise steeped in contradictory expectations: it, too, is framed by paradox and ambiguity. Consider the dyadic perceptions in the scenario. Women's studies is simultaneously thought to be safe and risky, soft and hard; a place for dialogue and disagreement; a space exemplifying harmony and one-ness as well as discord and difference; a biased, subjective area of study as well as an open-minded, analytical discourse; it is both like home and like hostile territory. Framed by classic subject/object dualisms, women's studies is simul-taneously beyond the pale and acceptable: it is both the witch/bitch of the acad-emy and the fair maiden/fairy godmother.

AN ARGUMENT FOR THEORY: THEORY AS PRAXIS IN INTRODUCTION TO WOMEN'S STUDIES

To reiterate, women's studies is thought to be "easy" because it is about everyday life, "soft" because it is about women, and therefore a seeming "waste of time" if required and obnoxious if challenging or "hard." Yet un-derneath expectations of "an easy A" are often internalized notions that women's ideas, art forms, bodies, and histories are inherently less important than matters of direct importance to traditional disciplines. Too, women's studies seems partial and biased in its overt focus on "women" because most of us teach "students who have been led to believe that all education within the university should be 'neutral' " (hooks 1989: 101). In other words, stereotypes, fears, and assumptions about women's studies and about women are part of the "dysconscious" baggage that students bring to the women's studies classroom. Joyce E. King (1994: 338) explains that

Dysconsciousness is an uncritical habit of mind (including perceptions, attitudes, as-sumptions, and beliefs) that justifies inequity and exploitation by accepting the existing order of things as given . . . Not only are [students] unaware of their own ideological perspectives (or of the range of alternatives they have not consciously considered), most are also unaware of how their own subjective identities reflect an uncritical identification with the existing social order.

Because oppression and domination are dysconscious, I structure the course around discovering, exploring, and describing how the politics of power per-meate "the whole social order," making sure to combine "a discourse of cri-tique with one of possibility" (Hernandez 1997: 10, 11).[2] Pedagogically, I aim to avoid passive learning in a "talking-head" learning environment. Theory pushes students' thinking beyond rote learning, especially if they must make cross-disciplinary connections and arguments. As Joyce E. King (1994) asserts, "Merely presenting factual information about societal inequity does not neces-sarily enable [students] to examine the beliefs and assumptions that may influ-ence the way they interpret these facts" (344). Thus, I understand women's studies to be inherently both "critical" and "deconstructive," whether at the introductory or advanced level. Patti Lather (1991b: 128–129) writes:

By "critical," I mean those stories which assume underlying determining structures for how power shapes the social world. Such structures are posited as largely invisible to common sense ways of making meaning but visible to those who probe below hegemonic meaning systems to produce counter-hegemonic knowledge, knowledge intended to challenge dominant meaning systems. By "deconstructivist," I mean stories that foreground the unsaid in our saying, "the elisions, blind-spots, loci of the *unsayable* within texts."

An introduction to women's studies course as a critical lens teases out students' a priori assumptions about gender, race, sexuality, disability, the nature of knowledge, and the structures of power. Consequently, a strong theoretical framework is requisite. Without theory, students' preconceived notions about knowledge and subjectivity as transparent, immediate, and unified are left unchallenged, and yet these preconceived, taken-for-granted notions undergird the social practices and beliefs I aim to interrogate in women's studies. As Adriana Hernandez (1997: 86) argues, "conceptions of knowledge turn into particular practices that constitute subjects to accept their place in society, conceiving it as 'natural.' " I aim to have students expand their own sense of capacity, to not accept their ascribed "places" in the social structure, and to push the limits set forth for them. Knowledge itself therefore must be denaturalized from the start. Hence, the course begins by delving into the intersections of knowledge and power: how knowledge, in its myriad forms (art, literature, science, philosophy) is never neutral, never innocent.

PUTTING THEORY INTO PRACTICE

The first half of WS 2013 investigates self–other, subject–object dualisms.[3] A "safer" place to start articulating this epistemological paradigm is "the past," since many students believe that "women's equality" (note that deconstructing the category "woman" is also necessary *from day 1*) has been fully achieved and that discriminatory practices against or negative ways of thinking about "women" are outdated, even "ancient." Thus, after initial readings that help explain the scope and purposes of women's studies,[4] we delve into Aristotelian oppositional thought with some additional insights from de Beauvoir, Hegel, and Fanon. I structure the course around investigating Valerie Walkerdine's (1994: 59) questions, "How is truth constituted, how is it possible, and what effects does it have? . . . The argument, in a nutshell, is that ideas about reason and reasoning cannot be understood historically outside of considerations about gender."

To illustrate the influence of subject/object, self/other dichotomies, the "epistemological dichotomy" that has been named "the most powerful gender totem" (Stone 1994: 224), we examine the history of the nude (female) in Western

art: this is not necessarily the most "safe" place to start the course, since art is
supposedly pure and not political. Moreover, *theoretical* discussions of nudity,
voyeurism, and objectification as they intersect with race, class, gender, and
sexuality are rare in our culture. Yet beginning with art can be (usefully) disturbing for students because it becomes apparent that in the world of "art" (as
opposed to craft), "Women do not beget culture; they mind it—both in the
sense of tending and in the sense of obeying. . . . Women are the objects out of
which art is made" (Pagano 1994: 256, 257).

Students read art critics and analyze slides from the fifteenth to the twentieth
centuries: odalisques and Venuses; women lounging, sleeping, frolicking, even
bathing, in gardens, fields, and lush interiors; rich, middle-class, and working-
class women, "exotic" foreign women, and slave women (sometimes all in the
same picture, allowing a complex analysis of how gender, race, and class intersect in ways of seeing and representation).[5] We also analyze representations
of slave men, working-class men, and "exotic" foreign men, which helps students understand (and many already do, whereas others have never considered
the fact) that the positions of subject and object, self and other shift and are
more complex than an overdetermined "male versus female" paradigm suggests. In other words, we explore some of the intricacies of compound identities.

Attention to complexity overwhelms some students and affirms others. Consider the range of student reactions to deconstructing simplistic categories:
"There are more different types of people than I had ever thought of"; "I don't
see a lot of the world or of different kinds of women and so this class helps to
identify different kinds of domination"; "I was challenged to think on a deeper,
multicultural level and I *loved* that. There are so many things that get left out
in most of my classes—it seems as if we only study the white male and an
occasional white woman, so it's challenging to begin to place everything on the
same level of importance, where it *should* be" (evaluations, spring 1998).

Students unconvinced by a feminist critique of art will often be more persuaded once lessons about how oppositions and hierarchy affect perception and
representation are repeated with different subject matter. As Michele Russell
(1982: 197) contends, "new ways of seeing and thinking must be reinforced."
We revisit the subject versus object paradigm in science (how women's health,
sexuality, and biology have been researched or not); in economics and work
(including pay inequities, employment opportunities open to women, "glass
ceilings," and so forth); in the ways violence permeates women's lives; in
women's attitudes toward their bodies (including racialized notions of beauty,
self-loathing, plastic surgery, eating disorders); and in media/advertising por-
trayals of women and women's implicit roles and rightful "place" in society.
Thinking about the many ways women's subjectivity is denied or limited can
be disquieting to students: "Really seeing discrimination in everyday things was
the most challenging thing. I had to change the way I looked at everything.
Things I'd never noticed before or had taken for granted were brought out in a
new light" (evaluations, spring 1998).

In exploring the many ways in which women are granted secondary status and made invisible, we also analyze how privilege and oppression are simultaneous and attend to the complexities of the category "woman." Thus, we discuss, for example, how whiteness, speaking "proper" English, practicing Christianity, being heterosexual, and/or not having a disability often mitigate other types of discrimination because these things grant one certain privileges and degrees of power. Peggy McIntosh's (1998) "White Privilege: Unpacking the Invisible Backpack" is useful for explicating embedded forms of domination and privilege, especially if students are asked to "unpack" not only their "backpacks" of racial privilege (or not) but also the "backpacks" of sexuality, ability, and religion. I, too, discuss how my knowledge as a teacher is partial and is located both by my identities and by my scholarly training.

Theory therefore provides a language to describe the complex realities and identities that women's studies explores. Hence, although "Others" have been defined and confined by language, bell hooks (1994a) acknowledges that language's "hurtful" qualities are also "double-edged" in that the oppressor's tongue and counterlanguages exist in the same realm. Questions of language and its influence upon our reality must not be overlooked simply because a course is introductory: all the more reason to discuss language! As Gayatri Spivak (1988: 77–78) contends, "We know no world that is not organized as language, we operate with no other consciousness but one structured as language—languages that we cannot possess, for we are operated by those languages as well. The category of language, then, embraces the categories of world and consciousness even as it is determined by them."

As one student put it, "I really liked learning about what things like 'social presence' and 'politic of domination' were *called*. I knew what they were, but didn't have the words to put with what I felt" (evaluations, spring 1998). Consequently, delving into the gaps of the unsaid, examining what society deems representable and unrepresentable, and learning to question a priori assumptions and givens underscore how theory can be a tool not only for analysis but also for refusal, reformulation, and exploration. One student wrote, "I learned that there are a lot of concepts I didn't know about. I am now able to label myself and find a lot of the concepts within myself and my family . . . [women's studies helps me because] I can now speak up and use and know the exact terms for my reasoning for what I want to say." Another commented, "The idea of who defines what society accepts was challenging. Who writes the definition of 'sex' or 'freedom' or 'woman'? Challenging society's view empowers me to begin to communicate about the injustices and to express what I deserve or want to achieve" (evaluations, spring 1998).

NAMING THE UNNAMED: PEDAGOGICAL CHALLENGES AND OPPORTUNITIES IN WOMEN'S STUDIES

Women's studies names and describes ideas, concepts, people, and topics that consistently remain overlooked: "the most interesting thing I learned was how we don't really learn or talk about women even though we are all women at a woman's university'' (evaluations, spring 1998). For example, students consistently respond with surprise and horror to the little-known but well-documented statistic that women are ten times more likely than men to experience violence from an intimate partner.[6] Women's studies breaks silences about family, economics, sexuality, and the body. It delves in gaps and fissures in the philosophical, artistic, literary, historical, and scientific canons. Women's studies explores social construction and social stratification. It also works to dismantle the "isms," including racism, sexism, heterosexism, ethnocentrism, and ableism.

Having words and language to name women's complex realities can be very powerful for students but can also induce disgust, fear, or reluctance to learn more. Michele Russell (1982: 196) describes the "heavy memory" that her African American female students face as they discuss and remember the history of Black women in America. Student commentary highlights how the rewards of learning to name are often mixed with some reluctance to further such learning: "Embedded forms of domination stood out to me because these have formed a blue print for my life and it is sickening''; ''The discrimination of women and minorities goes unnoticed because it is so much a part of how American society works. . . . The assignments have forced me to think about concepts that I may have been much happier avoiding but this in turn led me to learn more about myself and about how I really feel and think.'' Others wrote, ''It was all challenging to me—sometimes too challenging. But learning about breaking silences inspires me to be brave also''; ''I was forced to think about things I didn't want to think about because of their unpleasantness. My apathetic attitude has changed. I didn't realize I was so independent and so proud of my femininity and of feminist attitudes'' (evaluations, spring 1998).

Additionally, because women's studies challenges status quo silence about violence or sexuality, taking a women's studies course can put students at risk both emotionally and physically: a husband did not march ''his'' wife into my office to get a drop form signed for no reason (and other students faced pressure from family or spouses to drop the course—these situations are especially painful when one considers that women's studies is required for graduation). Feminist bell hooks (1994a: 3) describes the contradictions that liberatory learning meant to her as a child: ''To be changed by ideas was pure pleasure. But to learn ideas that ran counter to values and beliefs learned at home was to place one's self at risk—to enter the danger zone.''

For example, one student described the most challenging part of the course as ''my relationships with men, especially my father. Why? Thinking about it causes pain, but also grieving and healing.'' Another said, ''This is an extremely hard class to take especially if your views aren't as radical as the professor's . . . but Great Prof.!,'' showing how students often negotiate their feelings about the class and their outside life by keeping seemingly opposite claims in tension. Several students find discussions about sexuality difficult, especially in the context of the Bible Belt: ''Talking about homosexuality was difficult . . . because it challenged my personal Christian beliefs, but I was pushed to have my own

opinion, to question why I think the way I do, and effectively express it";
"Lesbianism challenged me the most because it was something I was not comfortable with"; "Women's liberation and lesbian issues were a challenge because they are completely against everything I've been taught: you definitely
made me think harder!" (evaluations, spring 1998). Interestingly, many of these
comments came from a class that was all "traditionally aged freshmen," as it
was a time slot set aside for a special residential program, which suggests that
a homogeneously younger group of students may have more difficulty with
"taboo" subjects than do classes with a more diverse age range.

Because women's studies delves beyond what is conventionally considered
"proper" or "rigorous" academic inquiry, women's studies teachers and content can be seen as abject, as embodying the "down there" of the academy or
of society. Placing women's studies within the context of social expectations
and assumptions can help alleviate teacher frustrations about student resistance.
Remembering that society continues to resist the idea that all knowledge is
positioned and political (a central women's studies concept) also helps to name
student fears or assumptions from the start. Denaturalizing "Knowledge,"
"Truth," and "Reality" requires that teachers offer multiple assignments and
readings that reinforce such concepts, which, heretofore, *did* seem perfectly
"natural" and "neutral" to many students. In other words, from the first day
of the class to the last, we learn and put into practice the idea of a critical lens
and of a deconstructive approach to culture.

With much humor and energy, I start each semester by listing "what peo-
ple/society generally think" when they hear the following words (we do one at
a time): woman/women, femininity, feminism, women's studies (note that I re-
move the discussion from what the individual students think to alleviate a sense
of blame or shame for what the class puts on the board). We discuss the veracity
of the lists that emerge on the board, and, generally, several students will re-
luctantly admit that ideas of femininity, for example, as pink, flowing, natural,
nice, kind, soft, and caring are "somewhat stereotypical." Sometimes, but not
always, a *few* students will (seem to)[7] resist such a list by yelling out contrasting
words to be included such as tough, hard, muscular, and assertive. We then
explore what stereotypes are, what their functions might be, how they come into
being, and whose point of view generally frames them.

We do nothing to change the lists right away, nor do we discuss them again
until much later in the semester—I do not expect to achieve a major epistemological shift or rupture right at the beginning of the course. I also discuss
from the start and reiterate throughout the semester that taking women's studies
can be uncomfortable or disquieting and that ideas that may be distasteful or
difficult for some students may be perfectly acceptable to others, and vice versa.[8]
I use this opportunity, then, not to introduce my "feminist agenda" (as many
expect) but to introduce the idea that knowledge is located, constructed, and not
necessarily transparent.

Learning that a priori assumptions and the status quo can be considered *con-*

structs rather than givens cast in steel can be exciting. A student commented that learning that "women are not paid as much as men for the same work challenged my thought and reasoning process because it doesn't make any sense," whereas another exclaimed, "These classes are empowering to us as women. They cause us to realize that the reasons why women have it so bad are STUPID" (evaluations, spring 1998).

Metaphors can be extremely useful pedagogically in making women's studies more "palatable" for students reluctant to "try" it. For example, I emphasize that women's studies is about stretching one's reference points and that stretching can sometimes be painful. I also describe women's studies to be like a dance class (we have an extensive dance program here), and the students' responsibility is to dance for a while with each "partner" (subject area or idea) before dismissing and/or accepting it. Students also come up with their own analogies to make women's studies fit their worldview or to help them explain it to their peers/families. One deeply religious young African American Christian student explained women's studies to her peers by saying, "Well, I guess women's studies is like [evolutionary] Biology where I learn about evolution even though I believe that God created everything. But this is what education is all about." Similarly, a colleague who teaches multicultural education courses uses the idea that learning to be open is what education is all about; this is what it means to be middle-class. She uses this idea to encourage students (many of whom are working-class but determined to enter the middle class through education) to risk seeing the world from a different standpoint—one that might challenge their assumptions or learned values.

WOMEN'S STUDIES: A CONVERSION EXPERIENCE?

Because many students see women's studies as a threat, I also describe women's studies as being like a pair of glasses (a critical lens) that they try on and wear for a semester. At the start of the course, students are often encouraged by the idea that they can take off or even discard these "glasses." By the end of the course I hope they will neither want nor be able to take off this critical lens; I aim to teach students to become cultural critics as well as agents of change.

In this vein, many students are also relieved when I make the disclaimer that the course will not be one in "conversion" to a feminist "lifestyle"[9]: I remain clearly focused on the idea that women's studies is an academic discipline. Challenging readings and rigorous assignments and tests are very concrete messages to students that the course is, above all else, academic. I make no apologies for rigor but, instead, discuss why I think an ambitious and intellectual course about women is important. As Adrienne Rich (1979: 242) comments, "women need to have their intellectual lives, their work, legitimized against the claims of family, relationships, the old message that a woman is always available for service to others." Concurring, bell hooks (1989: 51) remarks, "Students who want to learn hunger for a space where they can be challenged intellectually . . . [,] in short [such students want] a dialectical context where there is serious and rigorous critical exchange.'' Many students become excited by being challenged and stimulated, by being taken seriously as thinkers and writers: ''The best work to be done is in critical thinking, writing, and reading—I feel as if classes that *don't* challenge me in that way are underestimating my capacity to think intelligently'' (evaluations, spring 1998).

Moreover, I do not think of or teach women's studies as a unified discipline. ''Conversion'' myths about women's studies feed upon the idea that women's studies is a monolithic, ideological, and fervently (irrational) political ''renegade'' discipline (in other words, that it is undisciplined and not a dutiful daughter). I do not seek, ''[L]ike Pygmalion molding his wax woman,'' to make students over in ·my own image (Pagano 1994: 258). The goal of teaching women's studies is *not* to have students ''learn to produce 'correct' answers, to follow a kind of 'group think' that repositions them within a 'sisterhood' of oppressed women unified in their newly discovered rage at the 'patriarchy' '' (Lather 1991b: 139). Conversion claims also assume, like much critical pedagogy, that the teacher is fully emancipated and understands oppression better than any of her students—a rationalist assumption that I do not support (Ellsworth 1994: 308). As Lather (1991b: 137) suggests, such arguments and analogies ''assume an excessive faith in the powers of the reasoning mind. . . . Furthermore, they position the 'oppressed' as the unfortunately deluded, and critical pedagogues as 'transformative intellectuals' with privileged knowledge free of false logic and beliefs.''

Clearly, my theoretical beliefs and assumptions structure the course, but I design assignments that will push students to think beyond rote summary of my lectures or ideas and produce a diverse range of knowledges. For example, in-depth, take-home essay tests, for which students have two weeks to write and synthesize, push students to digest course materials but also to arrive at their own interdisciplinary, critical conclusions and analyses: ''On the tests and in class, we have been able to think critically and then write our own thoughts, opinions, and beliefs''; ''On the tests we had to pull everything learned and form one idea or argument [which] has improved my way of thinking and my organization''; and ''I enjoyed doing the essay tests because I learned and understood concepts very well afterwards. I have a tendency to memorize for objective tests and I don't remember what I learned. I will *not* forget what I have learned in this course'' (evaluations, spring 1998).

WHY WOMEN'S STUDIES?

In addition to the paradoxical and contradictory perceptions of women's studies that need to be considered, women's studies courses, like liberal arts courses or multicultural studies courses, can also suffer from a crisis of meaning. Women's studies may seem impractical, without immediate application, or lacking in "cultural capital" and thereby seemingly unworthy in the eyes of peers, parents, spouses, and/or future employers.[10] Consequently, students can resent a course from the start because, unlike a class such as Introduction to Statistics, Introduction to Women's Studies does not seem to have a "why" or a "what" to it.

Thus, a discussion of the pragmatic reasons to take women's studies can take place at the beginning of a course, debated throughout, as well as arrived at upon the close of the semester.[11] Many students come to the conclusion that, to their surprise, women's studies *is* "interesting," "really different and yet engaging," and that it "opens our minds" (evaluations, spring 1998). However, students also come to a wide array of conclusions about why women's studies *is* useful, pragmatic, and necessary, and I share past student observations and conclusions with my classes.

I close with student responses to the question, Why women's studies? not only because their voices and ideas are very powerful but also because they are inspirational: their words remind me why what I teach is important and also worthwhile. Their commentary is organized thematically.

1. Students identified *community resources* as useful:

   - "[Women's studies] helps you to know that you aren't alone and where to turn to for help, if needed."

2. Improved *writing and critical thinking skills* are commented upon frequently as well:

   - "Interdisciplinary work has really improved my way of thinking and organization";
   - "You are able to delve deep into your ideas and how you interpret concepts and how all of that relates to you";
   - "[Women's studies] teaches, even forces, us to think critically and learn more about different ways of life and different ways of thinking."

3. *Career and life success* was another theme that emerged:

   - "A [women's studies] course helps women promote themselves in a positive way. I feel that without this class, many women would never realize or even think about women's status in the world";
   - "It will help women better themselves and to overcome discrimination";
   - "This class has helped me to see the important things that I want to teach my daughter as she grows up";
   - "[Women's studies] helps you understand the real world before you get out there";
   - "[Women's studies] prepares us to excel in the world";

- "In today's society, especially the career world, you have to be strong and truly understand who you are. [Women's studies] teaches us more about women so we can express ourselves to say we are proud to be who we are."

4. A *stronger self-concept* and/or a *sense of social responsibility* are not as tangible "results" of women's studies but are clearly powerful ones:

- "It will help me in the future as far as looking at things differently, being more aware, and trying to change things";
- "This class helped me understand what being a woman in our society means, how I am viewed through others' eyes and that I have to stand up for my beliefs. [Women's studies] challenged me to look at things from my own perspective, not someone else's the way I have my whole life, and I also learned that I don't have to be silent and passive to be a woman";
- "This class will help me do my part to change the world and make it a better place";
- "I am better prepared to speak up against the hardships I plan to overcome";
- "The ideas of openness and standing up for myself without being afraid were very challenging but taking the class changed how I think about and talk about myself" (evaluations, spring 1998).

NOTES

Editors' note: Every effort has been made to provide current Internet information. However, readers are advised that Internet and e-mail addresses are subject to change.

1. All the evaluations are from the spring 1998 semester. The evaluations sheet follows:

In addition to your other evaluation form, I would appreciate your answering the following questions in some detail. I consider your ideas and opinions to be important and hope that you have learned some ideas and concepts of value this semester.

1. What is the most important or interesting concept or idea that you learned about this semester? Why?
2. What idea challenged you the most in this class and why?
3. This was a relatively work-intensive class: I have had high expectations for you regarding writing and reading as well as critical thinking because, as you know, I believe that you should be able to express your ideas and concerns in a persuasive and powerful manner.

- Have the assignments and/or the lectures helped you improve in the areas of writing, reading, and critical thinking?

4. Why do you think that TWU requires 3 hours of women's studies before graduating? How might this class help you in your future endeavours?

2. I emphasize to students from the start that although the first half of the course may seem a bit daunting or depressing, the whole second half is devoted to women's re-representations and refusals of dominant paradigms. However, I try to avoid overly simplistic analyses of power. We discuss, in the context of complex or compound identities, how coalition across difference and refusing a solipsistic view of social change are difficult and complicated. Without an "uplifting" emphasis, women's studies can become too much of what students have called "a real downer" that leaves them feeling hopeless against the status quo. Yet without discussing various kinds of "caughtness" that we face under what Foucault called "webs of power," women's studies risks being overly simplistic and eventually disappointing as well. Balancing the desire to inspire students and complicate their critical lens is never an easy task.

3. In the spring of 1998, I designed the course around overarching themes: "ideas about women: cultural symbols, philosophical constructs, social roles and expectations"; "issues of embodiment: invisible and visible bodies, sexualities, and kinds of violence"; and "women's re-representations of self: new artforms, new questions, new definitions— challenging, changing, creating."

4. For example, bell hooks' "Talking Back," Adrienne Rich's "Claiming an Education," and Alice Walker's definition of "Womanism."

5. For example, Linda Nochlin and John Berger can be very useful for an introductory level. bell hooks has written recently about contemporary art as well.

6. U.S. Department of Justice Web site: *http://www.usdoj.gov/bjs/abstract/vbl.htm*.

7. I would like to note that "resisters" may not necessarily be open to feminist analysis. They may believe that equality has been achieved, that men and women all have the same characteristics, and that such stereotypical perceptions are old and outmoded, or they may wish to disrupt the tidiness of the stereotypes on the board simply to make my life more difficult (or so they think). In addition, the resistance still usually upholds oppositional thinking, and thus students choose "opposite" or "masculine" characteristics to be included under the rubric of "femininity."

8. Patti Lather emphasizes the necessity of letting "students know they're not the only ones, or the first ones, to undergo a psychological upheaval (to whatever degree) as a result of participating in the course" (Lisa Dewey Joycechild as quoted in Lather 1998: 128).

9. Of course, misogyny and heterosexism, at the least, undergird such fears. However, I believe also that an effective class starts where students are but does not leave them there. In other words, women's studies fits in with Maria Lugones' (1990) discussion of "world-travelling": one has to depart from *somewhere*.

10. Discussing the relevance and importance of women's studies needs to occur within academic institutions as well as in public arenas. Otherwise, in this result-oriented age, the resources necessary to keep women's studies alive and expanding may continue to dwindle.

11. I generally do not open up discussion of "why" until one-third of the course has been completed. By then, many students are more engaged with women's studies. They may not exactly *like* it yet, but it starts to influence their ways of seeing, thinking, and acting.

SUGGESTED READINGS

Hernandez, A. 1997. *Pedagogy, democracy, and feminism: Rethinking the public sphere.* Albany, NY: SUNY.

hooks, b. 1994. *Teaching to transgress: Education as the practice of freedom.* New York: Routledge.

Lather, P. 1991. *Getting smart: Feminist research and pedagogy with/in the postmodern.* New York: Routledge.

Stone, L., ed. (with assistance of G. M. Boldt). 1994. *The education feminism reader.* New York and London: Routledge.

3

Conceptualizing the Introduction to Women's Studies Course at the Community College

Karen Bojar, Community College of Philadelphia

SPECIAL REWARDS AND CHALLENGES FACED BY COMMUNITY COLLEGE TEACHERS

Teaching Introduction to Women's Studies at an urban community college is a rewarding, exhilarating experience. My students have ranged in age from eighteen to seventy-eight, include African-Americans, Asian-Americans, Latinos, and European-Americans, and range from middle-class to very poor. They bring an incredible variety of experience to the issues we discuss.

The rewards are great, but so are the difficulties. Our students are also extremely diverse in academic preparation. Some have read widely and have highly developed academic skills; many have intellectual capacity but only limited opportunity to develop academic skills; and some are very weak. This diversity, both in ethnicity and in skill level, mirrors the demographic profile of the college as a whole, with one important difference: my students are overwhelmingly female. Since the course is not required for any curriculum, it draws only those with a strong interest, with an average enrollment of twenty-four students.

Roughly half of our students intend to transfer. Of those who do transfer, most will not become women's studies majors; for many, the introductory course will be their only women's studies course. When the course codeveloper, Elise Freed-Fagan, and I first contemplated our task, we despaired of achieving our goals within the limits of a fourteen-week semester. We wanted our students to develop a commitment to women's issues that they would pursue through independent reading and engagement in organizations devoted to women's issues. We hoped the course would change our students' lives and the lives of their children. This is quite a burden for a three-credit course, but for many of us women's studies is *a cause*, not simply an academic career.

Yet we are teaching academic courses, and if we want women's studies to be acknowledged as a serious academic discipline, we must ensure that our courses are academically rigorous and that our grading standards are consistent with academic standards at our institutions. This can result in some painful decisions for community college teachers. Our students are often ill prepared academically, and sometimes we are forced to give Cs to students we love rather than the As we long to give them for their courage and commitment to women's causes.

We also had to design a course that recognized our students' limited book budgets. Financial constraints have forced us into course-pack solutions rather than the range of texts we would prefer; these selections are further limited by the cost of reproduction rights for particular works. Along with limitations in financial resources, many of our students juggle family, work, and school responsibilities and thus have little time for extracurricular activities.

Our faculty also operate under severe time constraints with heavy teaching loads and many preparations for a range of courses. In addition to Introduction to Women's Studies, which I teach every other semester, I teach writing courses, interdisciplinary humanities courses, Introduction to Literature, and a labor-intensive service learning course. Although many of us bring a lifetime of reading in feminist literature and engagement in feminist activism, very few (are there any?) community college teachers can devote themselves to full-time teaching and research in women's studies. Despite my desperate attempt to keep up with the ever-burgeoning literature in the field, I always feel hopelessly behind—so many books to read, reread, and reassess.

In addition to the constraints under which our students and we operate, we have to deal with constraints stemming from the internal politics of our institution. Every institution has its own turf considerations resulting from arrangements developed over the years, and any new courses have to maneuver around these minefields. Our Introduction to Women's Studies was developed after Women in Literature and Women in History and was expected to cover different ground so as not to compete with these courses. Our course was designed to include material in the areas where the humanities and social and behavioral sciences intersect, material that is interdisciplinary in nature and generally included neither in Women in Literature nor in Women in History. We also focused on the diversity of women's experiences within the North American context, so as not to compete with a projected course on cross-cultural issues of gender. Thus, our particular interdisciplinary mix was determined by pre-existing institutional arrangements.

A further institutional constraint faced by many of us who develop women's studies courses is antagonism to the enterprise. Fortunately, although we encountered some fear that the course would be "propagandistic, pursuing a feminist party line," we encountered no extreme hostility. We answered our critics by pointing to the range of views as well as deep theoretical disagreements among feminist thinkers. Although all the writers we include share a commitment to equality for women, they disagree as to exactly what this means in practice, how best to achieve gender equality, the extent to which women's experiences and priorities vary, the extent to which men and women differ emotionally and intellectually, and the extent to which gender roles are socially or biologically constrained. Fortunately, our course was accepted as sufficiently pluralistic to avoid demands for the inclusion of antifeminist writers. In less politically liberal institutions, our answer might not have been considered acceptable.

COURSE GOALS: JUST WHAT CAN WE DO IN A MERE FIFTY-TWO HOURS OF CLASSROOM TIME?

It was difficult to be realistic when we developed goals; there is so much we hope to do in perhaps the only women's studies course our students ever take. First, we wanted to give our students a sense of women's studies as a field, a new field with fluid boundaries and major issues hotly contested. We wanted to introduce our students to some of the major thinkers and most influential works. Recently, I had the unnerving experience of reading a post on a women's studies Internet list that asked if teachers were still using Adrienne Rich's (1980) "Compulsory Heterosexuality and Lesbian Existence." Still using? Don't we have our classics, works that have changed the way we have conceptualized issues, changed the ways we have viewed the world? Although some of these works— as in any field—may have been critiqued and superseded by the work of later scholars, they retain their power and, of course, their historical importance. We certainly did not want to restrict our choice of works to the latest ones and create the sense that what matters in women's studies is what was published most recently.

Second, we certainly wanted to give our students a sense of the diversity of women's perspectives—in terms of class, ethnicity, age, sexual orientation, political philosophy. Although this goal is critically important in any Introduction to Women's Studies course, it is particularly urgent for community colleges, given the diversity of their student bodies.

Third, although we certainly want to introduce our students to women's studies as an academic field, the issues raised are the very issues women struggle with in their personal lives. We want students to use the information and perspectives introduced to them to reassess their relationship with family members, friends, and coworkers.

Fourth, we want our students to be able to enter the public debate about gender roles and to understand the powerful connection between women's studies as an academic discipline and feminist activism. Not everyone sees this as a priority. Catherine Orr (1998:4–5), in her remarks on the University of Minnesota's Women's Studies Program, states: "There was a conscious decision by the program's original members to distance themselves from the women's movement.... When the women's movement waned, the program had staying power." A women's studies program that tries to keep its distance from feminist activism is not my conception of women's studies and not the kind of approach I want to take. I want my students to learn through practice as well as theory. Thus, I include an optional service learning component in my course.

THE CONCEPTUAL FRAMEWORK

Once we clarified our goals, our conceptual framework began to take shape. We struggled to organize the course so as to give our students (most of whom have done very little, if any, reading in the field) a sense of the richness and breadth of women's studies yet present the material within a coherent conceptual framework. The range of articles included in anthologies often results in courses that appear like random grab bags of articles about women's lives. Yet how do we provide a conceptual framework that does not distort in its attempt to fit everything into one schema? Not so easy.

Unit 1: Historical and Social Context of Women's Studies as an Academic Discipline

We begin by introducing students to the striking parallels between the nineteenth century first wave of the American feminist movement and the "second wave" of the movement, dating from the 1960s. First wave feminism was influenced by the participation of its leaders in the abolitionist movement and by their subsequent disillusionment with former comrades who did not place the same value on voting rights for women as for African-American males. A similar disillusionment can be found among women veterans of the Civil Rights movement of the 1950s and 1960s; these women discovered that their male coworkers did not share the same commitment to gender equality that they had made to racial equality.

The anger of female veterans of the Civil Rights movement was not the only source of "second wave" feminism. The discontent of well-educated women confined to suburbia and denied outlets for their talents was another important current, first voiced by Betty Friedan (1963). We encourage students to consider the explanations offered for the growth of "second wave" feminism and try to account for the sudden explosion of feminist thinking and activism that occurred in the late 1960s and early 1970s. At first, I was uncertain whether to include a selection from Friedan's *The Feminine Mystique*, fearing that students would consider it hopelessly dated, but decided that its historical importance justified its inclusion and added the chapter "The Problem That Has No Name." Most of my students found the book still relevant—several decided to read it in its entirety—and one felt it described her life before her recent divorce.

Unit 2: Fault Lines in Women's Studies

After placing women's studies as an academic discipline in its historical and social context, we introduce students to some theoretical divisions in the field. The major theoretical divide is usually considered to be between those who focus on gender difference and those who stress sameness/equality. Both strands of second wave feminist thought challenge the notion of the male as the human norm—the unexamined assumption in all academic disciplines—although they draw very different conclusions. For example, psychologists such as Carol Tavris (generally considered an equality feminist) and Carol Gilligan (generally considered a difference feminist) analyze the ways women are expected to fit into unrealistic psychological roles based on theories of men as the norm. Tavris (1992) begins *Mismeasure of Women* by challenging the fundamental belief in the "normalcy of men and the corresponding abnormality of women" (17) and further challenging us "to expand our visions of normalcy" (20). Yet Tavris stresses dangers of overemphasis on difference and takes issue with Gilligan's stress on women's "different voice" and values. She explores the consequences of "difference feminism," which she thinks sentimentalizes women's capacities. Readings include selections from Tavris' (1992) *Mismeasure of Woman* and from Gilligan's (1982) *In a Different Voice*, which argues that men and women employ different criteria when making moral decisions—women according to an ethic of care, men according to an ethic of rights.

Students are asked to take a preliminary position and try to locate themselves along the sameness/difference continuum. This position will be rethought in light of the range of readings and issues explored during the course. Most report that the characterizations of women's different voice and values ring true to their own experience but generally recognize some of the potential dangers in such an emphasis on difference.

Race/Class Fault Lines

In the 1970s, feminist theorists argued that all disciplines had to be rethought from the perspective of women; however, the idea of a single standpoint of women has been challenged by women of color and by working-class women. Now the charge is leveled that, just as men have done, European American, middle-class women see themselves as the norm and fail to recognize the diversity of women's experience.

The issue was raised by bell hooks in 1981 in *Ain't I a Woman?: Black Women and Feminism*. In her more recent work, *Sisters of the Yam* (1993), she continues to charge that many white, middle-class feminists ignore the specificity of race. Alice Walker (1983) has raised similar concerns and coined the term "womanist" to express what she considers a uniquely African-American approach to feminist thought. Unlike Walker, hooks views the term "feminist" as valid for African-American women as she explores the nature of an African-American approach to feminism. Increasingly, Latina and Asian-American feminists have raised similar concerns. Generally, women of color who have raised such challenges to white, middle-class feminist thought have raised class as well as racial and ethnic issues.

In addition to texts by hooks and Walker, I always include Audre Lorde's (1981) classic "The Master's Tools Will Never Dismantle the Master's House" and Lorde's (1981) "An Open Letter to Mary Daly," where she explores the relationships between African-American and European-American feminists. I also include selections from *This Bridge Called My Back: Writings of Radical Women of Color*, edited by Cherrie Moraga and Gloria Anzaldua (1983), and *Making Face, Making Soul: Haciendo Caras* edited by Gloria Anzaldua (1990), which explore feminist issues from the perspective of Latina women. I am looking forward to including selections from the recently published *Dragon Ladies: Asian American Feminists Breathe Fire* by Sonia Shah (1998).

Generational Fault Lines

In addition to demands that it address cultural diversity, American academic feminism is also being challenged to incorporate the insights and experiences of a new generation of women now in their twenties and thirties. Naomi Wolf (1993) in *Fire with Fire: The New Female Power and How It Will Change the 21st Century*, advocates "power feminism," which she contrasts with what she considers the "victim feminism" of the organized women's movement. Wolf believes that women should embrace the pursuit of power and money, sex and beauty, and sees feminism as essentially a pursuit of power within the existing social system.

Most younger feminists (now often referred to as third wave) who have published books and attracted media attention are white and middle-class. Although they see themselves as very different from the older "feminist establishment," they share the assumption of many of an earlier generation that the European-American, urban, middle-class woman is the norm. Wolf, for example, clearly assumes that her audience is women in the professional-managerial class.

Not all younger feminists see the second wave generation feminists as "victim feminists," and some, like Susan Faludi (1991), have focused instead on continued resistance to equality for women. Increasingly, young women of color such as Veronica Chambers (1996) and Rebecca Walker (1995) are entering the debate, struggling to define feminism in a way they see as relevant to their generation. *Listen Up: Voices from the Next Feminist Generation*, edited by Barbara Findlen (1995), represents a wide range of viewpoints and cultural perspectives and demonstrates the intellectual and cultural diversity of a new generation of feminists now in their late teens and early twenties.

After completion of the fault lines unit, students are asked to stake out a position on the major theoretical issues: sameness/difference divide; race/class fault lines; generational fault lines. The theoretical stance taken has implications for debate on the issues. I also do the assignment, and we all share and respond to each other's papers. At the end of the semester, we rethink the initial paper, taking into account insights gleaned during the course. We then try to account for any changes in our perspectives. This is an ungraded assignment, as it usually involves incorporating much personal material.

Unit 3: The Private Sphere: Rethinking Sexuality, Gender Identity, and Family Ties

At this point, the focus shifts from the historical context out of which women's studies arose and the major theoretical divisions in the field to some of the significant issues feminist theorists have addressed. We decided to organize the course in terms of an analysis of the private and the public spheres, as the challenge to this distinction between public and private has been a major current in feminist thought.

Under the rubric of the private sphere, we have grouped together issues of sexuality, gender identity, and family dynamics. We explore the extent to which conventional ideals of beauty have shaped attitudes toward female sexuality, gender identity, and the life choices available to women. I include selections from Naomi Wolf's (1991) *The Beauty Myth*, which explores ways conventional notions of female beauty and body image have been harmful to women's physical and mental health. Wolf's analysis is, for the most part, limited to the experiences of European-American women and must be supplemented by an analysis of the ways European standards of beauty have shaped the experiences and self-concept of women of color, such as Patricia Hill Collins' (1990) excellent analysis of these issues in *Black Feminist Thought*.

Feminist scholars have analyzed the extent to which the images of female sexuality in pornography have contributed to the oppression of women. I include an interview with Andrea Dworkin (1996) in which she discusses her fight against pornography and her personal reasons for considering this struggle critical to achieving equality for women. Students generally find this interview more accessible than Dworkin's theoretical writings.

My students are usually most interested in exploring the dynamics of the family, and we discuss ways feminist psychologists have mounted a serious challenge to Freudian theories of the development of gender identity and family relationships. Feminist literature on motherhood greatly interests my students, most of whom are mothers. They have shown particular interest in African-American, Asian-American, and Latina feminist scholars' exploration of the ways family roles and the "ethic of care" associated with the maternal role have varied with race and class. They have responded especially well to Patricia Hill Collins' (1990) "Black Women and Motherhood," in *Black Feminist Thought*.

The feminist rethinking of the family has also involved a critique of the notion of heterosexuality as natural and inevitable. I always include Adrienne Rich's (1980) groundbreaking work, which questioned the assumption that heterosexuality is the human norm and has linked what she calls "compulsory heterosexuality" with the persistence of patriarchy.

Feminist scholars have also explored the once-taboo subject of violence within the family and have redefined rape to include spousal rape. Angela Davis (1981) in *Women, Race and Class* places rape, sexual extortion, battering, spousal rape, sexual abuse of children, and incest in a larger sociopolitical context. I also refer students to groundbreaking studies of rape and domestic violence such as Susan Brownmiller's (1975) *Against Our Will*, a work criticized by later feminist writers and scholars but nonetheless an important work that changed the way many view domestic violence.

The family, its traumas and discontents, and the burden of the caregiver role are issues of great interest to my students. Many are struggling with caregiving in their personal lives, and, among those who are employed, many work in low-paid caregiver positions, such as nurses' aides, home health-care workers, and mental health workers in assisted living facilities. The literature on motherhood and caregiving thus segues nicely into the next unit on workplace issues since so many women—particularly low-income women—have jobs that are, in some way, extensions of the caregiver role. Also much research on the impact of women in the workplace has focused on the extent to which labor force attachment can be successfully combined with motherhood.

Unit 4: The Public Sphere: Rethinking the Academy and the Workplace

Feminist scholars have challenged the dichotomy between public and private and in their analysis of the private sphere of the family have raised questions of justice and power usually thought to be political/public issues. Thus, the public sphere has been radically reconceptualized so as to include issues once thought to be exclusively private.

Feminists have brought a new perspective to a range of workplace issues. As always, I despair at the impossibility of including all aspects of the feminist critique of the workplace; all I can do is encourage students to do further reading, take further courses, and continue to explore their own workplace experiences and career ambitions in the light of feminist literature. Although from semester to semester selected readings on workplace issues shift from required readings in the course pack to the recommended reading list, there are some I always try to require.

I usually begin this unit with the struggle of women to enter traditionally male jobs. Possible selections include Kathleen Jamison's (1995) *Beyond the Double Bind: Women and Leadership*, which analyzes the "no-win" or "double-bind" situation (work vs. marriage, childbearing vs. career) as women seek to enter previously all-male careers. Jamison's focus is on professional women; the picture that emerges is considerably bleaker when one looks at the situation of working-class women. This terrain is well covered in "The Wages of the Backlash: The Toll on Working Women" from Susan Faludi's (1991) *Backlash*, which argues that the backlash against feminism during the Reagan years has impeded women's opportunities for employment, promotions, and better pay.

As feminist scholars have explored the consequences of women's entry into the workplace, they have debated whether women will change the workplace or the workplace will change women. Some have argued that what they perceive as feminist values of care and concern for community will transform the corporate world. They see no contradictions between such values and the demands of a market-driven economy. Such an optimistic viewpoint has been contested by other feminist scholars who have focused instead on potential for conflict: the current conflict over affirmative action, sexual harassment, and the continued resistance of employers to flex-time options or on-site child care.

Certainly, women's perspectives on these issues as well as their experiences in the workplace have varied in terms of race and class; such differences emerge most sharply in consideration of women's unpaid labor. Students are always somewhat surprised and intrigued by the extent to which unpaid labor such as housework has been the subject of academic feminists' inquiry. Angela Davis in *Women, Race and Class* (1981) and Linda Gordon in *Pitied, but Not Entitled: Single Mothers and the History of Welfare* (1994) explore the ways in which the social value accorded women's domestic labor has varied with race and class. Although Gordon's book does not easily lend itself to excerpting for a course pack, I rely heavily on her analysis of forces contributing to the development of the Aid to Dependent Children Program and the stigmatization of women on welfare. The welfare issue is particularly pertinent to my students, many of whom have been on welfare or have friends and family members receiving cash assistance. They are quick to pick up the irony that while traditionalists have argued that middle-class women should stay at home and raise families, often such attitudes change dramatically with regard to poor women.

Wherever they are on the socioeconomic ladder—welfare mother or corporate executive—women are responsible for domestic labor, whether they perform such work themselves or assume the responsibility for hiring nannies and domestic servants. I always include selections from Arlie Hochschild's (1989) *The Second Shift*, which argues that equitable division of domestic labor is still a distant goal. (My students do not think much has changed in the nine years since its publication.) I also always include selections from Mary Romero's *Maid in the U.S.A.* (1992), which explores housework as both paid and unpaid activity and considers the intersections of class, race, and gender.

I like to conclude this section with bell hooks' (1993: 41–52) "Work Makes Life Sweet," which traces her search to discover the work she has been "called" to do. My students are all searching for meaningful work, and, although I want them aware of the pitfalls, I also do not want them to despair of finding it. Students attend school in just such a search to find meaningful work, and we now turn our attention to the feminist critique of the educational establishment.

In our society there is an increasingly powerful connection between workplace and educational opportunities. Feminist scholars have turned their attention to the ways in which educational institutions have served or failed to serve girls. Feminism poses a challenge to standard pedagogy and the standard curriculum, as well as to how schools are structured—a fundamental challenge to the ways schools have served women and girls. Much of the research contending that teachers are more likely to call on boys and to praise boys for their ideas and girls for the form and appearance of their work has been challenged recently. I encourage students to do their own research by observations of male/female behavior in the classes they are taking this semester.

Feminist scholars such as Mary Belenky et al. (1986) have also explored women's "different ways of knowing," and feminist educators have studied what may be distinctly feminist styles of teaching. The work by Belenky, Clinchy, Goldberger, and Tarule can be seen as an example of "difference feminism," which brings us back to some of the theoretical issues earlier in the course. We find ourselves continually returning to the sameness/difference distinction as we explore feminist perspectives on a range of issues. Again I encourage students to do their own research and to analyze the teaching/learning styles of their classmates and instructors.

Unit 5: The Public Sphere: Rethinking the Civic and Political Sphere

The final set of issues grouped under the public sphere includes women's participation in political and civic life. Feminist scholars have broadened their definition of the political, bringing subjects once considered private, such as child care and domestic violence, into the realm of public debate.

Feminist scholars have also explored the role women have played in public life, particularly their rich history of civic involvement and voluntary activity. The highly gendered nature of women's participation in voluntary organizations has been explored, and considerable attention paid to the extent to which women have formed voluntary associations around their roles as mothers. Difference feminists such as Sara Ruddick (1992) have tended to celebrate maternalist movements and the "ethic of care" they have espoused. Others have called attention to the limitations of maternalist movements and the ways such movements have contributed to gender stereotypes. We consider the extent to which the maternalist ideology, which has been intertwined with so much of women's participation in public life, has aided or retarded the struggle for women's equality. A "must" read is Sara Ruddick's (1992) essay "From Maternal Thinking to Peace Politics," in which she modifies her earlier celebration of motherhood and maternalist social movements and argues for a "mother-respecting feminism," which can include men and women working together for social change.

The issues explored in this unit connect directly to the service learning option. Students have the option of substituting volunteer hours at an organization that serves women or advocates for women's issues and writing a brief report on their experiences or writing an academic essay exploring one of the issues discussed in one of the major units of the course.

COURSE REQUIREMENTS

This is the unpleasant part of the course. I would love to think that I conduct a reading group, that students are motivated solely by an interest in women's studies, and that messy subjects of grading and evaluation do not apply. Unfortunately, they do apply, and I continually struggle with working out a set of requirements that enhance learning, stimulate enthusiasm, and are academically respectable. Under the influence of my colleague and course codeveloper, Elise Freed-Fagan, I have moved in the direction of a series of short assignments rather than a major project. The mix keeps changing every semester, and I am still struggling.

The assignments include a journal in which students record their reactions to the readings and class discussions and an oral report in which students respond to one of the works in the course pack. The writing assignments include:

1. An initial position on the major theoretical issues—the sameness/difference divide, race/class fault lines, and generational fault lines.

2. A brief summary of their observations of differences in male/female behavior in the classes they are taking this semester.

3. A response to the book they chose to read in its entirety. This can be one of the books excerpted in the course pack or one of the books on the recommended reading list.

4. *One* of the following:

   - a six- to seven-page essay exploring one of the issues discussed in one of the major units of the course.
   - ten hours of volunteer service at a women's organization and a two- to three-page report on their experiences and observations.
   - a six- to seven-page bibliographic essay that evaluates the resources available to women's studies majors and feminist activists on the Internet.

I continually tinker with this mix and am resigned to the fact that my Introduction to Women's Studies course will always be a work in progress, modified in response to feedback from students and colleagues and my own evolving sense of what the course should include.

I constantly have to remind myself that this is an introductory course—a starting point. If I do a reasonably good job, students will be able to take further courses in areas I was unable to include or treated only superficially. I look at my syllabus in despair and see only the gaps. Where is the section on women's spirituality? On eco-feminism? On women in the military? I try to make students aware of what is missing and try not to drive myself crazy agonizing over what is omitted. Interestingly, I do not feel anything like this torment when I teach my Introductory Humanities course, which is supposed to cover the ancient world to the Renaissance in fourteen weeks. For so many of us, teaching women's studies is not a job, a profession, but a cause, a calling. Maybe if we are lucky, some of our students will feel the same way.

SUGGESTED READINGS

Bell, D. and R. Klein, eds. 1996. *Radically speaking: Feminism reclaimed.* Melbourne: Spinifex.

Findlen, B., ed. 1995. *Listen Up: Voices from the next feminist generation.* Seattle, WA: Seal.

Guy-Sheftall, B., ed. 1995. *Words of fire: An anthology of African-American feminist thought.* New York: New Press: Distributed by W. W. Norton.

Hirsch, M. and E. F. Keller, eds. 1983. *Conflicts in feminism.* New York: Routledge.

Moraga, C. and G. Anzaldua, eds. 1981. *This bridge called my back: Writings of radical women of color.* Watertown, MA: Persephone.

Shah, S. 1988. *Dragon ladies: Asian American feminists breathe fire.* Boston: South End.

4

Reading Women's Lives: A New Database Resource for Teaching Introduction to Women's Studies

Mary Margaret Fonow, The Ohio State University
with Lucy Bailey, The Ohio State University

Introduction to Women's Studies is the gateway course to the field of women's studies. Students learn who we are as a community of scholars and activists and make judgments about the validity of our endeavor. They also discover, many for the first time, the rich details of women's lives and experiences and learn how to make sense of this information. It has been described by many of our students as an "eye-opening" course and by a few as a "lifesaving" course, and the pleasure of watching this process of discovery, struggle, and survival keeps many of us engaged in teaching the course over the years.

At the same time the introductory course is a challenge to teach. Students come to us with little knowledge about the field of women's studies, and sometimes they come with preconceptions about the course that make them apprehensive about their decision to enroll. The majority of our students enroll to satisfy general education requirements, but some enroll to satisfy their curiosity about the field. Students say again and again, "This course is nothing like I thought it would be; it is so much better."

In this chapter we introduce and analyze a new resource developed and managed by the women's studies faculty at The Ohio State University (OSU) and published by Simon & Schuster. This resource is the CORE (Custom on Demand Resources) Program in Women's Studies—a database of women's studies classics, popular articles, and cutting-edge scholarship—which allows instructors, including non-Ohio State University instructors, to customize a reader for their own Introduction to Women's Studies course and even to add nondatabase

articles at extra cost. We also discuss the results of a study we conducted in the
spring of 1998 to measure student learning outcomes and student reaction to
Reading Women's Lives: An Introduction to Women's Studies, a series of readers
we designed from the CORE database.

INSTITUTIONAL CONTEXT

Ohio State is a large public research university with an undergraduate student
population of 37,703, over 90% of whom are from the state of Ohio. Women
are 49% of this population, and minority students are 17%, with African-
Americans (9%) the largest group. The average age of the undergraduate population is twenty-two years, and 80% of the undergraduates attend full-time. The
average American College Test (ACT) score of the first-year class is 24.

Women's studies at Ohio State is a mature program offering a comprehensive
graduate and undergraduate curriculum with course work in culture and representation; policy, politics, and social change; global issues; and diversity. Each
year about 1,700 students enroll in the introductory course, which meets both
general education and social diversity requirements. In the history of the program over 35,000 students have taken a course. The database was developed by
Ohio State University women's studies faculty, one of the largest in the country.
Faculty expertise covers a broad range including film, art, race, health and reproduction, work, public policy, feminist theory, feminist methodology, sexuality, politics and feminist movements, literature, global issues, biography,
folklore, and law. There is depth in feminist theory, visual arts, public policy,
social movements, Black women's studies, and area studies including Africa,
Asia, and Latin America. Faculty are balanced between the social sciences and
the humanities, with expertise in interdisciplinary and cross-cultural forms of
analysis.

CORE DATABASE IN WOMEN'S STUDIES

The CORE database contains over 300 articles, essays, documents, short stories, and poems selected by Ohio State faculty in eighteen topic areas in
women's studies.[1] A brief introduction places each piece in its historical context,
tells something about the author, and gives a sense of how the piece illuminates
key concepts, issues, and controversies in the field of women's studies. Following each piece are discussion questions that ask students to analyze and interpret
the selection and, in some cases, to connect it to other readings. The topics
include standard areas such as health, feminism and women's movements, and
violence as well as newer interests such as autobiography, science and technology, and the body. Rounding out the list are difference and inequality; education;
family relations; international perspectives; language; law and legal theory;
motherhood and reproduction; politics, government, and public policy; religion;
sexualities; representation and culture; and work, poverty, and economic policy.

Each topic area is introduced by a four- to five-page essay written by faculty. The essay provides a framework for thinking about the topic, orients students to some of the debates or controversies within the topic area, and calls attention to the ways diversity can be incorporated within the topic. The contributing faculty member was responsible for selecting, reviewing, and advising the editorial board on appropriate articles for the database. The overall project is governed by an editorial board chosen from faculty who teach the course and who reflect interdisciplinary and discipline-based training in history (Susan Hartmann), French and film (Judith Mayne), education (Elizabeth Allan), sociology (Mary Margaret Fonow), literature and black studies (Martha Wharton), and feminist policy studies (Nancy Campbell).

RATIONALE FOR THE PROJECT

There were both intellectual and practical reasons for this project. First, writing and reading are the very core of what faculty do, and many were dismayed by reports from the field that reading was somehow passé with students steeped in media images. Reading and good writing are interconnected and important to college learning. How could we avoid pitting these mutually pleasurable activities against each other? Perhaps an infusion of new types of reading that speak more directly to today's student would rekindle an interest in the printed word.

Our second concern was how to manage the large volume of published materials in the field of women's studies and in the women's movement while capturing the richness, complexity, and diversity of feminist interdisciplinary scholarship. We have found that our students benefit from exposure to a variety of materials. It helps them to understand the connections between the global and the local; to understand the implications of race, class, sexuality, disability, and other categories of difference in the lives and experiences of women; and to appreciate the variety of approaches to analyzing and interpreting women's lives and forms of activism. We also wanted materials that would demonstrate the efficacy of political, social, and personal action so that students would not be demoralized about the possibility of change.

Thirdly, we believe that students would begin to develop better critical reasoning skills if we provided them with materials that were more explicit about the various ways knowledge is constructed and interpreted across the humanities, arts, and social sciences. How do feminists construct, challenge, and defend knowledge claims? By incorporating different genres of inquiry from art criticism and literature to policy reports, social surveys, and journalism we hope to demonstrate that different genres use different tools of analysis and that each requires different forms of interpretation. Students, we hope, can begin to develop criteria for evaluating the adequacy of knowledge claims in light of the type of arguments being made or the mode of inquiry being used.

Finally, a database of high-quality articles would provide instructors with a choice of materials designed specifically for the topics and for the level of instruction typically found in the introductory course from which they could customize their own reader. In this format any instructor can change the readings each term to accommodate changes in the demographics and skill level of each class. Students do not waste money purchasing books with readings that are never assigned. Simon & Schuster has reduced a significant burden for the teacher by securing all of the reprint permissions for the articles in the database in advance and has a reputation for high-quality work. Most of the effort involved in putting together a course packet has been done for the instructor, and the finished product is more attractive by being bound in book form with its own cover.

The CORE database in women's studies has been used by our faculty to produce ten different customized readers for five faculty members. They found that the database combines the advantages of standardization and peer review with flexibility and choice. Faculty created readers that combine the classics in the field with more contemporary selections, that mix and match genres, that incorporate diversity, and that internationalize content. At the same time the instructors could play to their own intellectual training, strengths, and interests.

A reader can be designed to cover a few areas in depth or to provide an overview of a large number of topic areas. Many of the articles fit in more than one topic area. For example, "The Globetrotting Sneaker" by Enloe (1995) is currently listed under the Work, Poverty and Economic Policy topic. If an instructor did not choose this topic for a reader but wanted the Enloe article included, it could be placed under an area such as International. Because the introductory essays to the topics do not refer to specific articles, instructors can place individual articles where they like or create a collection of articles without any topic essay, taking full advantage of the flexibility in the system.

Furthermore, faculty can view the entire data set at their own convenience, including the full text of the 300 articles, on a CD-ROM available from Simon & Schuster. The publishers also have a complimentary sample reader containing the complete list of articles and selected texts, introductory essays, and discussion questions for three of the topic areas. (See information in note 1.)

Faculty have used readers as the only text in the course and in combination with other texts. For example, we combined Fonow's 1996 workbook *Women, Culture and Society* with a customized reader.[2] The workbook builds critical thinking skills, encourages discussion, and acquaints students with research models and facts about the status of women. In combination with the reader, the workbook exercises create an effective tool for students to integrate knowledge from the reader with real-life experience. The workbook covers ten of the topics found in the database.

STUDENT SURVEY

We have been using the CORE database at Ohio State since 1996. At the end of spring quarter 1998 we conducted a student survey to gauge the reader's

Table 4.1
Student Evaluation of Pedagogical Features

Questions	Strongly Disagree 1	Disagree 2	3	Agree 4	Strongly Agree 5
Recommend book (N=146)	5%	13%	21%	29%	32%
Variety was advantage to learning (N=146)	3%	3%	22%	41%	31%
Intro to articles helped me to understand why the article was written (N=162)	2%	7%	27%	36%	27%
Discussion questions stimulated thinking (N=150)	7%	20%	41%	21%	11%
Intro to sections provided good overview of the topic (N=149)	4%	7%	35%	33%	21%

effectiveness as a learning tool in three sections of the introductory course. Of the 151 respondents 87% were female, and 13% male, 77% were white, 21% were students of color, and 2% were biracial. Eight percent identified as either bisexual or uncertain about their sexual preference; 92% identified as straight. Respondents were primarily middle-class, with 35% listing family income of $41,000–$60,000. Finally, 64% of the students said they read 75% or more of the reader; 23% read 50%–74% of the reader.

Asked what three adjectives they would use to describe the reader to a friend, 56% said interesting; 23% said informative; 15% long; 11% thought-provoking; 9% educational; 9% diverse; 6% enlightening; 6% boring; 5% each "feministic" and powerful. Other adjectives used at least once were amazing, analytical, complex, depressing, mellow, provocative, shocking, and touching. Students were generally positive in their overall assessment of the reader, with 61% agreeing or strongly agreeing with the statement, "I would recommend this book to others" (see Table 4.1).

Students also liked the variety: 72% agreed or strongly agreed with the statement, "The variety of articles included in the reader (literary, research, personal narratives, magazine articles, etc.) was an advantage to my learning." Students' opinions about specific features of the readers varied. The majority (63%) agreed or strongly agreed that "[t]he introductions to the articles helped me to better understand the reasons the article was written," but 41% were neutral about the

Table 4.2
Student Evaluation of Diversity and Interest

Questions	Not at all 1	2	3	4	Very much 5
Increased interest in course (N=143)	5%	11%	24%	46%	13%
Think about issues from different perspectives (N=146)	1%	5%	23%	38%	32%
Addressed race and ethnicity (N=150)	0%	3%	25%	41%	31%
Addressed class (N=146)	0%	8%	25%	40%	27%
Addressed gay and lesbian issues (N=145)	0%	7%	30%	44%	19%

usefulness of discussion questions. One-third agreed or strongly agreed with the statement, ''The discussion questions stimulated my thinking on the topic.'' Our experience with writing and using discussion questions leads us to believe that their value depends on how the instructor uses them. Students do not take them seriously unless the instructor lays the groundwork. Over half (54%) agreed or strongly agreed with the statement, ''The 4–5 page introductions to the sections provided a good general overview of the topic.'' One-third were neutral about this feature of the reader. These essays are a good way to introduce the uniqueness of women's studies' perspectives on topics often covered in other disciplines to students with little knowledge of our field. The essays also provide coherency, making the connections between diverse topics and articles more apparent to students.

Most respondents (59%) indicated that the reader increased their interest in the introductory course (Table 4.2). There are indications that we are achieving some of the goals we established for the reader. One goal is to confront the notion that there is a monolithic feminist position on the issues and topics covered in the course. By including work by and about diverse groups of women from a variety of feminist perspectives we help students to see the complex dimensions of the issues we address. For example, the section on Violence presents a variety of feminist positions on pornography, such as Hill and Silver's (1993) explication of antipornography civil rights ordinances and the contrasting position of Duggan (1995) on the dangers of censorship. This section also includes articles, essays, and literary representations on intimate violence written by women from various racial, cultural, and social groups, including Dorothy Allison's (1988) heart-wrenching short story ''Mama'' and Zora Neale Hurston's (1926) enigmatic story ''Sweat.''

Another explicit goal for the reader is to increase student awareness of the variations in power and status among different groups of women in the United States and of the contributions of marginalized women to the creation of knowledge and interpretations about women's lives. To make this point we include a range of materials from Audre Lorde's (1984a) classic essay on difference from *Sister Outsider* to poet Judith Ortiz Cofer's (1993) narrative about her desire to convey a more complex portrait of Latin women through creative writing. We also seek to make visible the role of different groups of women in the struggle for justice and for women's rights, illustrated in a *New York Times* article by Carvajal (1996) about the oppressive working conditions of immigrant women and their activism to improve conditions for domestic service workers. In our survey 70% of the respondents responded positively to the question, ''To what extent did the articles help you to think about issues from different perspectives?''

The section on Difference and Inequality provides a framework for understanding how differences of class, culture, race, sexuality, and disability become the basis of exclusion, inequality, and struggle. Included in this section are analytic pieces on intersectionality such as Zinn and Dill's (1996) *Feminist Studies* article ''Theorizing Difference from Multiracial Feminism'' and writing on specific forms of difference such as King's (1993) reflections on disability. In addition, throughout the other seventeen sections we integrate attention to inequality and difference among women. The Health and Medicine section, for example, includes Linda Villarosa's (1994) introduction to *Body and Soul: The Black Women's Guide to Physical Health and Emotional Well-Being* and an article from *Canadian Woman's Studies* by Ramsay (1994) concerning heterosexist assumptions and practices in the health care professions and their implications for lesbian health. Almost three-fourths of the respondents responded affirmatively to the question, ''To what extent did the reader address questions of race and ethnicity?'' Sixty-seven percent thought class issues had been adequately addressed; for gay and lesbian issues the response was 63%.

A number of open-ended questions were designed to elicit information on learning outcomes.[3] We asked, ''What are the three most significant things you have learned from your reading assignments?'' The patterns we found indicate that students (1) broaden their understanding of feminism; (2) realize that sexism, inequality, and oppression exist and that a women's movement is needed; (3) gain an understanding of women's role in society and in history; (4) become more open to other viewpoints; and (5) find applications to personal life. The topics that appear to be significant to students are violence, eating disorders, suffrage, media, and diversity.

We also asked what students remembered from the reader about the meaning of feminism. For many students feminism means equality for all and rights for women—and that men can be feminists. For example, one student wrote that ''feminists are women and perhaps men who seek a fairer treatment for all people, regardless of their differences.'' Another wrote that ''[feminism] is not only [a] fight for the benefit of women but for the benefit of all being.'' A third student wrote, "To me . . . feminism means wanting equality. Wanting to make the table round so that anyone can sit down." Another theme involves empowerment and personal transformation. For some students feminism is standing up for yourself. "When I consider feminist I think of a person who is a strong supporter of the idea of women controlling themselves—physically, mentally and economically." Another student wrote, "I believe a feminist is anyone who believes in equality between the sexes and strives to make changes in their own lives." Some students believe that feminism is different things to different groups of women: "Feminists come in all shapes, forms and with different opinions and not all agree." Other students were relieved to learn that feminism and heterosexuality were not incompatible. "The reader has definitely changed my thinking about feminism. The article that comes to mind is the one about heterosexual feminism. Now, I perceive the word feminist as pertaining to any woman who acknowledges the progress her gender has made yet points to the future and says, this is where we have to go, what still has to be achieved."

For a few students the reader confirmed their negative assessments of feminism. One student responded that feminists were "people who would rather complain about the status quo than do something about it! That feminism is accepting of all views (accept [sic] ones that oppose theirs!)." Another student wrote, "Feminists are complainers." Someone did respond with "man hater, lesbian" as words that came to mind when that student thinks of feminism—a response, we hope, from one of the few students who did not read the book!

Two questions gauged students' understanding of difference. The first was, "In thinking about differences among women what ideas, poems, or stories about race, class, sexuality, or disability stand out in your mind?" The articles most frequently mentioned debunked welfare myths, discussed eating disorders among women of color, told about coming out, discussed problems and challenges of single motherhood, deconstructed stereotypes about Latinas, reconciled being heterosexual and feminist, debated gay marriage, and analyzed the experiences of women with disabilities. Writers cited most often were Walker, Lorde, Cofer, King, Frye, Thompson, Villarosa, Williams, Pharr, Kimmel, and Bray. "The reader helped destroy some stereotypes about welfare. Also I learned of the legal problems gay couples have." Another student wrote, "The welfare and coming out readings helped provide me with a view I'd never really thought of before, and again, helped me disassociate these people with certain stereotypes." "The thing that stands out in the topic of difference would be the womanist writing by Alice Walker that we read. Womanism seemed so much warmer and real than traditional feminism." The second question concerned their understanding of multiple and intersecting differences, and we asked for an example from the reader of a woman who was grappling with two or more aspects of her identity. The most frequently selected example was that of a Black woman coming out.

We also want students to gain some knowledge about the experiences of women activists and included selections covering a variety of issues from suffrage, to breast cancer activism, to lesbian organizing at the Fourth World Conference on Women. We asked students in our survey to discuss the personal and/or social value of studying women's activism and to identify activists or acts of protest from the reader that demonstrated the value of social change. The two most common responses to this question were that it was empowering to read about activism and that it was educational and enlightening to read about women's historical struggle for equality. The movements students were most likely to cite were suffrage (women getting the right to vote) and Take Back the Night (affirming women's entitlement to safe, violence-free mobility). The activists most frequently mentioned were Susan B. Anthony, Elizabeth Cady Stanton, and women during World War II. Getting one mention each were bell hooks, Charlotte Bunch, Alice Walker, Alice Paul, Sojourner Truth, "my mom," and the Guerrilla Girls (an anonymous group of activists who expose inequities in the display, sale, and distribution of art).

Finally, we asked what was learned of significance about the representation of women in popular media and cultural arts. Three main themes emerged: the objectification of women and the male gaze; the invisibility of women; and viewing the media as a place where women can express themselves and where they can reach other women. One student wrote, "I learned that women exhibited their art centuries ago, even when their lives were at stake. Art really must have meant a lot to them." Another wrote, "I learned about the objectification of women and the harm it can do, indirectly, in terms of social violence." Some saw the media as both objectifying women and also offering them an area of expression. "I realized how badly women have been portrayed in media but I also learned how women have moved forward through music and expression."

CONCLUSION

The reader helped us to meet many of the goals of the introductory course. Student responses show that their view of feminism has broadened, and they are more likely to hold a more complex view of feminism. Many students were able to see that feminism is a creditable mode of analysis that can be evaluated on the same basis as other systems of knowledge. One student wrote, "I'm keeping the book because it's a great reference base for future courses I take as well as interacting with others. I think it has great material."

Students liked the variety of materials. We think the variety increases the likelihood that students with different learning styles and preferences can be accommodated. Some students access the ideas embedded in the course through creative writing and personal narratives, while facts, statistics, and analysis are more important to others. One student wrote, "I like the reader because it's not some boring book written by one person. It's compiled with different articles by different people with different viewpoints. I like that." Students who dislike standard social science models of analysis nonetheless find something beneficial in the reader. "The stories that were real and connected to the reader were the most beneficial to my understanding of what and why this [eating disorders] went on."

Student responses regarding difference reminded us that this is the first time most of our students have been confronted with so much knowledge about so many different groups of women. At first they are just amazed that everyone is not the same, meaning not just like themselves. By the end of the course students seem to develop an understanding that women have multiple and intersecting identities and that inequality based on difference is still a fact of life. Eventually, they come to see that more than sexism is operating in the lives of women and that feminism is not the sole prerogative of white, middle-class women. At the same time some comments made us realize that we need to search for more materials about dominant groups and feminism. They want to know that they do not have to give up who they are in order to challenge the system. One student wrote, ''I thought it [the reader] made me understand more about why women are the way they are. That I am not the only one that thinks [in] these ways. I had articles that I thought my boyfriend should read and he was interested in them. But I thought there could be more in it about white middle-class women.''

The *Reading Women's Lives* database is an ongoing project. Each year the faculty will add thirty new readings. The database will grow as the field of women's studies grows and will stay on top of current issues and trends. The variety of selections, the special features, the flexibility, and the ease of using the database should appeal to instructors and students.

NOTES

Editors' note: Every effort has been made to provide current Internet information. However, readers are advised that Internet and e-mail addresses are subject to change.

1. For a complete list of citations for all the articles see the Simon & Schuster Web site at *www.sscp.com/womens_studies*, or for more information call at 888–847–1744 or e-mail at *women's_studies@prenhall.com*.

2. For information on the workbook *Women, Culture and Society: A Student Workbook for Introduction to Women's Studies* write Kendall/Hunt Publishing Company, 4050 Westmark Drive, P.O. Box 1840, Dubuque, IA 52004–1840 or call 1–800–228–0810. Web site: *www.kendallhunt.com*

3. All student comments are verbatim.

SUGGESTED READINGS

Bartholomae, D. and A. Petrosky. 1996. *Ways of reading: An anthology for writers.* Boston: St. Martin's.

Goldberger, N., J. Tarule, B. Clinchy, and M. Belenky. 1996. *Knowledge, difference, and power: Essays inspired by ''Women's Ways of Knowing.''* New York: Basic Books.

hooks, b. 1994. *Teaching to transgress: Education as the practice of freedom.* New York: Routledge.

Lather, P. 1991. *Getting smart: Feminist research and pedagogy with/in the postmodern.* New York: Routledge.

Part III

THEORIZING EXPECTATIONS

5

Border Zones: Identification, Resistance, and Transgressive Teaching in Introductory Women's Studies Courses

Katherine Ann Rhoades, University of Wisconsin, Eau Claire

"The whole aspect of femminism [*sic*]," laments a student in a journal entry recorded midway through an introductory women's studies course, "can begin to wear you out a little." This comment reflects one of the many concerns twenty freshman and sophomore women students expressed in journals they submitted as part of a qualitative research study that explored patterns of identification and resistance in a science-based introductory women's studies health course at a large public university in the Midwest.[1]

Because academic practice and research are invariably contextualized by the distinctiveness of the institutional setting where they occur as well as by the particularity of the student population involved (Luke 1996), this chapter begins with a brief introduction to the institution where the research was conducted, followed by a description of the research participants and the introductory women's studies course in which they were enrolled. This introduction is intended to lend a specific context for the ensuing data analysis, which first challenges existing models of identification and resistance in introductory women's studies courses and then suggests a conceptual revisioning of that process. The chapter concludes with a discussion of teaching strategies that link this revision with a transgressive teaching agenda.

INSTITUTIONAL CONTEXT

The university that served as the site for this research considers itself a world-class institution, a perception validated, in part, by its impressive standing on nearly every list ranking the nation's top public universities. It attracts many of the state's most academically promising students and is described by many equally promising out-of-state students seeking entrance to a competitive school as a "good but safe second choice." The university has been reasonably successful in attracting international students and also actively recruits racially diverse students, faculty, and staff. Nevertheless, it remains a predominantly white institution.

Given its proud history of progressive politics, the university generally has supported the Women's Studies Program both in spirit and in practice by applauding as well as funding its initiatives. Despite this relatively privileged position within the institution that houses it, the Women's Studies Program—like the majority of its national and international counterparts—faces mounting challenges. These challenges range from teaching a student body that is less political and more conservative and materialistic than students from any previous generation, to encountering increasing numbers of students who cling to a strong sense of individualism as they assert that feminism holds little, if any, relevance to their lives. The program is influenced further by wider campaigns fueled by increasingly vocal factions that express disdain toward the inclusion of diversity issues in education. Taken to its extreme, this disdainful commentary accuses women's studies programs of re-creating the very oppressions that they set out to dismantle (see Patai and Koertge 1994; Roiphe 1993; Lehrman 1993).

PARTICIPANT PROFILE AND CLASSROOM SETTING

All of the students who voluntarily participated in this research project were enrolled in the same introductory women's studies course, one of the university's most popular course offerings. Each semester 400 students enroll in this semester-long course, and as many as 1,500 others attempt to register after enrollment has reached capacity. The core course content is presented in two fifty-minute lectures each week. These lectures are accompanied by weekly fifty-minute discussion sections where approximately twenty students and a teaching assistant engage in lively sessions linking social, cultural, political, and economic dynamics of diverse groups of women to the topics at hand. Intersections of diversity among women in terms of race, ethnicity, sexuality, ableness, age, and other dimensions of difference serve as cornerstones for these discussions.

The course draws a diverse group of students. Many who are interested in women's studies enroll because it is a required course for students majoring in, or earning a certificate in, women's studies. A number of other students with wide-ranging interests enroll with the hopes of meeting science requirements without taking on the burden of what they fear will be a more taxing science course. Still others, both men and women, explain that they enroll because they are motivated to learn more about women's bodies.

Eighty students in the four sections I taught as one of the course's teaching assistants were invited to participate in this research study by writing journals describing their responses to the course, especially commenting on their reactions to feminism and the intertwining systems, including gender, race, class, and sexuality, that reside at its core. Participation in the study was optional, and students' grades were assigned before the journals were analyzed so the students could be assured that the content of their journals would not negatively influence their course grades. Students were assured anonymity and were encouraged to write an honest, fully descriptive critical commentary.

As a group, the twenty students who completed the semester-long project accurately reflect the demographics of the students who routinely enroll in this class and the university's student population at large, with two notable exceptions. No international students participated, and all of the participants are women.

Despite their shared gender, the students differed in other ways. Two-thirds were middle-class, and the remaining one-third were evenly distributed between working-class and upper-class backgrounds. They also varied in terms of regional representation, with close to two-thirds claiming roots in small to mid-sized communities mostly in the Midwest and the other one-third in metropolitan areas scattered across the United States or bicoastal urban communities. Two students were adult returning students, one of whom was a single mother. Four others identify as women of color: one African-American, one Asian-American, one Chicana whose parents are first-generation immigrants to the United States, and one Latina. Two students, one Christian and one Jewish, identify religion as salient to their identity. Sixteen identified as heterosexual, while two refused a label to define their sexuality, and two others identified as bisexual.

The journal data that this group of students produced were extensive, rich, and highly subjective, which was desirable given the research focus. Data analysis began with multiple readings of the journal entries after they were entered word for word into a computer file, which, in turn, facilitated identification of shared themes as well as variations to those themes. Journals as data sources are particularly helpful—as Patricia Bell Scott (1994) has also argued—because of their effectiveness at looking at multiple realities in a form that follows from a relatively unencumbered state of consciousness. As the analysis proceeded, the individual stories embedded in the journals became useful theoretical projects because they attempted to move beyond dominant discourses even as they were informed by them (cf. Tsing 1993). Finally, perhaps the greatest excitement resulting from a collective analysis of these individual journals comes from the data's effectiveness in unsettling as well as expanding the familiar models that have defined students' patterns of identification and resistance in introductory women's studies classrooms.

MODELS OF IDENTIFICATION AND RESISTANCE

In her review of the literature that had been produced by the mid-1970s, describing students' responses to introductory women's studies classes, Marjorie

Devault (1976) identified one widely accepted linear model used by women's studies educators to chart students' progression. The model began with periods of confusion, moved to acceptance of a new belief system, and culminated with students' reaching a position where they could reinterpret their past experiences and relationships according to this new belief system. The progression Devault summarizes is remarkably similar to Johnella Butler et al.'s (1991: 219) description written fourteen years later. Butler et al. describe the "identifiable series of moments of recognition" that women's studies students typically undergo after they experience a period of initial confusion:

Awareness of structures oppressive to women is followed by moments of empowerment in which patriarchal frameworks and perceptions are modified, redefined, or rejected altogether and replaced by a newly emerging view of the self and society. (1991: 219)

Two additional studies (Bargad and Hyde 1991; Lather 1991b) suggest a similar pattern of response but focus on different aspects of the process. Adena Bargad and Janet Hyde conclude from their study, which involved collecting quantitative and qualitative data from 189 students enrolled in three different introductory women's studies courses, that the students from all three courses perceived themselves as actively committed to feminism by the end of the semester. Patti Lather, on the other hand, argues for a more flexible model and suggests that at any given point in the process some students may align with resistance rather than feminist identification. Though Lather's framework includes the familiar process of feminist identity development beginning with ignorance and ending in liberation, it does allow for students' resistance to oppositional knowledge. Further, Lather acknowledges what others fail to consider by drawing attention to the complexity of negotiating new meanings that challenge the scripts and cultural models students have relied on to frame their gendered lives. By accounting for acceptance *and* rejection Lather introduces more variation in responses than the other models, but her framework retains preordained stages of feminist identification that fail to account fully for the variety of student responses.

The following analysis challenges the previously discussed models, which characterize the process of feminist identification in introductory women's studies classes as a prescribed progression from ignorance to enlightenment. Contrary to these models, this study's findings suggest that identification and resistance function less as oppositional pillars supporting a predictable continuum and more as partners in a tango performed on a shifting stage upheld by varying relations of power, privilege, and oppression, which, in turn, are anchored within specific historical contexts and cultural scripts.

BORDER ZONES AND SKIRMISHES

One major theme of the student journals emerged from repeated accounts of feeling excluded from the course content, particularly the feminist aspects of it.

An interrelated theme extended from the detailed and often painful expressions of personal discomfort and cognitive dissonance that accompanied this sense of exclusion. A closer analysis of these major themes reveals that the students conceptualized their introduction to women's studies course as representing a border zone. Entry into this zone often meant that they had to renegotiate previously held worldviews and reconsider dominant constructions of femininity, coming face-to-face with how these constructions may affect their daily lives, sometimes by limiting their choices or curtailing their options. Faced with this border zone and its perceived entry requirements, the students engaged in a number of skirmishes as they both identified with certain aspects of the course and heartily resisted others.

The absence of any sense of a unified process in the students' responses suggests that their experiences represent a dynamic cycle that falls beyond the reach of the previously discussed models of feminist identification in introductory women's studies courses. The students' patterns of identification and resistance in this study may be read as similar in design, though certainly not in intensity, to anthropologist Renato Rosaldo's (1989: 211) description of the acculturation of immigrants into a dominant culture as they "both comply and deviate, bobbing and weaving between assimilation and resistance." One of the more powerful examples of this acculturation process comes from Gloria Anzaldua in *Borderlands/La Frontera* (1987) when—writing from a Chicana lesbian perspective—she describes the new mestiza (a person of mixed ancestry) as coping with her position by developing a tolerance for contradictions and ambiguity as she learns to be Indian in Mexican culture and to be Mexican within an Anglo point of view. She accomplishes this by learning to juggle cultures and ultimately strengthens her identity by weaving together disparate and overlapping cultural strands.

These images of negotiating differences at border zones are an instructive way to conceptualize the tango students perform when faced with theories and practices in introductory women's studies courses that disrupt their worldviews and unsettle their place within them. In the discussion that follows I draw on data from the student journals to illuminate the concepts of border zones by explaining some of the skirmishes that take place there. This discussion serves as an introduction to the final section, which focuses on how teaching strategies infused with understandings of these processes may assist students in negotiating the cultural drift that they often experience in introductory women's studies courses.

STORIES FROM THE BORDERLANDS

In at least half of the twenty journals, students begin by describing their initial fears of taking a women's studies course. The following is among the more descriptive:

I was sure that the class would be filled with four or five hundred raging, die-hard feminists who would men bash telling of all the evils men have created. I guess you could say I was a little nervous.

Ten other students echoed this student's nervousness. Referring to feminists as "big time radicals" and "brutes" who "live and breathe" feminism, the students registered fears of, and disdain for, what they perceive as an alien, angry, overpowering, and dangerous feminist image. Taken together, their descriptions construct feminists as a large, undifferentiated, angry mass of women who are out of control ("raging"); hateful toward men ("male bashers") and yet masculine ("brutes"); and zealously and exclusively committed to feminist causes ("die-hard," "live and breathe"). These comments, typically focusing on negative appraisals of feminism in terms of public displays of appearance and behavior, bespeak a remarkably similar, internalized cultural stereotype of feminists that stands in direct opposition to students' allegiances, however controversial and incomplete, to dominant constructions of a feminine ideal (Bauer with Rhoades 1996).

Students also described how their initial fears about the class were quelled. For example, one student explained, "I felt better when someone told me that I can be a feminist and still shave the hair on my legs and under my arms." At least half of the students questioned how aligning with feminism would undermine their femininity. One adult returning student who is a single mother asked but did not answer:

Can feminists be feminine? Can they wear makeup, enjoy wearing a skirt or something cute or pretty vs. 1960s or all cotton? Can feminists be mothers who like to hug and cuddle their kids? Can they enjoy being in a relationship with a man where romance feels good?

This student by implication placed feminism in opposition to femininity, heterosexuality, and mothering. In doing so, she reflected the concerns expressed by the other students who viewed feminists as militant, brutish, excessive, and unstylish in light of their understandings of conventional feminine standards. Underlying these concerns is an abiding fear that by accepting feminist views they will threaten what they have come to believe is the very essence of their femininity. They believe such a step would, in turn, banish them from what they consider the "privileges of womanhood" that they have come to value.

The students described various other skirmishes that they engaged in as they attempted to make sense of where they stood relative to the course. For example, close to two-thirds of the students offered complaints about course materials that encouraged them to extend their analyses beyond an individual focus. Their journal entries dealt with this theme in ways similar to the following example:

I can't help to wonder what good can come about by constantly complaining about the present day state of things. This is just one aspect of what I consider to be blatant feminism in many of the articles that are assigned for our readings.

These same students contested the value of applying feminist lenses to examine broader sociopolitical issues, particularly those that move beyond white, middle-class, heterosexual perspectives. As they attempted to deal with differences, students "can't help to" (to quote the preceding student) rely on received conventional cultural models, which often work against the analysis of issues considered to be socially marginal. One student poignantly explained:

At first I was disbelieving of the readings and the lecture, because I thought people were overreacting and finding excuses to be angry. Then I thought about it a little more, and I think that I am reluctant to believe certain things because they are so awful and there seems to be nothing I can do about them.

Faced with similar feelings of discomfort, other students evoked a rhetoric of individualism widely promoted by contemporary Western culture to ease their concerns. Unfortunately, this rhetorical position often limits their understandings of how their lives are embedded in interlocking, socially constructed relations of class, race, gender, and heterosexuality that are enacted in specific fields of power, culture, and history. This position also leads them to hold themselves, rather than social structures, historical contingencies, and cultural constructions, responsible for the dilemmas they face. It further prompts them to reject the feminist notion that the "personal is political" and to subscribe instead to a "personal is personal" philosophy. Moreover, while all twenty students upheld a liberal feminist agenda of gender equality, only two identified with feminism either as a theoretical position or as a collective social movement. For example, one student wrote:

I am now more convinced than ever that I am not a feminist. Before I took this class I never classified myself as a feminist, and then I did, and now again I don't. This doesn't mean that I do not care about women's issues and rights, but just that sometimes I think that some people take things just a little too far. Women shouldn't desire to conquer the world, only to share it equally with men.

This student's commentary summarizes several of the themes arising from the data. First, nearly all of the students simultaneously embrace the personal promise of gender justice that they believe feminism offers while rejecting the feminist label and the transformative implications that it strives to represent. Therefore, they expect individual equality irrespective of gender, but they refuse engagement with an ethos that calls for a sense of collectivity—even as individuals—among and between women. Second, half of the students perceive feminism as antifeminine; these students describe notions of femininity that most feminists would argue sustain, rather than reduce, their oppressions. Finally, students often dismiss feminism as exclusionary. From this perspective, feminism becomes a position that not only fails to speak to their experiences but also is excessive; in the words of the student just quoted, feminism takes "things just a little too far."

All of the students of color explained how their gender functions as one etching intersecting a more complex identity pattern. One Chicana described how feminism has given her a way to understand oppression in terms of being both a woman and a Chicana. However, she also expressed fears that if she professed her feminist leanings, the women in her family would criticize her. She explained, "Even though I'm not a radical feminist, if my mother and aunts knew what I was thinking they would think I'm trying to act white or be a lesbian or something." Overall, this student and the other students of color expressed ambivalence about how feminist ideas contradicted aspects of their cultural background. She explained:

I am a Chicana, not only must I deal with racism but I must also live in a sexist world. I come from a family with strong conservative views compared to other families in the U.S. . . . . Machismo is very prominent and sometimes can not be seen but it is there. I never really thought about important feminist issues in high school. But I always knew that women were oppressed in our society. I saw it in my own home. It was not until I broke away from home that I began to think about my identity. I must say that my first real exposure to feminist ideas was when I left home for college. It is here where I am learning and trying to understand feminist ideas.

Like the other students in this introductory women's studies course, this student did not follow an easy path of feminist conversion, nor did she sequester herself in a rigid camp of resistance. Unlike some of the other students, she was able to use new information to question the terms of her gendered and raced experiences, an ongoing process that in itself is a goal of feminist education.

Several conclusions central to the subsequent discussion of teaching strategies emerge from these borderland stories. First, the majority of the students described conflicting desires, on one hand, to refuse conventional notions of femininity and, on the other, to achieve these impossible ideals. They tended to reject feminism primarily because they concluded that it is antifeminine. Further, they calculated the risks of aligning with a movement that combated feminine stereotypes as high. Second, nearly all students described how they felt alienated from feminism because they considered it to extend beyond the reach of their experiences. This was particularly true for the women of color, who described aspects of feminism as opposing cultural expectations for women within their communities. Finally, other students suggested that because they do not fit what they consider a particular monolithic feminist prototype, they feel socially alienated and excluded from feminist groups.

TOWARD A TRANSGRESSIVE TEACHING AGENDA

Throughout this chapter I have argued for a revision of existing models that describe students' identifications and resistances in introductory women's studies courses as following a predictable, linear path toward enlightenment. The revision I suggest, based on the preceding data analysis, is grounded in the understanding that many students feel like outsiders when they enter a women's studies course for the first time. This outsider status requires them to negotiate symbolic border crossings as they confront theories and practices that invite a reexamination of their received social understandings. The dynamic process encircling their border negotiations involves numerous border skirmishes as they actively engage in identifying both with and against new knowledge.

The teaching strategies I describe have been useful to me as I have attempted to help students negotiate the introductory women's studies borderlands and the skirmishes that inevitably occur there. These strategies are neither preventive nor curative but rather mechanisms to help students understand and appreciate the process they are experiencing as they are exposed to oppositional knowledge. They are offered as illustrations gleaned from my own teaching practice, which has been influenced considerably by the research findings presented in this chapter. Though these strategies are not necessarily transferable to all teaching situations or institutional contexts, they may stimulate ideas that will be helpful in other situations and contexts.

The following examples represent a few strategies from a vast repertoire of pedagogical efforts that I consider beneficial in creating a classroom climate that celebrates the excitement of grasping new ways of understanding and being in the world and simultaneously acknowledges the discomfort that often accompanies this celebration as new understandings rub against the familiar. Such a classroom climate promotes a transgressive teaching agenda that, in the words of bell hooks, not only promotes excitement and pleasure but "moves against and beyond boundaries" (hooks 1994a: 12).

NAMING THE MYTHS AND STEREOTYPES

At the beginning of each introductory women's studies course that I teach, I ask students to tell me what they have heard about women's studies and feminism, and I write each response on the board. If the students are reluctant to speak at first, I offer a few examples to prime the discussion, and I add to the list if key concerns are missing at discussion's end. We then discuss each response, analyzing the possible origins of the myth or stereotype and considering the social and cultural implications each conveys. I ask students to bring the list of myths and stereotypes to the final class so we can discuss them again after they have had a chance to experience a women's studies classroom for themselves. This final class discussion is invariably one of the richest and most lively of the semester because it provides a platform for students to ponder the changes they have experienced throughout the course.

CONVERSING "WITH" INSTEAD OF TEACHING "AT"

I begin every course syllabus with a statement that emphasizes my expectation for discussion and reflection. Discussion makes each of us confront beliefs different from our own. The rigidity born of lack of reflection is many times worn away as we become aware of the beliefs of others and reflect on our own beliefs. I highlight this concept at the first class session to underscore my conviction that any classroom offers the promise of becoming a committed community of learners who will engage actively in a series of lively conversations. I further emphasize that I teach for questions rather than answers, and I remind students that I will always ask for opinions that challenge and extend our discussions in the hope of sharpening our critical thinking skills to strengthen our positions as shrewd social analysts. I also talk about the excitement of extending our understandings even as I acknowledge the potential pain of such an extension. I urge students to embrace contradictions and to view confusion as a gateway to knowledge. These gestures help to clarify some of the characteristics of border crossings that require negotiation of the familiar with the new, in ways that can be celebratory, agonizing, or both.

OPENING PARACHUTES AND LIFTING SOCIAL ROCKS

Though it may seem trivial, I am convinced that it is important to remind students that our minds, like parachutes, work better when they are open. Encouraging this sort of openness works together with fostering conversations that represent a multitude of perspectives. Openness and conversations serve as survival gear for border crossings, but they must also be conducted with an awareness that classrooms can never be entirely "safe places" that operate outside power relations. To illuminate these power relations, I urge students to examine the theories that attempt to explain and contain their lives. I challenge them to use, make, and question theories as a way of pursuing understandings of power and knowledge. I explain that many of our social institutions and cultural codes operate in ways that hide mechanisms that privilege some groups and individuals over others. I suggest that they lift up these social rocks and look underneath them to discover the fierce activity that takes place beneath the surface. These activities encourage students to gather and analyze information about the interconnections between gender, race, and class and the myriad of other socially constructed identity markers that frame their lives. They also engender understandings of how privilege and oppression are influenced by these interconnections and how social institutions often play vital roles in perpetuating privilege and oppression.

In conclusion, these strategies represent small measures designed to challenge students to explore the borderlands surrounding introduction to women's studies courses and to analyze the history of their own struggles, privileges, and oppressions. Developing a transgressive teaching agenda that pushes against and beyond boundaries compels women's studies educators to appreciate that the processes of identification and resistance are never static or complete because maps of meaning and ideological positions are invariably taken up and lived in different ways with changing investments and intensities. These awarenesses provide a provocative rhythm for the dance that students and teachers perform as we ''do'' women's studies in the borderlands of introductory courses.

NOTE

1. The students' journals were part of a larger one and one-half-year ethnographic study of women's studies students and the politics of ''empowerment'' (Rhoades 1996). Additional sources for the study included data from interviews with students, faculty, and administrators; analysis of documents relating to the university's women's studies program; and participant observations in women's studies classrooms. The journals serve as the primary data source for the ensuing analysis, but the discussion and conclusions are also informed by the entire study.

SUGGESTED READINGS

Downing, D. B., ed. 1994. *Changing classroom practices: Resources for literary and cultural studies*. Urbana, IL: National Council of Teachers of English.
Gore, J. 1993. *The struggle for pedagogies: Critical and feminist discourses as regimes of truth*. New York: Routledge.
hooks, b. 1994. *Teaching to transgress: Education as the practice of freedom*. New York: Routledge.
Luke, C. and J. Gore. 1992. *Feminisms and critical pedagogy*. New York: Routledge.
McLaren, P. 1995. *Critical pedagogy and predatory culture: Oppositional politics in a postmodern era*. New York: Routledge.
Shor, I. 1992. *Empowering education: Critical thinking for social change*. Chicago: University of Chicago.

6

Revisiting the "Men Problem" in Introductory Women's Studies Classes

Glyn Hughes, University of California, Santa Barbara

Outside women's studies classrooms, discourses of white masculinity under siege are proliferating with devastating consequences for women and people of color. Indeed, in each of the most reactionary domestic political events and trends of the past five or so years the social group most united in the support of reaction has been young white men, from the 1994 "Republican revolution," to California's propositions 187 and 209. Yet, against the backdrop of globalized labor markets and diffusing corporatization, the manifest destiny of being young, white, and male in the United States now seems to many like a cruel promise; in the face of this uncertainty, it makes a kind of sense that white guys could feel powerless, experiencing social policies like affirmative action and political projects like feminism (and "identity politics" generally) as antagonistic to their self-actualization. Nor is it any surprise that Hollywood films like *Falling Down*, the four *Lethal Weapon* movies, and *Die Hard* depict the angry return of the vanquished white male (usually at the hands of affirmative action, immigration/greedy foreigners, or an uppity woman). At the same time, though, a new, highly commodified, kick-ass "feminism" has emerged on the popular culture horizon. Here, seemingly more transgressive images like those in *Buffy the Vampire Slayer* and *Terminator 2* blend with the Spice Girls and Nike ads to imply that liberation requires only individualistic attitude adjustment as opposed to reconfiguring institutional power relations.[1] These are just some of the features of gender relations as they appear in a few registers of contemporary U.S. social life, but they are enough to evoke the daunting stakes faced by students and teachers of women's studies.

As an institutionalized manifestation of a political social movement, women's studies occurs both within and against these trends. At the University of California, Santa Barbara (UCSB), where, as a Ph.D. student, I work as an instructor and teaching assistant, Introduction to Women's Studies courses fulfill a range of undergraduate general education and special subject requirements, including writing, social science, literature, and ethnicity. Though the Women's Studies Program is small relative to other departments at UCSB (with only three full-time faculty as of fall 1998), the integration of its curricula with university requirements brings a diversity of students and student expectations into our introductory classes. Yet our introductory courses (one humanities-oriented and the other a social science) are where we attempt to make feminism compelling to students with a systematicity that they have probably never encountered before. For their part, many students register for such a course with the expectation that it is going to deal with something other than "feminism," which they understand as bra-burning, street-demonstrating radicalism despite their firm beliefs in the "equality" of women and men; and, perhaps most significantly for this chapter, usually at least 10% of our Introduction to Women's Studies students are men.

Although the challenges could be conceived in broader terms, this chapter focuses on pedagogical issues raised by the presence of male students in the Introduction to Women's Studies classroom. Feminist pedagogies often assume that women's studies or feminist analysis is best taught when female students are unencumbered by gendered power relations in the classroom itself. By extension, women's engagements with feminism are most productive not only when women are enabled to make connections between their personal experiences and the social politics of gender but also when the classroom is maintained as a space in which they can witness their shared experiences as women. When male students enter the women's studies introductory classroom, however, women's studies teachers are challenged with the task of pursuing feminist goals through objectives other than gender exclusivity—though some teachers respond to the challenge by ignoring the men as much as possible. Given the troubling cultural and political scene of gender relations in the United States, and in particular those enticing discourses of male suffering, it seems to me the *risks* of actively including men in Introduction to Women's Studies are, by and large, outweighed by the political *potential* of doing so. As my goal here is to further the political efficacy of feminism through women's studies, I treat the presence of men in Introduction to Women's Studies as an educational opportunity (as opposed to a burden) for positive feminist engagement, an opportunity that is most adequately addressed by methodologically and substantively grounding Introduction to Women's Studies pedagogy in U.S. Third World feminism.

Men who show up in women's studies classes differ from one another in so many ways that it can create problems to collapse them into the label "men":

some show up accidentally, some to meet women, and others out of a sense of social obligation to challenge oppression; by other measures some are queer, nonwhite, or from impoverished families. When I refer to men in this chapter, however, I mean to evoke the social positioning of straight, white, middle-class men because, generally speaking, that identity configuration remains the most consistent guarantor of privilege in this country. Yet, as I imply later, no identity absolutely guarantees a corresponding consciousness or practice. When I am talking about "men" in this chapter, then, I acknowledge the slippage between the white male as exemplar of privilege and the variations of privilege that individual men bring to women's studies.

FROM WOMEN'S SPACE TO FEMINIST SPACE

The very presence of men in the Introduction to Women's Studies classroom makes impossible the preservation of "women's space." Consciousness-raising groups—methodologically grounded in women's space—have been the generative sites for the foundations of much of what we value as feminist theory and practice. Nonetheless, in women's studies classrooms, "women's space" has historically come to represent *middle-class, white* women's interests, and so there are already reasons to question the term's exclusivity. Few women's studies teachers *today* would dispute the importance of constantly challenging this exclusivity. Power-laden gender differences are *the* reason for a certain guardedness with respect to male incursions on women's spaces. However, it is also the case that feminist challenges to the exclusivity of (white) women's space have already demanded that curricula integrate dialogically the epistemologies, voices, and experiences of women whose sense of their own sexual, racial, or class positionings/politics makes their life experiences inseparable in many ways from other struggles in which, incidentally, men are often their allies. Through a consideration of the "men problem," I argue for the fostering of a classroom space that moves beyond "women's space" toward a *feminist* space characterized by constant (re)negotiation and an attentiveness to the voices and experiences that continue to be attacked and marginalized in society in general.

In 1988, invoking her essay of six years prior, Renate Klein asserted that the "men problem" was "even more urgent" than it was in 1982, especially in the United States (1989: 120). In the essay itself, she asks this not quite rhetorical question:

Wouldn't it be wonderful if we could just treat men as a "non-problem" and either not admit them into our women's studies classes or, if their presence is outside our control, not let them intrude an inch on our interactions and work? (Klein 1989: 114)

Klein here seems to view men as, at worst, disruptive and destructive and, at best, noncontributors who, unfortunately, have to be tolerated. In her longing, then, Klein voices a just-under-the-surface sentiment in women's studies that actually heightens many men's sense that "rightly or wrongly, they perceive themselves as the innocent targets of women's hostility" (George 1992: 28). Additionally, the dystopia of male presence rationalizes women as a coherently delimited group positioned unproblematically in uniform opposition to men. Indeed, the longing for a (re-)centered, pure women's space embedded in Klein's question suggests a link between the "men problem" and the *problem* of women's space as it has been articulated by nonwhite/middle-class/straight feminists. Chela Sandoval, for example, has remarked that hegemonic feminist classifications operate "as sets of imaginary spaces, socially constructed to severely delimit what is possible" (1991: 5–6). The point here is that, despite men having generally greater access to privilege than women, the projected dismissal of men from the women's studies classroom is epistemologically linked to the purging of *all* difference. In this sense, calls for "women's space," when they occur in denial of the differences among women, also obscure *connections* between men and women at the register of privilege. That is, the exclusion of men often (though by no means always) also enacts more general mechanisms for repressing the effects of privilege by scapegoating men as the unique embodiments of it.

These observations suggest at least two grounds on which women's space forecloses coalitional possibilities with men as potential "allies" in the women's studies classroom. First, calls for a pure women's space jeopardize the possibility of discussing the positive allegiances with men that for U.S. women of color have been expedient, necessary, and even rewarding in their struggles against an array of interrelated oppressive forces. Relatedly, keeping men out is a way for straight, white women to avoid confronting their own allegiances with men in terms of privilege. In light of these conflicting positionings, teacher expectations can make a lot of difference (in both senses of the term).

Consequently, when women's studies men are figured as *necessarily* nuisances, the possibility of expecting that they will both learn and *contribute* to the learning process cannot be taken seriously—by either the instructor or the students.[2] Given the preponderance of discourses in U.S. culture aimed at convincing young men of their victimization by the likes of feminism, how might Introduction to Women's Studies avoid resonating in that way for the men in the class? The rigidity often accompanying insistences on "women's space" (even when men are present) is precisely what many of our male students *hear* and then dismiss when they are presented with feminism, certainly, in part, because they are predisposed to hear in certain ways; and these reactions might also predispose teachers to see male students as always already a problem. In turn, men's negative reactions to/from (hegemonic) feminism become further evidence not only that they do not belong in women's studies but that it has nothing to offer them. This seems like a circularity worth escaping. But before I discuss some of the other mechanisms that are similarly troubling, I want to complicate a certain parallel that I have implied: to the extent that hegemonic feminism constructs both men and women of color as its Others, what are the dangers of equating the two in the interest of greater inclusivity?

Unlike Klein (1989: 106), who asserted that "there is no room for men in women's studies, none whatsoever," Madonne Miner (1994: 465) sees a benefit to having men in women's studies "if only because, in this one class, women move to center stage and men find themselves on the margins." From her admittedly "small and racially homogenous [white?]" survey of ten men, Miner (1994: 453) found that "men in Intro experience the effects of minority status: they feel highly visible, subject to stereotyping and a loss of individuality." My own experiences of women's studies corroborate the symptoms that Miner identifies, but we need to be mindful that similar symptoms can be caused by different diseases. In the classroom, conceptualizing the experiences of men as analogous to minority experiences in dominant discursive spaces casts men as victims in a hostile environment; it seems to equate male pain and minority oppression, which, incidentally, is the same sort of logic that allows "reverse discrimination" to have such currency as a reason to dismantle affirmative action. Thus, a clearer distinction between men's Intro experience and minority experiences in hegemonic spheres is crucial for developing teaching strategies that effectively address the experiences of men in Introduction to Women's Studies.

Most of the men in Miner's (1994: 456) study were disturbed that they seemed to be "capturing a larger awareness share" in women's studies; for example, many of them "commented that they knew their absences would be noticed. . . . The men felt the spotlight on them." It is an important point that the silence, cynicism, squirming, or lashing out that such attention often prompts *does* result from a sort of forced reckoning with power, but I would argue that it is because feminist spaces deprive men of the ground of cultural *privilege* that sustains the hierarchy of gender relations. The otherwise familiar presence of this ground helps to construct certain expectations in men, senses of entitlement—to speak, to be heard, to be valued, to be at the center, to be perceived as an individual. Minority experiences of dominant spaces, on the other hand, do not tend to involve the same sense of betrayal at the hands of a system that they thought was their own; they do not have to leave their hegemonic privilege at the door. Instead, minorities confront, once again, a wall of privilege invisible to those it protects.

This distinction raises the question of how and whether to center men's interests in the women's studies classroom, which has historically militated against such centerings. Whereas most women know the risks of speaking in male-dominated (or otherwise masculinized) classroom settings—because the classroom is not without the power relations that define the social generally—men's struggle to find a voice can exist because their reliance on those power relations has been undermined. Then again, none of this is to say that we should ask a man to speak for all men, but I do think we should view their silences as suspiciously and cautiously as we do their outbursts. In fact, the most productive pedagogical strategies might try to anticipate these responses ahead of time and be prepared to name them, to resist their owners' attempts to diagnose themselves as only victims in a sort of leveling gesture that equates any sense of powerlessness with systematic oppression.

However, having made the distinction clear and having deconstructed women's space, I am not at all saying that "we" should abandon concerns about gendered power relations in the classroom or the possibility of making the classroom a coalitional, feminist space. To illustrate how both of these important objectives remain possible, I will have to say more about what I mean by feminist space as something different from women's space. This is an analytical distinction, of course, because one of feminism's main lessons concerns the interconnection of bodily identity and social experience, even as one way of understanding feminism is as an attempt to delink the two. Thinking in terms of feminist space is useful here because it helps "us" to imagine men as potential participants in feminist delinking activities while at the same time reminding "us" that feminist practice/pedagogy exceeds socially inscribed identity; as such the practice/pedagogy cannot be guaranteed to emerge from a secure women's physical space. It will be important, therefore, to imagine spaces that can be created independently of the biological identities that inhabit them.[3] For men, I think, feminist spaces can simultaneously conjure the theoretical possibility of the separation of the penis (the body) and the phallus (socially structured power), and they can provide a challenging context for exploring the relationship between the two as they manifest in practices.[4]

BEYOND ESSENTIALISM AND PLURALISM . . . FROM OPPRESSION TO PRIVILEGE

For a variety of legitimate reasons, including overwork, job insecurity, institutional constraints on time, and pedagogical staging (i.e., women need to learn to identify as women and with women's oppression before creating coalitions with, say, men), many feminists find themselves teaching versions of feminism that they themselves do not quite buy. As a result, rigid identity politics still occasionally work their way into our classrooms—particularly in Introduction to Women's Studies, the *only* sustained exposure to feminism some students will ever get. But—and this should not be underestimated—for many people, (white) feminist separatism remains *the* stereotype of feminism in general, and the persistence of this stereotype constricts the possibilities for coalition, much the same way that the identity politics stereotype of men as always only nuisances too often works as a self-fulfilling prophecy.

It seems, therefore, that much of the political solution to the "men problem" is already embedded in the work of U.S. Third World feminists. I leave it as an open hypothesis, then, that whenever men as a category appear troublesome to the project of Introduction to Women's Studies, it may be a sign that there is more work to do in exploring the ways that privilege works *within* gender categories. When well-meaning, privileged folks are accused of essentializing outward from their own social positions, they commonly respond with additive or assimilationist gestures—"Sure, it says 'all *men* are created equal,' but women and people of color should certainly feel included!" Similarly, the vast majority of white feminist theorists now "recognize the problem of difference," according to María Lugones (1991: 38), but "whether they *recognize* difference is another matter." What still happens all too often, especially in introductory classes, where there is a certain urgency to create an initial unity of oppression, is that a disclaimer is made about the actual lack of inclusion only to be followed by no further engagement with the facts of difference (Lugones 1991: 38).

Perhaps an even more common pedagogical approach in the late 1990s is to essentialize the category woman initially, only to problematize and de-essentialize it later through an exploration of other axes of difference. But even this more evolved strategy may not be adequate. By way of illustration, consider Gayatri Spivak's response to Ellen Rooney's statement that she views the "essentialism/antiessentialism" approach as a necessity:

Rather than make it a central issue, work it into the method of your teaching so that the class becomes an example of the minimalizing of essences, the impossibility of essences; rather than talk about it constantly, make the class a proof of this new position. . . . it seems to me that one can make a strategy of taking away from them the authority of their marginality, the centrality of their marginality, through the strategy of careful teaching, so that they come to prove that that authority will not take them very far because the world is a large place. (Spivak and Rooney 1993: 18)

Spivak's remarks reframe the challenge as one of determining what teaching methods might produce a solidarity of *doing* antiessentialism in opposition to systems of oppression. Similarly, Chela Sandoval (1991: 23) posits the "differential consciousness" of U.S. Third World women as the basis for "a kind of anarchic activity (but with method), a form of ideological guerrilla warfare . . . in a highly technologized and disciplinized society." For Sandoval, the transformative potential of U.S. Third World feminism is in its two-part methodology of reading "the current situation of power and of self-consciously choosing and adopting the ideological form best suited to push against its configurations, a survival skill well known to oppressed peoples" (15). Sandoval's work moves us closer to the "method" referred to by Spivak earlier. It evokes the feminist space of the classroom as a *process* of inquiry, not a pluralist celebration of difference or a search for some surefooted position at which everyone in the class might, finally, arrive. That is, it involves a vigilant inquiry into "the modes the subordinated . . . (of any gender, race, or class) claim as politicized and oppositional stances in resistance to domination" (Sandoval 1991: 11).

In Introduction to Women's Studies, we would, of course, remain focused on the ways that social power works through gender relations. Even though the questions asked about how to work against that power would likely result in white men (or men generally) "capturing a larger awareness share," putting the spotlight on men would never involve the dichotomizing absolution of the others in the class, who would be challenged (perhaps by analogy) to think about whiteness, class privilege, heterosexuality, and attractiveness. These potential, temporary centerings of identity categories other than woman are key elements of feminist space as I have been discussing it. In that sense, feminist space does not prescribe the centering of women as such. Instead, feminist space is some-times most "feminist" when it decenters women, when, for example, it shifts the burden of social change away from women and onto men by overtly mark-ing/centering masculinity.

As I have indicated, invocations of patriarchy as the external Other to Western feminist calls for unity generate stumbling blocks for men in women's studies, because they propose a certain predestined connection between the penis and the phallus, something that does not resonate for men already tempted by nar-ratives of the besieged white male. In that same conversation with Ellen Rooney, Gayatri Spivak navigates the twin traps of patriarchy studies and liberal plural-ism by articulating practical guideposts for teaching self-reflexive critiques of privilege.[5] I quote her at length as a preparation for thinking in terms of concrete tactics in the final section:

> This idea of a global fun-fair is a lousy teaching idea. One of the first things to do is to think through the limits of one's power. One must ruthlessly undermine the story of the ethical universal, the hero. But the alternative is not constantly to evoke multiplicity. . . . That leads to pluralism. I ask the U.S. student: "What do you think is the inscription that allows *you* to think the world without any preparation? What sort of coding has produced *this* subject?" I think it's hard for students to know this, but we have a re-sponsibility to make this lesson palliative rather than destructive. This is not a paralyzing thing to teach. In fact, when a student is told that responsibility means proceeding from an awareness of the limits of one's power, the student understands it quite differently from being told, "Look, you can't do all of this." I will share with you what I have learned about knowing, that these are the limitations of what I undertake, looking to others to teach me. I think that's what one should do rather than invoke multiplicity. (Spivak and Rooney 1993: 19)

This is an important passage to bookend this theoretical discussion because it shows that feminist teaching of privilege requires that *all* students engage in self-critique. But even as there is no sure footing for students, teachers are here also called to model the vulnerability necessary for coalition to really begin to happen. As a white male teacher of women's studies, I take this passage as a call to *interactive* teaching, to borrow a phrase from Lugones (1991). In that spirit, perhaps this is a good place to consider some actual pedagogical tactics.

IN PRACTICE

My experience with Introduction to Women's Studies has been as a discussion leader/facilitator. Although all the reflections in this chapter have to be taken up differently by readers facing a variety of institutional constraints and positions as well as classroom demographics, the following tactics could be reworked for use by teachers in a variety of pedagogical roles, including lecturing.

Checking the ("White") Box: Privilege versus Minority Experience

This sequencing of activities demonstrates to students that privilege operates as a sort of blindness to the effects of socially inscribed identity. Students are asked to write down all of the words that describe who they are—I assure them that they will not have to show this paper to anyone, so they should feel free to be honest. Without making any initial link to their lists, we talk for a bit about how being confined by labels can be disconcerting for anyone. I then solicit comments from students about whether there is any difference between the experiences of white folks and people of color in checking the race/ethnicity box on, say, a job application form.

After some discussion, many of the white students continue to insist that the violence they feel in being marked in such a way is equal to that of nonwhites; some argue that these boxes create racism by making it a relevant issue at all. At this point I urge students to revisit their lists, pointing out that privileged categories in binary systems are, more often than not, considered irrelevant to those in positions of privilege. White students tend not to mention their race on the list; men tend not to mention their gender; and straight people tend not to mention their sexuality.

White discomfort in checking the box can be discussed as the trauma of having to confront privilege as opposed to the trauma of being a minority. While this may spark a sense of powerlessness in the "victim," it is not at all the same as oppression. I ask students to consider how these different experiences shape their interactions with each other and with course material throughout the term.

Paired Readings

Students often find it useful when faced with daunting challenges to see others succeeding at the same task. One of the more effective sequencings that I have experienced in this regard is María Lugones' (1991) "On the Logic of Pluralist Feminism" and Minnie Bruce Pratt's (1984) "Identity: Skin, Blood, Heart." Lugones asserts that, "in hearing the 'What Chou Mean *We*, White Girl?' question, white/anglo women theorizers did not really hear an interactive demand, a demand for an answer . . ." (1991: 39).[6] Pratt's essay offers an "answer" not only to this question but to Spivak's request for an interrogation of the "sort of coding [that] has produced this subject." Pratt is particularly deft at linking up the intimacies of her self-doubt and privilege with both personal and social histories. In so doing, she provides a crucial reference point for translating introspection into action.

Modeling Struggles with Privilege

It is also true, however, that students often find it useful, when faced with the challenge of doing antiprivilege work, to see that others have *struggled* and *continue to struggle* in their efforts to do the same. It undermines one's message to claim, on one hand, that oppositional consciousness and feminist spaces are *processes* while presenting oneself as having already arrived on the stable ground of authority. In Spivak's terms, the instructor should exhibit what it is like work from the limits of one's power, to show what it is like to learn from others.

As a white *male* in women's studies classes, I have learned that disclosure of this sort walks a fine line between generous offering, inappropriate centering of suffering men, and, relatedly, excessive self-deprecation. Yet walking the line is both difficult and necessary; and at strategic moments it is something to be specific about in the classroom, because the thickness of privilege that tends to cohere at the intersection of whiteness and maleness can sometimes be productively scrutinized in the women's studies classroom. Indeed, there is quite a difference between centering men because they are feeling left out and centering men to talk about the dialectics of gender privilege and oppression.

In a classroom discussion of connections between mass media, body image, and eating disorders, a man who had not yet spoken observed that women should resist media messages by not worrying about their bodies so much, and they should not be bothered with guys who try to hold them accountable to unrealistic beauty ideals. His comment was met with fidgety silence. Playing devil's advocate, I offered, "Well, let's talk about that. Why can't women just 'get over it'?" It didn't work very well, because the whole gesture really kept the burden of answering on the women, who had already spun out their opinions as much as they could tolerate in that mode. In retrospect, this classroom moment was an opportunity to shift the burden away from women through a focus on male privilege. In anticipation of this moment, I could have been prepared with stories of conversations with my women friends, many of whom have spent years working out sustainable resistances to the cultural impositions of body image (with varying degrees of "success"). I might have wondered aloud about why the intensity of my socialization to be a heterosexual male in this culture rarely entered the dialogue. Perhaps the class could consider how gender privilege tends to occlude discussions of (straight) men's investments in women's preoccupations with their appearance. The discussion might then have turned to what sorts of male practices might undermine the negative effects of women's body image. For instance, we might have explored ways that hegemonic channelings of sexual desire might be rechanneled; how the gendering of fat prejudice, for example, is both different from, and related to, women's "obsession" with fat; and we certainly might have thought more creatively about tactical interventions for conversations in which fat prejudice emerges.

Cataloging Interventions for Everyday Life

One positive implication of reconceptualizing women's space as feminist space is that it shifts the focus from bodies to practices in a way that, incidentally, creates coalitional opportunities. Focusing on practices can be liberating in a sense for both men and women because it suggests the possibility for change without undermining the possibility for critique. Along these lines, I have made it a habit in the past few years to collect stories of successful, practical interventions that can be linked to thematic issues in Introduction to Women's Studies. For example, during a unit on gender segregation in the workplace, the assigned reading for the course offered that networking among (white) men in job settings creates exclusionary effects on promotion rates for women and people of color. To illustrate how it would look to intervene in such networkings, I tell the following "true" story:

During a smoke/coffee break at a social movement organization retreat, one male manager approached another in a secluded smoking spot. In what he perceived as neutral chit-chat, the first man complained to the other about the "bitch" who's running the meeting, and about how he was distracted by the breasts of another woman. After the break, the second man proceeded to relay the conversation to the entire group. The group, in turn, began to ask questions about how gendered power differences might be affecting the organization's functioning.

The story illustrates that privilege cannot be sustained if members of the privileged group refuse to entertain the assumptions of mutual identification upon which the maintenance of social privilege relies. The refusal itself creates the possibility for oppositional solidarity to emerge.

Students generally enjoy such stories—perhaps initially because the stories are scandalous—but their interest usually goes beyond that; they eventually develop stories of their own, especially later in the term as they begin to try out some of the tactics themselves. In addition, students are remarkably skilled in evaluating the effectiveness of various tactics. While those evaluative discussions are useful, it is perhaps more exciting to know that the entire class is involved in building repertoires of oppositional tactics for use beyond the class.

CONCLUSION

Introduction to Women's Studies courses, when taught in ways that are compelling to men, can be a point of resistance to the mass-mediated, hegemonic masculinity, which imagines (and thereby conjures) the solidarity of other men clustering around kindred discourses of their own victimization by "race extremists," "the gay agenda," and, of course, "feminazis." This particular victimization is a face of privilege, one self-righteously oblivious to its effects on Others, even viciously constructing them as the enemy. We need to take their victimization away from them—or, as Spivak says, we need to "make a strategy of taking away from them the authority of their marginality." We need to replace it with a set of skills: how to recognize one's own privilege at work; how privilege affects space and then how to know when one's presence is appropriate; how to listen intently from a position of self-doubt. We might also not *deny* their sense of victimization so much as we name the real sources of that powerlessness while also refusing to let them settle on the notion that they *alone* (or to some *greater* degree) are the victims.

I have tried to emphasize that the trick to getting men to engage feminism productively is to make them members of the class by forming coalition out of something that everyone can participate in: the critique and dismantling of privilege. Feminist space, according to this criterion, is a *process* effected by modeling vulnerability and a shift away from oppression studies as an end in itself toward pragmatic studies of privilege that take their cues from compassionate listenings to stories of oppression.

NOTES

I am grateful to Rachel Luft (1997), who shared with me her important research on women's studies students' attitudes toward feminism; to Barbara Schulman and other participants in the February 1998 discussion, "Men's Participation in the Women's Movement and Feminism," sponsored by the University of California, Santa Barbara (UCSB) Associated Students Women's Commission; to Maurizia Boscagli, Susan Dalton, and Shirley Geok-lin Lim for their varied assistance; and especially to Laura Scott Holliday, without whom this chapter could not have been written: she edited, advised, and consulted with wonderful generosity.

1. See, for example, Cole (1995).

2. By suggesting that men students could be contributors to women's studies, I imply a space for men as *teachers* of Introduction to Women's Studies classes, although it is a position I do not want to endorse wholesale and in advance. Certainly, no man should ever accept such a nomination by his women's studies colleagues as anything but a tentative venture that should be undertaken with relentless self-critique (by which I mean something very different from positioning one's need for support at the center of things).

3. Throughout the entire chapter I use the words "we" and "us" to refer to an imagined community of women's studies teachers and students and to acknowledge the complex webs of identity and solidarity that imagining such community evokes. In fact, as I wrote this paragraph, I realized that at times it may have been unclear to some readers whether I was referring to us *people* in women's studies (I was) or us *men* in women's studies (I was not)—a disjuncture that testifies to the complexity of these webs.

4. Challenging though it may be for everyone, from a feminist perspective, Introduction to Women's Studies is certainly "safer" than those masculinist spaces where most college-aged men put the finishing touches on a subjectivity destined for the top.

5. Hazel Carby's essay in which she critiques the notion of patriarchy for lacking "cross-cultural reference points" (1986: 223) is also relevant here.

6. Lugones is referring to Lorraine Bethel's (1979) essay by the same name.

SUGGESTED READINGS

Lugones, M. 1990. Playfulness, "world"-travelling, and loving perception. *Making face, making soul/Haciendo caras: Creative and critical perspectives by women of color*, ed. G. Anzaldúa, 390–402. San Francisco: Aunt Lute.

Messner, M. A. 1997. *Politics of masculinities: Men in movements*. Thousand Oaks, CA: Sage.

7

"Is This Course Just about Opinions or What?" Scripted Questions as Indicators of Group Development in an Introduction to Women's Studies Class

Toni C. King, Denison University

In this chapter I discuss three questions posed by students in my introductory women's studies class, Issues in Feminism: (1) "Is this course just about opinions or what?" (2) "Can't you make them take this seriously?" and (3) "So, Professor King, is *all* knowledge constructed?" Each of these questions is discussed and explored for its meaning in relationship to the group development issues arising in the class. As I discuss classroom dynamics, I share how attending to the developmental phases of the class as a group informed my framing of a class assignment to help students reach resolution of issues threatening to undermine student participation and course objectives. I conclude by offering some impressions about how my womanist identity influenced my pedagogical choices.

HOW AND WHERE I ENTER

I am an African-American female with a Ph.D. in organizational behavior, preceded by a master's in counseling. Courses that I have taught over the past five years have included graduate and undergraduate courses in multicultural theory; race, gender, and institutional change; and women and organizations, to name a few. My research has focused on women's development and "recovery" from race, class, and gender oppression.

Recently, I accepted a position at a small liberal arts college in the Midwest as an associate professor of Black women's studies. In this capacity, I teach one of the two sections of the course Issues in Feminism 101. This course meets for one hour and twenty minutes twice a week. Last semester was my first experience with this course. I am two weeks into my second semester as I write this chapter. As one who is learning the emotional terrain of the introduction to women's studies class, I am finding myself listening to students' comments and questions, and the kinds of issues they raise, as well as how they raise them. I consider their comments and queries as "scripts" that reflect underlying and potentially recurring themes. With a script the actors may change, but the script can be repeated. So, too, in the women's studies classroom, the students may change, but the scripts representing larger thematic issues may reemerge.

According to Belenky et al. (1986), the connected knower uses subjectivity as a primary method of understanding the world. This concept applies to my personal reflections on the ways that the "class as a group" appeared to orient itself to the women's studies classroom, contest the norms of this classroom, and resist the implications of the knowledge presented in this classroom. As a connected knower delving into the multiple ways of understanding what my experiences are telling me, I have chosen to explore the introductory women's studies classroom from the perspective of group development.

PHASES OF GROUP DEVELOPMENT IN THE CLASSROOM

Group dynamics theory defines a group as a body of individuals existing within a specific period of time and space, interacting for a common purpose. Group dynamics theories indicate that groups develop from stages of relative dependence on the leader, to stages of relative independence, and finally toward stages of interdependence and shared leadership (Bion 1961). Such paradigms also acknowledge that movement through these major stages varies significantly from group to group and context to context relative to the internal and external events affecting the group.

It is also important to emphasize that group dynamics theory makes a clear and emphatic distinction between individual-level dynamics and group-level dynamics. Research and theory hold that there are individual responses and processes occurring within a group; yet simultaneously there is a "collective level of consciousness" deriving from issues germane to the group in its entirety. Primarily, it is to this "collective" or group level of dynamics that I am referring throughout this discussion. At the same time, I use individual perspectives (student perspectives and issues as well as my own perspectives and experiences) to explain and explore the individual issues, needs, and concerns constituting the intricate interaction of individual and group phenomena.

Phase 1: "Is This Course Just about Opinions or What?"

During the first week of classes, a white male student confronted me with the question, "Is this course just about opinions or what?" As I had heard this question in some capacity last semester, this time the question had the ring of familiarity to it, which allowed me to respond and explore its imperious challenge from the vantage point of having had one entire semester of Issues in Feminism under my belt.

In contrast, last semester, everything was new to me, and I grappled with my own anxieties about teaching a subject I had not taught before in a context I had not taught in before. In fact, I had three ''new preps'' and was making the transition from having taught primarily at large state universities to the current liberal arts setting. The deja vu experience that this question prompted compelled me to sift through the memories of last semester, reconsidering this question about ''opinions.'' In reflecting, I hypothesized that this question was an indicator of an early phase of group development. Early group behavior is characterized by student dependency on the (leader) instructor for guidance and clarity about the group norms. This stage would include students' needs to determine appropriate behaviors for earning inclusion as well as for attaining social and concrete rewards (e.g., approval from the instructor or grades, respectively). I surmised this question expressed the need for clarity, reassurance, and the requisite information to feel confident about how to approach the class as well as a need to know what skills and competencies acquired in other educational settings might also be applied here. At an organizational level, I felt this question represented the issue of how this class compares to other classes within this institution in terms of the criteria for success. That is, does it differ, and if so, in what ways?

I also heard a subtler, metalevel question of whether the professor would play a role in making the norms and expectations explicit, or would it be incumbent upon students to ''decipher the codes'' of performance. Finally, I feel this question called forth yet another level of dynamics in that it reflected the initial challenge to the group leader. Group dynamics theory postulates that an effective challenge to the group leader is a prerequisite for resolution of the dependency issues characterizing early stages of group life. Until successful resolution of empowerment in relationship to the leader is achieved, the group will be stymied in realizing its potential. Effective resolution of dependency issues requires the group leader to respond to the challenge to her or his authority in a way that supports development of individual and group trust and agency.

In the context of an introduction to women's studies course this particular question, however, not only challenges the instructor's credibility as an appropriate bridge between the ''traditional worldviews'' of Western or Eurocentric cultural assumptions and feminist cultural assumptions but also challenges the field of women's studies as a legitimate mode of discourse and scholarly inquiry. Thus, the women's studies professor is also responding to this broader challenge. Students who themselves question the legitimacy of the field of women's studies need an answer that contextualizes women's studies as a scholarly field of endeavor. They need an authentic response that both differentiates women's studies and the pedagogical processes it uses while at the same time links or places these processes within the context of learning.

In response to this question, I become a mediator of the contested contextual domain demonstrated by students' need to understand how we will learn and how we will demonstrate our learning from a more woman-centered (feminist) orientation. In addition, I must translate what "ways of knowing" will be rewarded and promote students' confidence in the criteria of evaluation as well as trust that these criteria can be administered fairly.

The issue of fairness is generally framed by another series of questions that may be spoken or simply be acted out during the duration of the course: Will men be treated fairly in comparison to women? Will there be articles/readings that have the effect of male bashing? Will the professor engage in, allow, or collude in male bashing? Will students be sanctioned or penalized for disagreeing with authors or with the professor? Will some "unfair" advantage be had by students who make it known that they are feminists?

I see these concerns as indicators of a critical shift in power that is symbolized by the presence of women's studies courses. Such a shift places women at the center of discourse within a particular classroom context but does not necessarily undo existing patriarchal power structures within the larger social order. Still, this placing of women's experiences at the "center" is a new enough experience for many men and women students within the introductory course that they question how this shift might create the abuses of power all too familiar in patriarchal hegemonic societies. At this particular university, the intensity of this feeling that something other than male experience is (temporarily) at the center is felt all the more deeply because this university *requires* students to take a women's studies *or* a minority studies course to fulfill a general studies requirement. For some of these students who choose the introductory course, resolving their questions and concerns about the "criteria" and norms of performance particular to this context becomes a salient dynamic.

Phase 2: "Can't You Make Them Take This Seriously?"

As I struggled to facilitate and empower students for serious engagement, several women students approached me during my office hours with concerns about the course. During our discussion, they questioned my pedagogical processes and critiqued the class as one in which I had not been effective in getting male students to take the class seriously. I feel their collective question, "Can't you make them take this seriously?" represented some group-level issues occurring in the class as a whole.

Group dynamics theory indicates that stages of differentiating from the leader may be characterized by conflict between group members as well as conflict between the group and the leader. Literature identifies many such conflicts as "fight/flight" (Bion 1961). These dynamics are signaled by an issue, person, or group becoming the site of conflict. The group will either demonstrate overt conflict (fight) or passive conflict (flight) such as avoidance. One classroom example includes student needs to "protect" male students from the usurpation of power or the threat of attack by those perceived as radical feminists. I use the words "perceived as radical" because I have seen students apply these labels regardless of any student's acknowledging a radical feminist identity, in spite of clarification and definition of radical feminism(s) and even before reading assignments that draw upon radical feminist ideas.

Last semester, little resolution pertaining to "the threat of radical feminism" occurred until the final weeks of the course. Although male students acquired a measure of safety and trust, some continued to project the ideation of "radical" onto the more outspoken women in the class. I think this was one way that some male students handled their own gender-related anxieties, which included, but were not limited to, age-appropriate male/female relational dynamics; concerns about being less knowledgeable and less able to comprehend some issues due to their gender; feelings about women whose presentation of self transgresses their expectations or gender schema for "appropriate" behaviors; fears of saying or doing the wrong thing in class; or internal dissonance arising from learning about gender inequities in society. These concerns also affected classroom dynamics and may have contributed to the judgmental comments made by both male and female students about the "dangers" of radicalized feminist orientations.

The very bright, articulate, well-read in feminist literature, and outspoken women students who experienced this form of peer rejection struggled to continue to have a voice within the class. Yet, I could sense their growing apprehension and disillusionment. Some weeks into the course this group of students approached me after class for a lengthy discussion and critique of the class and my role as instructor. Their disappointments were shared with justifiable outrage as follows:

- "They [the male students] don't take the subject seriously, and you're not making them respect the field of women's studies."
- "The men in the class have more opportunity to speak." (This class was *two-thirds* male.)
- "We don't feel safe, the male students all sit together and snicker at us as though there is something wrong with us."
- "They are not mature enough for the kind of teaching that you are doing. How can you spend so much time focusing on their views when they don't understand the issues?"
- "The other women don't seem to understand where we're coming from, and we're also isolated on the campus because we identify ourselves as feminists."
- "They think we are man haters."

During the students' consultation with me in which they aired their grievances, my response was to listen quietly and take notes about their concerns. I wanted them to know I was "taking *them* and their concerns *seriously*." Although overwhelmed by the expression of their collective concerns, I managed to express appreciation for bringing their concerns to me. I also indicated that my office was always open to them and that it might be a good idea for us to talk again during the semester. Overall, this was a very uncomfortable period of teaching women's studies for me. While some students showed no signs of disapproval, and others seemed to be thriving, I was acutely aware that some of my more advanced women students felt that I had fallen from grace.

In my view, several dynamics accounted for the concerns expressed by the women students in the incident I just described that are particular to this class. They include a larger than usual class size of thirty-nine (classes generally did not exceed twenty-five) and the numerical majority of male students. In addition, this class included a group of twelve fraternity members who had apparently registered for the course together. The male majority combined with the dynamics of fraternal cohesiveness contributed to the classroom climate. I would surmise that, experientially, the male students represented a "traditional" male presence to women in the course, ultimately embodying some interesting contradictions for "this type of class." For example, some women students, especially those who had taken other women's studies courses, may have expected a classroom in which women's physical and intellectual presence was central or even "dominant." The subject of women's studies in an environment involving more male students could easily feel "less safe" for exploring the personal and political implications of women in society.

Finally, I feel that in a liberal arts setting such as this, in which students are "traditional" undergraduates, many students within the introduction to women's studies course will have had limited experiences that they construct to be related to gender differences, gender inequities, or institutionalized sexism. As one young woman who fits this profile said early in the course: "I just don't understand what all the fuss is about. I have never been discriminated against because of my gender. So what? . . . if we study these issues! I just don't see women suffering *because* they are a woman!" All of these dynamics are present and play a role in impeding the kind of discussions that seriously engage students and help them ground theory within their experiential framework.

To counter dynamics suppressing open engagement and energized discussion, I developed numerous assignments to be submitted on the day that we would be discussing the readings. In this unusually large class of thirty-nine students assignments each week required an inordinate amount of reading, grading, and feedback on my part. However, I was gratified to see students develop in their abilities to think critically about issues in these written assignments and contribute more thoughtfully in small group discussions and, to a lesser extent, in discussions of the class as a whole. While the group of women students who had approached me earlier with concerns about the course did not return to my office, they approached me after class a few weeks later to inform me that they felt "the class [specifically, "the guys"] was settling down." In general, however, the ability to move through this stage of group dynamics is facilitated by students' acquisition of the information and the intellectual tools (theoretical perspectives and analytical methods) that will support them in engaging each other.

Phase 3: "So, Professor King, Is *All* Knowledge Constructed?"

About two-thirds of the way through the course, I knew we were about to begin our descent and prepare for landing when a white male student raised his hand after my presentation of a framework for understanding gender role "transgressions." When I acknowledged him, he posed the question: "So, Professor King, is *all* knowledge constructed?" I was thrilled at his question, as it was the kind of thinking that he or other students could internalize and apply in other classes. This student's question also modeled male openness to inquiry into gender-related social issues.

I felt this question signaled the beginning of the final phases of group development, which are characterized by a deeper level of work with respect to the task of the group (Bion 1961). My experience of the student's question was that it evidenced a new level of respect for women's studies because it provided him with an alternative way to assess information and knowledge. In addition, it was not lost on me that he had raised this question, in spite of the fact that he was sitting with a group of young men who always sat and talked together when my construction of small groups did not mitigate against it. This student's question is one example of the kind of incidents that confirmed my view that the class was increasing its capacity for inclusion and voice by empowering all class participants with the tools for inquiry, critical thinking, and analysis.

Only during the final weeks of class, however, did I begin to feel real resolution taking place. During the final three weeks of class, students were called upon to make group presentations. These presentations allowed them to see each other present scholarly work on women's lives and through this process develop a sense of shared responsibility for gender issues. I carefully developed an assignment that I hoped would create *self-inquiry* for students at the same time that they were asked to investigate women's experiences (see Appendix A: Student Presentation Assignment). Before giving the assignment, we discussed the idea of "gender role transgressions." It appeared to me that the unspoken issues and power dynamics within the classroom centered around unconscious and preconscious beliefs about what it means for women to transgress social norms. I felt that the idea of "radical" feminist identities students had been grappling with was one constructed in the minds of some students—that such women were transgressing the appropriate (though unspoken) gender roles for women. The assignment was a group project in which students were to illustrate in the most creative manner possible an example of gender role transgression. In support of this example, the group was required to explain the manner in which knowledge was constructed to view this behavior as a "transgression" against the existing patriarchal social order.

The assignment itself felt risky at some level. Indeed, my presenting the assignment (in spite of the earlier preparation through class discussions of a framework for gender transgressions) functioned as an external threat and elicited strong fight/flight behaviors from many students (even some who were typically quiet). According to group dynamics, a group may be progressing through stages of group development when an incident of internal or external threat creates in essence a form of regression to a previous and less rational stage (Bion 1961). In this case, group members were relatively stronger and more empowered than during the initial stages of the class and therefore quite confident in challenging this assignment as not clear enough, not structured well enough, and too demanding for them to do in groups within the amount of time remaining during the semester. I responded by affirming my belief in their abilities to meet the challenge. However, upon meeting continued resistance, I gently, but firmly, pulled rank and stood by my decision.

Ultimately, students found the assigned project quite engaging. The first presenters did a superb job setting the tone for the remaining class sessions, which were characterized by high motivation, individuality, and creativity. Students saw both men and women "take the subject of women's studies" seriously. More specifically, women students received affirmation that men did indeed have the capacity to understand and to apply scholarly inquiry to women's lives. While this would be a difficult assignment to fulfill without demonstrating some capacity for understanding women's experience, the assignment allowed both an appreciative and playful (creative) approach to analyzing patriarchal consequences in women's lives.

Resolution vis-à-vis the development of the class as a group was further signaled by the fact that during the very busy weeks as we neared semester's end, attendance at all classes was high, and there was a feeling of excitement and anticipation. In fact, the women students who had earlier complained by asking, "Can't you make them take this seriously?" were highly engaged by this assignment. One of these students, after making a particularly strong presentation about standards of beauty for women of color, addressed me directly in the hallway after class. Her comment was a simple one, yet it touched me deeply. "That was for me—and for you," she said.

In general, the students attended very well to the presentations of their peers and completed the presentation reaction sheets quite thoughtfully throughout the three weeks' duration of these presentations. Group development theory considers the final stages of group development as those evidencing group cohesiveness. Final stages of group development are characterized (in both behaviors and group ethos) by high engagement in the work or tasks of the group, high interest in both one's own work and the work of other group members, enhanced capacities for collaboration in pairs or small groupings, and a sense of anticipation that the group is capable of producing something of a transcendent nature (Bion 1961). In my judgment, this class exhibited these characteristics.

WOMANIST ORIENTATION: INDIVIDUAL AND COLLECTIVE
AFFIRMATION AND HEALING

I conclude by offering some impressions about how my womanist identity influences my pedagogical orientation and strategies in the classroom. My definition of womanist refers to a philosophy and praxis that is life-promoting (versus life-negating), is wholistic, and derives from a highly personal spirituality emanating from one's personal and collective identity and shaped by Africentric belief systems. Womanist approaches emphasize issues of survival, liberation, and wholeness that include concern for and about Black people and Black women in the context of a pan-humanist cosmology that promotes the "highest good for all of life" (Nobles 1972).

Out of my experiences as an African American woman, being attuned to the communal value of oral tradition shapes my awareness. Hence, as I became privy to the individual student transformations shown in students' writing assignments, I began to ponder how the class as a whole might benefit from this knowledge. I wondered how students might come to witness one another in the process of serious engagement in the study of women's lives, whether this contested domain and the multiple issues within this classroom that impeded group development might make use of the anxieties and resistances, and how healing of some of the issues, polarities, and projections could begin.

I believe that this view of the classroom, in which the very sources of anxiety could be used in the service of course goals and objectives, derives from my womanist orientation. Such an orientation supports me in diunital thinking, described by Linda James Myers in her text *Understanding an Afrocentric World View*. Such thinking is characterized as the process of moving toward the "union of opposites" (Myers 1988: 13). This process begins with self-awareness, moves through awareness of self and "other," and culminates in the conscious search for a new or "third" space. This new space is one that facilitates or creates the integration of polarities that allows inclusiveness of self and other without homogenizing differences.

It is this third space that I sought to facilitate by developing an assignment that created opportunities for class members to build communal ties by demonstrating their collective engagement in the work of the course. At the same time, I developed the assignment to fulfill the group-level needs for increased interdependence, empowerment vis-à-vis course material, and a degree of cohesiveness that would enhance the development of a safe climate for deeper levels of discussion. My purposefulness in developing the assignment is connected to my experience of the tradition of "witnessing" as it is employed within Black communal settings, particularly within Black church contexts in America. While witnessing has many meanings (e.g., evangelical, testimonial), I am referring specifically to the process of affirming to self and others the blessings received from God in one's life. It is an age-old tradition stemming from the most rudimentary beginnings of the Black church in America and is culturally congruent with the primacy of oral traditions within Black cultures throughout the diaspora.

WITNESSING: TOWARD A UNION OF OPPOSITES

What I know of witnessing at the experiential level is that it implies speaking from the particulars of one's experience, speaking from "the heart," and speaking courageously in spite of what others might think or say. Communally, this process serves to create a wholistic story woven of individual contributions that culminate in a collective narrative. What emerged was an assignment to illustrate gender role transgressions that was structured to provide a classroom forum that met these characteristics.

To address the idea of speaking from one's own understanding and one's own analysis of the issues, this assignment required students to convey how their particular social location influenced both their interest in, as well as how they saw, this issue. Students were also required to address more than one level of analysis. Throughout the semester we had used a framework that posed three general levels from which to view an issue as a means of maintaining a more complex understanding of multiple social forces at work. The levels include (1) individual-level factors (intrapsychic issues), (2) contextual-level factors (specific situational variables), and (3) societal-level factors (sociocultural variables). The requirement to draw upon more than one level of analysis was very useful in promoting critical thinking and helping students avoid common traps of focusing solely on individual choice and agency as the cause of behavior.

The process of witnessing through student presentations helped move the class toward shared meanings and understandings, ultimately creating both an individual and collective identity in relationship to the issues examined. Yet students were allowed, by the very nature of how each group approached the assignment, varying levels of recognition of sexism within society. Thus, this assignment did not ask for a "tight" consensus in which all agree to the same extent but allowed a relatively loose consensus that acknowledged varying levels of transgression against a socially constructed patriarchal social order. At the same time that a loose consensus was allowed in keeping with a both/and rather than an either/or perspective, the assignment made sexism increasingly visible, and thus the global nature of sexism itself was "witnessed" by the collective (class). Finally, by having a common task to complete in a public manner, students witnessed each other's scholarship and saw "others" from many different social locations focus on issues relevant to women's studies (see Appendix B: Presentation Topics).

Underworld as "Third Space"

In conclusion, I view the introductory women's studies course as one that has tremendous potential for influencing student "opinions" about the field of women's studies. I feel that my role is to facilitate border crossing and the kind of playful world traveling referred to by Lugones (1990) for students who are taking the introduction to women's studies course. Opportunities for border crossing among students help them experience a both/and epistemology that defies the dualism of traditional education. They learn to value subjectivity, multicultural perspectives, and the many ways that logic can be constructed. It is to these multiple learning agendas that I respond during the semester. I can only hope that as I learn more about the deep structure of the "scripts" that emerge in these classes, I will become more able to clarify and assist in this most significant negotiation.

APPENDIX A: STUDENT PRESENTATION ASSIGNMENT

This assignment is based on the following three premises. First, according to postmodern theories, knowledge is "constructed." Second, according to leading sociological and organizational theorists, the cultures of societies and the cultures of institutions are structured to preserve and perpetuate themselves. Finally, issues in society concerning women develop when knowledge is constructed to preserve the status quo of male power. Any challenges to the constructed social arrangements constitutes a "transgression." Transgressions can occur at the *societal/institutional level* (e.g., major institutions such as religion, health care, education), the *contextual level* (norms within a particular setting such as one's own family, school, church, a particular organization or even within a marriage, friendship, relationship etc.) and, at the *individual level* (an individual's gender schema or internalized beliefs, attitudes, feelings or perceptions).

You may work *individually or with one or two others* within the class (groups of no more than three). You are to prepare a "presentation" to the class which *illustrates constructed knowledge and subsequent social arrangements* and *which illustrates a real or imagined transgression* (imagined refers to a possible transgression that might realistically occur). *Your instructions for this presentation are*:

1. Using Chapters 6–14 of the *Women's Realities Women's Choices: An Introduction to Women's Studies* text (See Hunter College Women's Studies Collective, 1995), demonstrate your ability to clearly identify an example of constructed knowledge and/or specific cultural arrangements aimed at preserving the existing power structure. Clearly identify the level of analysis you are examining and illustrating.

2. Use creativity and resourcefulness in illustrating your example. Show us rather than tell us (mime, photography, music, advertisements, video taped segments from real life, skits, or television, dance, art).

3. After the illustration, briefly explain your example of "constructed knowledge" as well as the implications for how the related "cultural arrangements" operate to constrain both men and women. In addition, indicate what you see as a solution(s).

You will have only 10 minutes. I recommend 5–7 minutes for the illustration and only 3 minutes for the wrap-up following it. There will be a penalty of 10 points for presentations which exceed the time limit.

Note: Students were also required to submit an individually written assignment to accompany this presentation assignment.

APPENDIX B: PRESENTATION TOPICS

The following topics were addressed by students in completing the assignment outlined in Appendix A.

Women and Education	Contemporary Japanese Women
Women in the Church Hierarchy	Black Female Beauty
Women's Rugby	Women Healers
Sex Discrimination at Work	Women in Medicine
Women in Politics: Hillary Clinton	Women in the Military
Women and Violent Crime	Women's Bodies in Contemporary Dance
Women and Marriage	Women in Advertisements
Constructed Knowledge and Siblings	Nuns, Lesbians, and Unmarried Women in India

SUGGESTED READINGS

Bennis, W. G. 1962. Goals and meta-goals of laboratory training. *NTL Human Relations Training News* 6: 1–3.
Bion, W. R. 1961. *Experiences in groups and other papers*. New York: Basic Books.
Nobles, W. W. 1972. African philosophy: Foundations for black psychology. *Black psychology*, ed. R. L. Jones. New York: Harper and Row.

8

Students' Fear of Lesbianism

Margaret Duncombe, Colorado College

Numerous scholars and public polls have documented the "I'm not a feminist, but . . ." phenomenon in which women who hold beliefs associated with feminism do not self-identify as feminists[1] (e.g., Kamen 1991; WMST-L 1993; Misciagno 1996; Boxer 1997). Taylor and Rupp (1996) argue that the linkage of feminism and lesbianism is one reason young women reject the feminist label. On my own campus, a survey conducted in spring 1997 by the Feminist Research Methods class members found that, across constituencies, many did not label themselves feminists because they did not want to be seen as fitting a set of negative stereotypes—"extreme," "strident," and "lesbian." Furthermore, respondents who did accept the feminist label were quick to point out they were different from the feminist norm, that is, not strident, not extreme, not lesbian.

Colorado College is a small, private, coeducational, liberal arts college. Colleges such as mine provide an intimate learning and social environment for students, but they also provide a "hothouse" environment in which finding and being accepted by a group of peers are overly important. The college uses a modular calendar where students take and faculty teach one course at a time. Because classes are small (twenty-five or fewer), and classes usually meet at least two to three hours each day, this calendar intensifies the intimacy of the learning environment. Students make friendships quickly but find themselves changing friends every three and a half weeks. This calendar makes "who is taking what course" one of the first conversation topics whenever students get together. Many of my Introduction to Women's Studies students report they have to defend their enrollment against charges of man-hating[2] and political correctness. About 15% of the student body at Colorado College is affiliated with a fraternity or sorority. Although there is a bisexual, gay, and lesbian student group, and although the college includes sexual orientation in its non-discrimination policy and provides domestic benefits, fraternities and sororities help to define a campus culture that is definitely heterosexual.[3]

Colorado College is one of the "liberal" institutions in an otherwise quite conservative town of about 350,000 people. In recent years, Colorado Springs has become home to a large number of national evangelical Christian organizations. Inclusion of gays, lesbians, and bisexuals is a hotly debated local topic; although the college traditionally does not take a position on local politics, both the faculty and the student government took official positions opposing Amendment 2, a 1992 ballot initiative to deny gay and lesbian civil rights.

Women's studies is an accepted part of the Colorado College curriculum. Most women's studies courses fulfill an "Alternatives to the Western Tradition" general education requirement. Students can major or minor in women's studies. As of 1998, there is a tenure-track line in women's studies, and approximately thirty-five faculty teach courses in, or cross-listed with, women's studies each year. Despite these signs of institutional vigor for women's studies and despite institutional support of lesbians, the association of lesbianism with feminism at Colorado College makes Introduction to Women's Studies a less attractive course and engenders students to describe themselves as "not feminists, but . . ."

Unlike Marilyn Frye's (1992) rhetorical question, Does one have to be a lesbian to be a feminist?, the reverse question is relevant at colleges such as mine, Can one be a lesbian and an effective teacher of Introduction to Women's Studies? Eisen and Hall (1996) argue that lesbianism has moved from "the closet" to "the cover," but in recent years I have found myself wondering whether my identity as a public lesbian was a detriment to my hopes for the introductory course and my women students. In this chapter I describe how I, as a lesbian faculty member, do respond to students' expressed rejection of lesbianism, and I "think through" what might be better, more efficacious ways of responding. I organize my discussion around two polarities: whether I deem my response to be positive or negative and whether the response is personal or pedagogical.

NEGATIVE/PERSONAL: ANGST

The negative personal response is hurt and despair. I see myself as an impediment to my advocacy of feminism and women's studies. This sense of failure leads, on one hand, to all kinds of workaholic behaviors as a method of compensation—if I just work harder, do more, appear smarter, students and colleagues will see past my lesbianism and appreciate my commitments in both the college and the wider community, and my sections of Introduction to

Women's Studies will suddenly have double-digit waiting lists. On the other hand, the hurt leads, in the extreme, to objectifying nonfeminists as know-nothing homophobes, a form of rejecting my rejectors. There is no doubt that homophobia[4] is alive and well in the United States (Rosenberg, Miller, and Leland 1994), and Colorado Springs is subject to some of its most virulent rhetorical forms, so my characterization of my rejectors may not be wrong. Nonetheless, such responses exacerbate my inability to contribute to the college and help its members embrace feminism and women's studies. I am often exhausted, and I am often angry, especially angry at the need to prove to students that emotional and erotic bonding with women is not hatred of men.

NEGATIVE/PEDAGOGICAL: LESBIAN INVISIBILITY AND FEMINIST INVINCIBILITY

Fueled by what I have called negative personal reactions, my teaching in Introduction to Women's Studies is often designed to convince students that their heterosexuality is OK, that my lesbianism does not matter, and that feminism is *right*, that is, that the varieties of feminism are powerful interpretations of women's situations. These are worthy teaching goals; nevertheless, I deem them negative when used in the extreme and when used to avoid confronting students' fear of lesbianism and the feminist label.

I go out of my way to convince students that heterosexuality and feminism are compatible and to distinguish the institution of compulsory heterosexuality (Rich 1980) from the individual practice of heterosexuality. In particular, I do not push very hard for students to reconsider their felt experience of innate heterosexuality in light of the societal coercions of institutional heterosexuality. While I am ''out'' to all my students, I do not talk about my personal life, and, for the most part, I do not teach texts that describe lesbian lives. In upper-division courses I do devote considerable teaching energy to the role of homophobia in perpetuating the gender-role system (Pharr 1988), but this is downplayed in the Introduction to Women's Studies course. If I have students whom I know to be lesbians or gay men in class, I am somewhat more vocal about heterosexual privilege so that these students need not reveal their sexual orientation unless they want to. I should do this more than I do because closeted lesbian and gay male students surely take Introduction to Women's Studies.[5] These students, perhaps more than their ''out'' peers, could benefit from an explicit challenge to homophobia and heterosexual privilege.

I structure my classes to show students that feminism is such a powerful—and right!—analytic tool that they ought to embrace it. Students do not have to agree with me to do well in my class, but I feel I have failed to effectively present the material if students reject the power of feminist analysis. Particularly with issues of domestic and sexual violence, I hammer hard the power of feminist analysis. Indeed, this is some of my best teaching. I am an old hand at structuring an argument, and often I can structure the argument in such a way that students have a hard time disagreeing. Rather than agreeing with me, however, students shut down and withdraw intellectually from the discussion. Maher and Tetreault (1994: 117) observe that there is a "tension between female undergraduates' desire for heterosexual fulfillment in relation to men . . . and the narrative of women as sexual victim often encountered in feminist theoretical work." Given a perceived tension between their wishes for fulfillment and feminist narratives, introductory students embrace their own wishes and reject feminism. Thus, a teaching strategy designed to attract students to feminism, in fact, may drive them away from it.

POSITIVE/PERSONAL: ANALYSIS OF HETEROSEXISM

A more positive response to students' expressed rejection of lesbianism is to realize that their rejection has nothing to do with me. Students do *not* reject me, a particular lesbian; indeed, students who take my classes are, for the most part, respectful of me and willing to learn from me. Rather, students' rejection of lesbianism is a fear that they will be thought of as lesbians if they embrace the feminist label or if they are too passionate about the materials in Introduction to Women's Studies. For my students, my being a lesbian is perfectly acceptable; what is not acceptable is for them to be deemed, called, known as lesbians. Anderson (1994: 152) argues that this attitude of tolerance of homosexuality in others but rejection for self is pervasive in the secondary schools from which most of our students come; he reports that "[a] Harris poll released in June 1993 reported that 86% of high school students said they would be very upset if classmates called them gay or lesbian."

Women are accused of being lesbians when their behavior challenges the gender system (Pharr 1988). Gaard (1996: 115) found that "when a woman is harassed and does not respond in the way the harasser wants, one way to escalate the attack is to shift the harassment from antiwoman to anti-lesbian remarks." Blinde and Taub (1992; see also Lenskyj 1990; Krane 1996) report that women athletes are often falsely accused of being lesbians, and they argue that accusations of lesbianism serve to define sports as an exclusive male arena and source of privilege. Male athletes, those most directly threatened by increasing attention to women's athletics, are those most apt to accuse women athletes of lesbianism.

Lesbianism itself is not necessarily a threat to the gender system. Women who live psychologically and economically independent of men challenge the hegemony of patriarchy, but women-to-women sexuality can be incorporated into male domination of women. For example, Andrea Dworkin documents the inclusion of lesbian practice in heterosexual male practice and pornography (Szikla 1996: 6). Smith-Rosenberg (1975) and others have documented that intense emotional and erotic relationships between women coexisted with Victorian patriarchy. If lesbianism can coexist with patriarchy, why is there so much stigma attached to the lesbian label? The accusation of lesbianism functions to reinforce the gender system more than to enforce heterosexual sexual practice.

Another way to understand that students' fear of lesbianism is not about lesbianism per se is to examine what students are really afraid of. The rejection of lesbianism is a culturally provided rhetoric by which students (among others) articulate their fear of feminism. In other words, my initial formulation that students' fear of lesbianism led them to reject feminism needs to be inverted: students' fear of feminism leads them to articulate a rejection of lesbianism. Every culture provides culturally acceptable modes of discourse. Lesbian-bashing is one culturally provided discourse for reaffirming one's compliance with the gender role system and for rejecting challenges to that system.

Lisa Marie Hogeland (1994) argues that young women have very good reasons to fear feminism. Thus, young women have very good reasons to articulate a rejection of lesbianism. Feminism decenters men and as such is a violation of deeply held gender norms, a violation that exposes young women to risks, at a minimum, of disapproval by male friends, family members, and love interests:

Young women may believe that a feminist identity puts them out of the pool for many men, limits the options of who they might become with a partner, how they might decide to live. They may not be wrong either: how many young men feminists or feminist sympathizers do you know? A politics that may require making demands on a partner, or that may motivate particular choices in partners, can appear to foreclose rather than to open up options for identity, especially for women who haven't yet discovered that all relationships require negotiation and struggle. When you live on Noah's ark, anything that might make it more difficult to find a partner can seem to threaten your very survival. (Hogeland 1994: 20)

Feminism also decenters individualism and makes it difficult for students to believe that they will be able to craft a life and relationships independent of the gender system. Waxman and Byington (1997) use a line from Paul Monette's memoir, "Is this more than you want to know?" to describe student resistance in the classroom. Bauer and Rhoades (1996) quote from journals in which students complain that feminism paints too negative a picture. One of the students interviewed by Maher and Tetreault (1994: 117) made explicit her fear of feminist knowledge: "When I was eighteen I was sexually assaulted and . . . one reason it took me so long to get into Gender Studies was that I didn't want to have to deal with that." Hogeland (1994: 21) says:

Women have real reasons to fear feminism, and we do young women no service if we suggest to them that feminism itself is safe. It is not. To stand opposed to your culture, to be critical of institutions, behaviors, discourses—when it is so clearly *not* in your immediate interest to do so—asks a lot of a young person, of any person.

Such an analysis of what is really going on in students' articulated rejection of lesbianism makes me sad, but I need not take their rejection personally. I am not being rejected; rather, the role of activist, change agent, societal critic is being rejected. Even so, I am not completely comfortable with this analysis. It strikes me as incredibly arrogant and self-serving to claim that I know what is really going on for my students. This analysis of students' often unknowing capitulation to heterosexism is as dismissive of students as the more explicitly negative dismissal of them as "know-nothing homophobes."

POSITIVE/PEDAGOGICAL: DIRECT ENGAGEMENT

As a teacher, my responsibility is to put my analysis of heterosexism, what I think is really going on in students' articulated rejection of the lesbian label, on the table for discussion. Rather than skirting the issues, I should confront them directly. There are at least two teaching agendas in such a project.

Explicit Discussion of Homophobia and Heterosexism

In the introductory course, the power of the lesbian label must be confronted directly. I should argue that the threat of being called a lesbian is a vehicle of social control that constrains women's choices. I might have students write an in-class essay about a situation in which they were called lesbians—what were they doing, who labeled them, what was their response? When do they use the lesbian label? What do they hope to accomplish? Another teaching strategy would be small-group discussions of Suzanne Pharr's (1988) argument that sexism will not be dismantled until *every* woman is willing to be called a lesbian (regardless of the gender of her sexual partner/s). Parallels from other resistances to oppression may help students understand this point—for example, Danish Gentiles wearing the "Star of David" during the World War II Nazi occupation of Denmark.

I should structure my classes to examine the ways in which heterosexism affects heterosexuals as well as lesbians. Adrienne Rich's (1980) essay on "compulsory heterosexuality" could be used as a text.[6] Students should discover that their acceptance of heterosexual privileges and their search for individual solutions reinforce a system of oppression; their so-called liberation requires the continuing subordination of other sisters. These are not easy lessons for students, and I expect they will resist. The danger is that their resistance will trigger the negative personal and pedagogical reactions I discussed earlier. My hope is that by being explicit about my teaching strategies and anticipating resistance, I can avoid overpersonalizing student reactions to lesbianism.

Explicit Discussion of Sexuality

Both lesbianism and heterosexuality need to be made visible in the Introduction to Women's Studies classroom. Lesbianism should be explored so that students have an opportunity to correct the misinformation presented in the wider culture, to unlearn their homophobia. Effective ways to do this are student panels of lesbians, bisexuals, and gay males (Fonow and Marty 1991; Nelson and Krieger 1997). Patricia MacCorquodale encourages students to write questions or comments that they submit anonymously. MacCorquodale normalizes the activity by explaining that she is asking for input ''so there will be a chance for you to ask the things you probably really want to say and know, but I know it's difficult for you to ask them in this big group context'' (Maher and Tetreault 1994: 60).

As important as discussing lesbianism as a separate topic is mainstreaming lesbianism in the class, for example, showing the film *Choosing Children*[7] or using Barbara Smith's (1983) narrative ''Home'' as part of a ''family'' discussion; including discrimination against lesbians in a discussion of work issues; and including hate crimes against gays and lesbians in the discussion of violence.[8]

At the same time lesbianism is included, heterosexuality has to be discussed explicitly so that it is not so ''normal'' as to be taken for granted and not in need of discussion (WMST-L 1995). Fonow and Marty (1991) suggest using panels of heterosexuals to parallel panels of lesbians. Naomi Wolf's (1992) piece from *Ms.* entitled ''Radical Heterosexuality'' would be especially helpful in modeling for heterosexual women students the kinds of demands they might make of men they hope to live with. Wolf's analysis is perhaps more effective than a similar piece by Marilyn Frye (1992) because it is brief, accessible, and predicated on the assumption that ''you *can* hate sexism and love men'' (Wolf 1992: 29). Frye (1992) is skeptical of this assumption, and, as a result, heterosexual students in the introductory course sometimes find her description of ''willfull virgins'' beyond what they can envision for themselves. Students need to understand the feminist tenet that ''the personal is political,'' and they need to be inspired to make explicit political choices in their personal lives.

"SAFE" CLASSROOMS

Much of the literature on ''teaching tolerance'' assumes that the kind of frank consciousness-changing discussions I have advocated here cannot take place unless students feel ''safe'' in the classroom. For example, Carla Rensenbrink (1996: 265) argues that a fifth-grade teacher's lesbianism made a positive difference because of her ''efforts to create a safe place in which her students can be 'who they are' ''; the teacher describes her classroom in this way: ''it's safe to be who you are here, and you can be anything you want—and I think part of that is me being a lesbian and they knowing it and so what? It's like anything is OK; everyone is OK'' (266). I can hardly argue against the wisdom of creating an environment in which ''everyone is OK,'' but I reject the position that ''*anything* is OK.'' Heterosexism, racism, classism, and so on are not OK, and no one should be given permission to say hurtful things. Maher and Tetreault (1994: 122) interviewed an African American student who questioned the wisdom of feminist pedagogy because "it assumes that everyone's opinion is valid, so that the feminist classroom becomes a safe place in which students can say 'stupid things.' " Swearingen (1996: 152) acknowledges that creating a safe classroom is a double-edged technique: "Because of the comfort zone that has been so carefully crafted and encouraged, the students say things that would be less likely to be said in other classes. . . . [T]his comfortable situation also allowed statements to surface that were homophobic, racist, and sexist." Swearingen (1996) and McMahon (1997) argue that rather than challenge such remarks directly, teachers should ask questions that will move students toward recognition of their prejudice, to allow them, in Waxman and Byington's (1997) words, to become "border-crossers."

By implication the "safe" classroom is one in which anything is OK, and students (and, presumably, faculty) feel comfortable saying "stupid" things they would not say in "unsafe" classrooms. Creation of such a "safe" space is clearly troublesome for the women's studies teacher. No classroom is uniformly safe for all students (Disch and Thompson 1990: 76); the danger of seeking to make our classrooms safe is that we will further exacerbate existing privilege imbalances and make the classroom safer for white students, for male students, and for heterosexual students and less safe for students of color, for female students, for lesbians, and for gay male students.

Fonow and Marty (1991: 407) change the definition of "safe" from one in which anything is OK to one in which anything can be said (and challenged):

Ethical considerations demand careful attention to the creation of a safe environment in which all participants can discuss sensitive topics. Gay students and instructors will be exposed to the homophobic reactions of nongay students, who need to have the freedom to reveal their prejudices and lack of knowledge in order to have them challenged. For real learning to occur, confrontations with students about their homophobia must be dealt with directly in a way that does not shame or humiliate the offending student and at the same time repairs the damage done to the self-respect of gay, lesbian, and bisexual students. It is important not to reproduce in the classroom the racism, class privilege, sexism, and heterosexism found in society.

This conception of "safe" is more useful, although still fraught with danger. In particular, I question my ability consistently to walk the tightrope of not shaming or humiliating the offending student at the same time I repair the damage to the self-respect of offended students.

Some authors advocate letting students challenge peers rather than insisting that faculty always be the ones to do so. For example, Disch and Thompson (1990: 77) say that "[w]hen our teaching is successful, students confront each other about distorted attitudes rather than leaving the confrontation up to the teacher." Students may be more willing to be challenged by a peer than by a faculty member, so perhaps peer criticism is more effective than that from a teacher. Nonetheless, I am not comfortable relying on students to manage the tightrope described by Fonow and Marty in the previous quotation. Students may not be willing to consistently take on this task, and I do not think faculty have the right to demand that they do so.

Fonow and Marty (1991) argue that students' prejudices are most effectively challenged if given voice in the classroom. Even if this is true, their strategy of allowing students to reveal their prejudices underestimates the incredible hurt of hearing peers/acquaintances/friends make prejudicial remarks. Personally, I cringe every time I hear a student describe heterosexuality as "normal" even when I recognize that the context is normal, meaning frequently occurring or typical. Rather than encourage students to give voice to prejudiced statements, faculty would do better to model a dialogue with prejudiced attitudes using quotations from the news, popular culture, or even a hypothetical, made-up bigot. Staged dialogues allow the prejudiced attitude to be challenged without damaging any of the face-to-face relationships of the classroom. Staged dialogues permit students to see the parallels between their own attitudes and those criticized by the faculty member without being publicly identified with the attitude and thus without being publicly shamed or humiliated. If attitudes do change as a result of classroom challenge, staged dialogues allow the challenge to occur without the dangers of allowing students to voice homophobic (racist, classist, etc.) remarks. I wonder, however, whether prejudiced students will change their attitude as a result of such classroom challenges; it seems naive to assume that people willingly give up privilege just because they are made aware of it.

Rather than "safety," the best we can offer our students is that their ideas will be listened to attentively, taken seriously, and responded to civilly. Students should be told the issues for class discussion are ones they and the faculty member care passionately about and ones about which there will be heated disagreement. I always tell my students on the first day of class that I am a woman of strong opinions, but that I am not necessarily always right. I tell them that my responsibility is to question their taken-for-granted assumptions and that I hope they will be willing to question mine.

Teachers should exhort class members to listen carefully to what is being said rather than too quickly assuming what is being said, and teachers should be prepared to offer listening exercises. Role-playing activities in which students must articulate a position not their own or other active learning exercises may be useful.[9] Class members should devise a set of guidelines for discussion of controversial topics. Many faculty have had success using the guidelines developed by Lynn Weber Cannon (1990); others find that devoting part of the first class session to students' developing their own guidelines sets the stage for effective discussion. At a minimum, class members should agree to carefully consider the remarks of others and to think about how to extend the discussion rather than attack or make points before they speak. If some students blurt responses and thereby dominate the discussion, the class will have to resort to raising hands or devise some other way of distributing the right to speak.

My classroom is inherently political. The topics I include, the examples I use, the texts I assign, the remarks I take up, and the remarks I let pass all make my classroom political; it cannot be otherwise. I have never taught a class that could not have been done better. I suspect I never will. Teaching is a struggle. What I have done in this chapter is to think publicly about the tensions that define my struggle at this point in time: where is the balance point between respecting students' narratives of their lives and validating what, as an old-fashioned sociologist, I learned to call "false consciousness"? What is the point at which a "safe" classroom becomes a complacent classroom? How much do I reveal of myself to my students and how much do I risk their rejection?

NOTES

I am grateful to Frances Kendall, Gwen Kirk, and Margo Okazawa-Rey for conversations and resources that helped me deepen my thinking about these issues. An earlier version of this chapter was presented at the Women in Higher Education Conference (January 1998).

1. Patricia Misciagno (1996) calls women who are activists in feminist causes without identifying with the feminist label "de-facto feminists."

2. See Cataldi (1995) for an analysis of the charge of man-hating.

3. See Boswell and Spade (1996), Sanday (1990), and Martin and Hummer (1989) for a discussion of the role of fraternities in enforcing hypermasculinity and heterosexuality.

4. Nelson and Krieger (1997) review the work of Hancock (1986), who distinguishes a *fear* of gay men and lesbians (homophobia) from a prejudicial attitude toward gay men and lesbians, which might be better labeled "homonegativism" or "homoprejudice." Although I am sympathetic to this distinction, in this chapter I follow common usage and use "homophobia" to refer to negative attitudes toward lesbians and gay men whether these attitudes have their origin in fear or not.

5. If I do not know a student to be lesbian, bisexual, or gay before the class begins, I do not usually discover this as a result of class discussion, written work, or office conferences. Unlike Patai (1992; see also Patai and Koertge 1994), who describes a form of lesbian intimidation or heterosexual closeting in women's studies classes, my experience confirms Maher and Tetreault's (1994: 161) observation that lesbian students in the women's studies courses they observed usually stayed in the closet.

6. Richardson and Taylor's (1993) introductory textbook, *Feminist Frontiers III*, includes an edited version of the original *Signs* article; this edited version also includes an afterword of critical comment and response. *Signs* itself published a critical comment by Martha Thompson (1981). Both critical comments raise the question of whether heterosexuality can be rehabilitated for the feminist project; while this is an important question, including it in the introductory course may be a "turnoff" for students trying to imagine a heterosexual *and* feminist future for themselves.

7. *Choosing Children* was produced by Margaret Lazarus and directed by Debra Chasnoff and Kim Klausner in 1995. It is available from Cambridge Documentary Films.

8. See Fonow and Marty (1991), Crumpacker and Haegen (1993), and Schieder (1993) for useful discussions of teaching resources and pedagogical practices for inclusion of lesbianism in the women's studies classroom.

9. Many students will be familiar with these exercises through peer mediation training in their secondary schools. Human relations departments at colleges and universities are sometimes prepared to teach active listening skills. There is an extensive conflict resolution literature that may be helpful in suggesting exercises that can be adapted to the classroom. See for example the chapter on ''Building Trust and Cooperation'' in Moore (1986). Schniedewind (1993) provides several activities that teach ''feminist process'' in the women's studies classroom.

SUGGESTED READINGS

Cannon, L. W. 1990. Fostering positive race, class, and gender dynamics in the classroom. *Women's Studies Quarterly* 18: 126–134.

Fonow, M. M. and D. Marty. 1991. The shift from identity politics to the politics of identity: Lesbian panels in the women's studies classroom. *NWSA Journal* 3: 402–413.

Hogeland, L. M. 1994. Fear of feminism: Why young women get the willies. *Ms.* (November/December): 18–21.

Pharr, S. 1988. *Homophobia: A weapon of sexism.* Inverness, CA: Chardon.

Rich, A. 1980. Compulsory heterosexuality and lesbian existence. *Signs* 5: 631–660.

Wolf, N. 1992. Radical heterosexuality . . . or how to love a man and save your feminist soul. *Ms.* (July/August): 28–31.

9

"When I Look at You, I Don't See Race" and Other Diverse Tales from the Introduction to Women's Studies Classroom

Lisa Bowleg, University of Rhode Island

"Gee, I feel like we're being bombarded by the writings of Black lesbians." So wrote a White female senior in her reading journal in one of my two Introduction to Women's Studies courses during the fall 1997 semester. Although I had taught in the undergraduate Women's Studies Program at Georgetown University since 1994, this was my first time teaching an Introduction to Women's Studies course. Initially, I was elated with nostalgia at teaching the course that I had taken as a student at Georgetown exactly ten years earlier. I hoped that my Introduction to Women's Studies course would affect students in the same way that my first course had affected me. Specifically, I wanted to challenge students to think about what it meant to be girls and women in our culture and to explore throughout the entire course the intersections of gender with identities such as race, ethnicity, socioeconomic class, sexual orientation/preference, physical disabilities, and age, to name just a few. Yet, my student's quote about the bombardment by topics and materials relevant to women who are not White or heterosexual clearly illuminates the expectations that many of my students had for the course. Specifically, students expected to learn about women who were like themselves. This quote and others like it set the stage for much of what the students and I would experience throughout the semester as we confronted issues of diversity not in one class period, but in every class.

Each of the classes met twice a week for an hour and fifteen minutes. Although required for women's studies major, Introduction to Women's Studies is offered as an elective for all students at the university. Each section of the course had fourteen students, most of whom were juniors and seniors. I estimate that most of the students were nineteen or twenty years old. The first section of my course was the most diverse. This class included one African American male student, two African American female students, and one Latina student. The rest of the students were White and predominantly middle-class. None of the students self-identified as other than heterosexual. The second section of the class consisted entirely of women. With the exception of a Latina woman who identified as bisexual, all of the other students were White, and no others identified as other than heterosexual. Although one student self-identified as working-class, most of the others identified as middle-class.

This chapter focuses on my students' expectations about the legitimacy and relevance of issues of diversity in the Introduction to Women's Studies curriculum. Specifically, I explore how my students, who were predominantly White, middle-class, able-bodied, young, heterosexual, and female, perceived and responded to topics, course papers and journals, reading assignments, and class discussions that focused on women from diverse perspectives rather than from a solely White, middle-class, able-bodied, young, and heterosexual perspective. Additionally, I explore how the aforementioned dynamics become manifest when the professor is "other." In my case, I am a Black, middle-class, openly lesbian, Caribbean-born professor who teaches students whose demographic backgrounds and life experiences often differ quite markedly from my own. Throughout the chapter, I highlight specific experiences and anecdotes from my course; analyze these issues and dynamics; and discuss what we as teachers can learn from my students' and my experiences in fostering an appreciation for diversity in the classroom.

FEMINISM AND CATHOLICISM ON CAMPUS:
STRANGE BEDFELLOWS INDEED

Founded by the Jesuits in 1789, Georgetown University is the nation's oldest Catholic university. Although students need not be Catholic to attend the university, the indomitable presence of Catholicism permeates many aspects of student life. For example, because the Catholic Church forbids premarital sex, there are no campus sites at which students can obtain birth control or condoms. Women who believe that they may be pregnant face a wall of silence, fostered by policies that prohibit university staff from discussing abortion as an option or referring students to an abortion provider. Gay, lesbian, bisexual, or transgendered students are becoming increasingly visible on campus. Much of this visibility is due to a 1988 settlement of a decade-old lawsuit initiated by the campus' gay, lesbian, and bisexual student group (a group whose very existence is antithetical to church teachings) that charged that the university had discriminated against students on the basis of sexual orientation by denying the student group the same funds as other student groups. Consequently, Georgetown's religious foundation fosters an environment that, despite pockets of progressive activism, is predominantly socially conservative. Not surprisingly, many Georgetown students tend to hold relatively conservative positions on issues such as abortion and rights for women, lesbian, gay, bisexual, and transgendered people.

"IF SOMEONE CALLED ME A FEMINIST, I'D BE INSULTED": INTRODUCTION TO WOMEN'S STUDIES, DAY 1

Historically, Georgetown University has been inhospitable to feminists and women's studies. In a recent address to the fourth annual National Association for Women in Catholic Higher Education (NAWCHE) conference, Dr. Margaret Stetz (1998), an associate professor of English and Women's Studies at Georgetown, chided the university for its disrespect of women's studies. Stetz noted that this disregard for women's studies was manifest through status indicators such as the absence of women's studies courses from the core curriculum, the small, two-office women's studies space, and the prevalence of poorly paid or low-paid, part-time adjunct faculty to teach core women's studies courses.

At the student level, Georgetown's disrespect for women's studies is so effortlessly transmitted that "entering students learn disrespect for Women's Studies because that is what is modeled for them by [Georgetown University] itself" (Stetz 1998: 2). In my courses, many of the students brought their preexisting contempt for women's studies as well as their unexamined social identity privileges to the first class. Yet, whittling away the students' initial disdain for women's studies proved fairly easy, especially in light of the strength of the antifeminist backlash on campus. The semester got off to a rousing antifeminist start when two students calling themselves the Women's Guild (1997) published *The Guide: A Little Beige Book for Today's Miss G* with financial backing from an off-campus conservative women's group and distributed it to all female first-year students. Among the gems in the nineteen-page manual was the introduction, in which the authors claimed that "the fight for equality [for women] is largely a thing of the past—after all, two Supreme Court Justices, the Secretary of State, and Attorney General all wear heels" (1). *The Guide* assiduously derided campus feminists for overestimating the prevalence of rape and eating disorders and encouraged women to "conquer the world (and men) [with] a dash of grace, a flash of charm, a modest flirtation" (19). Presumably because campus contemporaries had written it, *The Guide* swiftly and adroitly enlightened my students about the importance of feminism and women's studies on campus, as well as beyond it.

So, whereas at the beginning of the course several students readily admitted that they would have been insulted or uncomfortable being called a feminist, the antifeminist sentiments pervading Georgetown's campus in *The Guide* and student newspapers, combined with course material, encouraged students to recognize and think critically and analytically about gender-based prejudice, oppression, and discrimination. However, educating students to critically and analytically recognize the ways in which they were socially privileged and how this unexamined privilege bolstered systems of oppression against people (women in particular) who were members of racial or ethnic minorities, low-income or poor, disabled, old, or gay, lesbian, bisexual, or transgendered remained a challenge.

"THE AMPERSAND PROBLEM": BUILDING THE MULTICULTURAL INTRODUCTION TO WOMEN'S STUDIES COURSE

Day 1 of the course began with an overview of the Introduction to Women's Studies curriculum. As Dr. Stetz (my first women's studies professor) had done, I invoked the Pandora's box myth as a metaphor for the journey on which students had embarked. After an explanation of the tenets of women's studies, I emphasized that the course was designed to explore topics relevant to gender in general and women and girls in particular, framing the lives and experiences of girls and women within the context of other identities such as race, ethnicity, age, class, sexual preference/orientation, culture, and physical abilities. To this end, I had chosen the anthology *Women, Images and Realities: A Multicultural Anthology* (Kesselman, McNair, and Schniedewind 1995) as one of my required texts and had included a readings packet of articles by diverse and multicultural women. I explained to the students that they should not expect to find a "diversity section" on the syllabus, but rather that they would read the voices of diverse women throughout every section of the course. Thus, in the "What Is Women's Studies?" section they read Ferreira's (1995) "Finding My Latina Identity through Women's Studies," and in the section on "Heterosexism" they read Appleby's (1993) "Disability and 'Compulsory Heterosexuality.' "

Spelman (1997) has critiqued feminists for what she calls "the ampersand problem," namely, the tendency for many feminists to elevate gender to a level that obfuscates other important identities such as race and ethnicity. Yet a mere three classes after having read and discussed Spelman's article, I had a student remark in her journal upon reading of Rosa Park's role in the Civil Rights movement that Rosa Parks was relevant to the Civil Rights movement but had absolutely nothing to do with women's rights. For this student, feminist attempts to celebrate the achievement of one of American history's most courageous women was, as she put it, "a stretch." This inability to simultaneously recognize the intersections of sexism and racism is troublesome at best because it fosters the misguided notion that racism is more fundamental than sexism (Spelman 1997).

WILL THIS BE ON THE TEST? THE RELEVANCE AND LEGITIMACY OF DIVERSITY IN WOMEN'S STUDIES

With time, students can be enlightened about the relevance and legitimacy of studying women's issues. Indeed, the fact that they choose to enroll in a course for which they often have ambivalent feelings suggests that, on some level, they view the subject of gender and women as worthy of their time and tuition. They soon encounter the "click experience" in which they link their personal experiences as women within a larger political system of patriarchal domination. This is the easy part. Acknowledging the relevance and legitimacy of focusing on diverse and multicultural issues, however, is much more difficult. Take the midterm paper that I assigned, for example. Pursuant to my stated emphasis on the importance of diversity, I assigned what I thought would be a stimulating, albeit fairly simple, assignment. The instructions were straightforward: "Find a woman with whose background you differ and are unfamiliar (that is, no close friends or family members). You may choose a woman who is significantly older, or one who is from a different racial, ethnic, cultural or religious background than yours; a woman who has a physical or mental disability; a woman who identifies as bisexual, lesbian or transgendered; or a woman from another socioeconomic class. Interview this woman using the five questions provided." Simple enough, right? Not quite.

While many of the students embraced this assignment with relish, others were reluctant to do it. One student had a particularly aversive reaction to the assignment, noting that she saw all people as people first and resented being asked to focus on diversity. "After all," this student pleaded, "we're all just people." I explained to her, as I had to the other students, that one of the values of this exercise lay in having the opportunity to learn how people evaluate multiple identities. Specifically, just because a student chose an interviewee on the basis of race would not necessarily mean that the interviewee considered race to be a salient identity. Rather, she may have identified one or more identities such as class, culture, or religion as being a more significant definer of her life as a woman.

Another reason for some of my students' difficulty with the midterm paper was that they lived lives that were fairly insulated from diverse others. Mostly, they lived and socialized with people who looked like them and shared their class backgrounds. Many of the students admitted that they did not know anyone of another race, class, or sexual orientation to interview. Other students noted that they were reluctant to seek out someone unknown or different from themselves to interview. In reflecting on the nature of the racial and class chasm on campus, students suggested that this "was just the way things were at Georgetown." With rare exceptions, students of the same race or ethnicity ate together in the university cafeteria and socialized at the same events. Some students mused that this voluntary racial segregation was a "natural state," others felt disturbed by it, and still others had committed to fostering a multicultural network of friends.

My students' difficulties in finding multicultural others to interview and their reservations about doing so have important implications for the personal-political nexus that we so frequently discuss in Introduction to Women's Studies courses. It is not enough for people who have (by choice or circumstance) no social interactions with people from diverse backgrounds to simply acknowledge the importance of diversity in theory but not in practice. Similarly, it is imperative that people from dominant groups who teach students the importance of valuing multiculturalism practice in their personal lives what they teach in the classroom. Feminist bell hooks (1994a) has called for an "engaged pedagogy" that would require teachers to self-disclose their personal experiences relevant to the academic material. Echoing hooks' theme, Rosenberg (1997: 80) calls on White teachers who teach about race to "consider how much, what, and when it is appropriate for us as educators to share with our students our own process around understanding ourselves as White."

WHEN MORE IS LESS: PERCEIVING RACE AND MULTIPLE IDENTITIES AS DEFICIT

"My question is: What does all of this business about multiple identities have to do with the Women's Movement" wrote one student in her journal. "If asked to describe myself," she continued, "I would provide my name, age and maybe my major—that's it. We need to focus on the things that unite us as women, not just the differences." This student's attempt to ignore cultural differences among women was emblematic of a larger social phenomenon operating in my classes, namely, that the White, middle-class students had the privilege of seeing themselves as generics (that is, as "just people"), while the people of color in the class were keenly aware that they were "Black people" or "Latina people." Kimmel and Messner's (1992: 2–3) reflection on a dialogue between a Black and White woman at a feminist theory seminar aptly captures the issue:

"When you wake up in the morning and look in the mirror, what do you see?" [the Black woman] asked. "I see a woman," replied the White woman. "That's precisely the issue," replied the Black woman. "I see a Black woman. For me, race is visible every day, because it is how I am not privileged in this culture. Race is invisible to you."

This invisibility of race, particularly the White race, has emerged as a recurrent theme in several of my women's studies courses at Georgetown. Many of my students who are White readily acknowledge that people who are not White have a race but appear unaware that White is also a race and that White people derive a host of privileges by virtue of their skin color alone. McIntosh (1989: 76–77) has likened white privilege to an "invisible package of unearned assets that [White people] can count on cashing in each day, but about which [White people were] 'meant' to remain oblivious." Not surprisingly, when confronted with the unearned privileges that they derive on the basis of their race, many students report feeling discomfort and guilt. For educators, the challenge is to validate the students' feelings while simultaneously guiding them to an awareness of their privilege and how they wield it and encouraging them to recognize that sexism cannot be eradicated without a concurrent fight against other forms of oppression.

A section of the course entitled "Ties That Bond and Divide: Women's Similarities and Differences," in which we focused on racism, classism, and anti-Semitism, acutely revealed the discomfort that students felt about discussing these issues, particularly racism. Although they all decried racism as an oppressive force, many students conceded that the topic of racism made them uncomfortable because of their guilt as White people and because it simply was too difficult to discuss. In an attempt to create some psychological distance, I shifted the discussion away from the students toward their analyses and critiques of the readings. This was partially successful in the sense that some students readily grasped the messages that the women of color conveyed. Yet, other students remained absolutely baffled. "What does Parker [1978] mean when she says that White people who want to befriend her must first forget that she's Black and second never forget that she's Black?" some students asked. "That's a contradiction." Precisely.

It was also clear that several of my students subscribed to the deficit model of race. Specifically, they perceived people of color as being disadvantaged solely by virtue of their race. One student remarked, "You know, when I see a Latina or other woman of color on the street, I want to say 'hello' just because I know how hard her life has been." Embodied in this comment is the notion that any race other than White is a burden fraught only with the challenges of living in a racist society. Yet, perceiving non-White race only in terms of racism deprives people of color of the many unique and distinct ways in which our cultures enrich our lives. The converse of the race-based pity perspective was another student's comment to me, "You know, when I look at you, I don't see race." Shocked by the comment (after all, we had already spent several weeks discussing the significance of intersections of gender with other identities), I explained to the student that my race was not only a very important part of my identity but one that defined a myriad of experiences that I have had as woman, and indeed, as a human being. Her desire to obliterate my race tells much about the embodiment of whiteness as norm.

CLASS IN CLASS: EXPLORING SOCIOECONOMIC PRIVILEGE

Class has long been a taboo topic in the United States, yet "we experience class at every level of our lives" (Langston 1988: 102). Class and class privilege are particularly important in light of the tendency for class to be so easily conflated or confused with race and ethnicity.

Compared with their race privilege, many of my students had some notion of the ways in which they were privileged by class. Georgetown's tuition is so expensive that students would have to actively ignore their socioeconomic advantage or that of those around them not to recognize the benefits that accrue to middle-class and upper-middle-class people. This notwithstanding, many of my students had an understanding of their class privilege that was superficial at best. Moreover, students seemed quite confused about how class functioned in their lives. For example, having acknowledged her upper-middle-class background, one of my students noted that upon graduation she would lose her class advantage because of her parents' decision to terminate financial support. Another student from a working-class background (and the beneficiary of numerous federal student loans) explained to the former student that graduating debt-free was certainly indicative of class privilege, as was having parents with an ample cash reserve if circumstances necessitated.

The students were not alone when it came to middle-class solipsism, however. Although I belong to more subordinate social category groups than dominant groups, the middle class is one of the dominant groups to which I belong. My membership in this group affords me a host of privileges denied working-class and poor people. My recognition of my class privilege prompted me to be hypervigilant about the readings I selected on class and the examples that I used to elucidate points and principles from the readings. My examples, however, were not always successful. In the class on work, for example, I would unwittingly and inevitably invoke examples of women working in offices rather than in factories or as domestic workers. To confront this solipsism, I did as hooks (1994a) has advised and openly shared the manifestations of my middle-class bias with my students. My invitation to students to help me overcome this bias in my class examples proved to be an ideal pedagogical tool. Not only did my invitation impel students to think critically about the role of class throughout the semester, but it had the added benefit of making the course material less threatening as my students observed me grapple with my own biases.

TEMPORARILY ABLED: DEALING WITH DISABILITY

Despite its gains in terms of acknowledging racial, ethnic, class and sexual diversity, the feminist movement has "fail[ed] miserably" in acknowledging disability (Green 1995). As such, it was very important to me to include articles written by, and a film about, women living with physical and mental disabilities. Inherent in this decision to feature women who are frequently absent from feminist discourse was a challenge analogous to Pat Parker's (1978) assertion about friendships between White and Black people, namely, how do non-disabled people forget that some women have disabilities while simultaneously never forgetting the disabilities?

Articles such as King's (1997) "The Other Body: Reflections on Difference, Disability, and Identity Politics" and Chan's (1990) "You're Short Besides" adroitly introduced students to the physical, sociocultural, and psychological realities of the lives of women living in a culture in which people in general and women in particular are judged by their physical attributes. Students responded to these articles with great interest and empathy. However, like most non-disabled people, the students were reluctant to consider that they were, for the most part, *temporarily* abled. Moreover, the fact that none of the students in the class had any visible disabilities further served to distance students from the topic. Instead, most of their concerns centered on their discomfort in interacting with people with physical disabilities in greeting them or respecting their autonomy while simultaneously offering assistance. They comprehended that issues relevant to women living with disabilities were feminist issues but appeared to have a difficult time relating disability-relevant issues to their own lives.

COMPULSORY HETEROSEXUALITY AND WHY DOES SEXUAL ORIENTATION MATTER?

For the most part, students in both of my courses had fairly liberal attitudes about gay, lesbian, and bisexual issues. These students have come of age in the post-Stonewall era in which the gay, lesbian, bisexual, and transgender movement, despite some significant setbacks, has also made some significant gains in promoting gay and lesbian visibility. During the semester that I taught the course, for example, comedian Ellen DeGeneres established her place in television history as the first openly lesbian leading star on a television show. Moreover, although none of my students openly identified as lesbian, gay, or bisexual, several of the students reported that they had friends or relatives who were openly gay, lesbian, or bisexual.

Since issues relevant to bisexual people are rarely included in the Introduction to Women's Studies literature, I selected a group of articles from the anthology *Bi Any Name: Bisexual People Speak Out* (Hutchins and Kaahumanu, 1991). For the most part, students readily apprehended the implications of the heterosexual/homosexual dichotomy. Similarly, students comprehended (albeit with some reserve) Rich's (1980: 631) assertion that we live in a culture in which heterosexuality is usually assumed and rarely questioned, an assumption that serves as a "political institution which disempowers women." Most students, however, remained flummoxed by Rich's notion of a "lesbian continuum" on which a myriad of women-identified experiences would fit.

Despite the ease with which they embraced issues of sexual diversity in the course's section on "Sex and Sexuality," a few students remained stymied by the writings of lesbians outside the context of a class devoted to sex and sexuality. The student's comment about the "bombardment" of writing by Black lesbians aptly demonstrates this. Of the nineteen articles included in the "Talking and Shouting Back: Feminists Respond to Patriarchy" section of the course, only three were written by openly identified Black lesbians. Moreover, all of these essays focused on issues beyond race and sexual orientation. Yet this student perceived the inclusion of writing by three Black lesbians as an assault (note the use of the word "bombarded"). Her remarks tell much about how power and status condition students' reactions to assigned readings and class discussions. This student's membership in at least three dominant group categories—White, middle-class, and heterosexual—provided her with the status to critique the legitimacy and relevance of work by members of non-dominant groups. Indeed, it is highly unlikely that she would have lamented the "bombardment" of readings by White, heterosexual women. Moreover, her sense of being attacked by the number of readings by Black lesbians has a historical resonance in which the number of non-dominant group members is often distorted out of actual proportion and perceived to be a hegemonic threat. As such, my student's comment is evocative of what many ethnic and racial minorities have long known: a conversation between two people of color is a conversation; a conversation among three or more is perceived as fomenting a revolution.

Several students also seemed perplexed by the importance of labels given to identities such as gay, lesbian, bisexual, or transgender. Indeed, they labored to understand the fuss made about these labels and seemed more interested in adopting a "who cares who you sleep with" or "why does it matter" mind-set than critically examining what it means to identify or be perceived as a sexual minority. Initially, I was astonished at this mind-set. After all, the fact that a person could be bashed for "looking gay" or engaging in public displays of affection with a same-sex partner soundly refuted the argument that the sex of one's romantic or sexual partner was irrelevant. I soon learned, though, that many of their notions were due to the false-consensus effect. Simply put: because they held such tolerant attitudes about gay, lesbian, and bisexual people, they consistently exaggerated the number of people who shared their attitudes. Moreover, few students were aware of the extent of institutionalized bias against gay, lesbian, bisexual, and transgendered people. Few of the students knew of the existence of same-sex sodomy laws in many states or about the absence of hate crime legislation and antidiscrimination protections in employment, housing, and public accommodations for gay, lesbian, bisexual, and transgendered people.

THEY'RE TALKING ABOUT MY LIFE: THE INTRODUCTION TO WOMEN'S STUDIES TEACHER AS "OTHER"

With the exception of my middle-class and educational privileges, I differ from my students on virtually every important social identity dimension. Overwhelmingly, my students are White; I am Black. My students are, for the most part, U.S.-born and bred; I am Bahamian-born and lived in Nassau until the age of eighteen. Most of my students identify as heterosexual; I identify as lesbian. As such, I am the "other" on an individual as well as academic level.

Thus far, I have discussed my students' expectations vis-à-vis diversity. Interestingly, other than my nostalgia about teaching Introduction to Women's Studies for the first time, I had not previously considered my own expectations in teaching a course in which women like myself (i.e., women who, with the exception of class, live on the margins) would be center-stage. Specifically, I had not considered the emotional toll that being the prominent "other" (both as subject matter and as teacher) would have on me as I taught material to students who, for the most part, possessed the luxury of not having to think about living life as a non-dominant other. To most of my students, learning about the lives of diverse women was a scholarly endeavor; to me, I was teaching about my life.

There was the experience of being a Black female lecturer on a campus where most of the professors (particularly those in tenure-track or tenured positions) are White, male, heterosexual, and middle-class. I had long since grown accustomed to having students (even seniors) inform me that I was the first Black professor that they had had at Georgetown. What was new for me was the introspection that this knowledge fostered as we discussed a topic as seemingly innocuous as "Our Work: Tales from the Workplace, the Home, and School." When a student observed the demographic constitution of the faculty at Georgetown, she had departed from course material and was instead talking about my life. Other discussions hit even closer to home as I shared my experiences with heterosexism and racism. One class, "Racism, Classism, and Anti-Semitism," remains especially fixed in my memory. As I sat straining to initiate discussion among a typically loquacious group of students, I despairingly realized that my race may have served to silence student discussion. I had attempted to create a classroom in which all points of view were welcomed. Yet, those students who were fearful of insulting me as Black person or having me perceive them as racist opted for the safest route: silence. More troubling was the notion that this upcoming generation of feminists perceived the topics of race and racism to be so insurmountable. I left both classes that day feeling dejected and hopeless about the possibility of White women and women of color ever being able to candidly confront and discuss the complexities of race and racism.

LEARNING FROM THE DIVERSE TALES IN THE INTRODUCTION TO WOMEN'S STUDIES COURSE

My reflection on my students' expectations about diversity and women and my experiences in my course have yielded several lessons from which I believe other teachers of Introduction to Women's Studies may benefit. First, women's studies educators must make serious efforts to integrate issues and topics related to diversity throughout the entire syllabus rather than placing them in a designated section of the course. Confining multicultural issues to one section sends students a clear message that material on women who are not White, middle-class, heterosexual, able-bodied, or young is not as important as material on women from dominant groups.

Second, teachers must assiduously examine the ways in which they are privileged and how this privilege consciously or subconsciously influences dynamics within the classroom, particularly with students who are members of historically marginalized groups. Unexamined privilege may manifest itself in countless ways that alienate students and hinder learning. For example, using readings or examples that only deal with heterosexual women reinforces heterosexual hegemony, makes women who are lesbian or bisexual invisible, and robs heterosexual students of the opportunity to consider how social norms concerning sexual orientation function together with sexism and other forms of oppression as institutions of power.

Third, educators must make a concerted effort to find films and articles on diverse women. A plethora of wonderful anthologies and articles exist. It is also a good idea to involve students in this effort by inviting them to bring to class articles on class topics that reflect diverse perspectives. Fourth, teachers should not allow students, particularly those from dominant groups, to remain safe in their unexamined privilege. Articles such as those by McIntosh (1989), Rich (1980), and King (1997) unsettle and challenge students in a manner that is essential to critical thought, analysis, and learning. Last (and repetitively), but hardly least, teachers of Introduction to Women's Studies must earnestly endeavor to practice what we teach. Students will not learn to value diversity if we do not ourselves value it in our own lives through meaningful social interactions with women who differ from us in race, ethnicity, class, age, culture, sexual orientation/preference, and ability. Simply put: the act of acknowledging and appreciating diversity among women begins at home.

SUGGESTED READINGS

McIntosh, P. 1989. White privilege and male privilege: A personal account of coming to see correspondences through work in women's studies. *Race, class, and gender: An anthology*, 2d ed., ed. M. L. Andersen and P. H. Collins, 76–87. Belmont, CA: Wadsworth,

Rosenberg, P. M. 1997. Underground discourses: Exploring whiteness in teacher education. *Off white: Readings on race, power, and society*, ed. M. Fine, L. Weis, L. C. Powell, and L. M. Wong, 79–89. New York: Routledge.

Spelman, E. V. 1997. Gender and race: The ampersand problem in feminist thought. *Issues in feminism: An introduction to women's studies*, ed. S. Ruth, 22–34. Mountain View, CA: Mayfield.

10

Inter-Racial Teaching Teams, Antiracism, and the Politics of White Resistance: Teaching Introduction to Women Studies at a Predominantly White Research Institution

Audre Jean Brokes, St. Joseph's University, and France Winddance Twine, University of Washington, Seattle

In this chapter we explore the risks, difficulties, and benefits of teaching Introduction to Women Studies from an international, multicultural, and antiracist perspective. We focus in particular on the resistance both to us and to the course content that we, as a U.S. inter-racial team, experienced from U.S. White women of working-class and middle-class backgrounds. We describe the strategies that we employed and the structural adjustments that we made to both respond appropriately to this resistance and preserve what we regard as the integrity of the course.

We are a U.S. Black/American Indian woman from a largely working-class background (Twine) and a U.S. White, middle-class woman (Brokes) who collaborated for three years on the cornerstone Introduction to Women Studies course at a large, predominantly White research university, which we will call "The University." The University is 20.3% Asian, 3.3% Black, 3.8% Hispanic, 2% international, 1.1% American Indian, and 69.5% all others,[1] and we found that the racial/ethnic makeup of our classes closely approximated this university average.[2] Although most of the students were women, men made up between 10% and 15% of the 200+ students enrolled in the course each term. A large lecture course with weekly discussion sections, Introduction to Women Studies required a teaching team of four individuals: a principal instructor and three graduate teaching assistants. At the time of our collaboration (1994–1997), Twine was an assistant professor of women's studies, and Brokes was a graduate student in philosophy and women's studies at The University. We began working together collaboratively after Brokes initially served as a graduate teaching assistant for Twine. At a later time, Brokes also served as principal instructor of the course.

TWINE'S INITIAL CONCEPTION OF INTRODUCTION TO WOMEN STUDIES

When Winddance Twine assumed responsibility for Introduction to Women Studies in 1994, the course already had a history at The University. It was one of two introductory courses required for the women studies major, and it also functioned as a "service" course—a popular elective for nonmajors. Perhaps as a result of certain common stereotypes of the field of women studies and of feminist and interdisciplinary studies in general, the course was perceived by many students as not intellectually rigorous. It was seen as a place in which one could, with comparatively minimal effort, receive a relatively high grade. In addition, the course was largely, if tacitly, perceived as a place in which U.S. White women could expect to be affirmed as U.S. White women. This perception is perhaps best explained by the fact that, though given a good deal of attention, the issues of race and racism were not accorded a central and essential place in the overall university course curriculum. In addition, some versions of this course made the U.S. experience central and/or were not consistently or explicitly antiracist.[3] As a result, many U.S. White women expected to see reflections of themselves in much of the course content.[4]

Twine revised the course curriculum radically. The course took on an international focus, and U.S. White women were decentered; that is, although both social and political issues confronting U.S. White women and tools of analysis historically employed primarily by U.S. White women were included in the course, neither was given central weight or attention. Instead, such topics and tools appeared as only one element among several others in the course. The new format preserved the interdisciplinary character of the course and its focus on women's lives in the sense that it primarily examined how gender differences and gender inequalities are culturally constructed and maintained in social institutions (e.g., education, the medical industry, the beauty industry, families, the media, and work, including sex work). But Twine placed central emphasis on understanding the ways in which the intersections of nationality, race, class, sexual orientation, and physical ability create and maintain differences and inequalities *among* women as well as between men and women. In particular, the role played by race and racism in perpetuating these inequities was emphasized. Some of the specific topics addressed in the course as it was initially conceived by Twine were alternatives to a binary gender system in India, sex work, media representations, issues surrounding the division of labor, and gender activism among American Indian and Mexican American women. Like almost all subsequent teaching teams for the course, the teaching team on which Twine and

Brokes initially served was inter-racial and interdisciplinary, although all of the participants had training in women's studies and/or feminism.

SITES OF WHITE RESISTANCE AND FORMS OF RESPONSE

As a result of Twine's 1994 modifications of the course curriculum, we expected a certain amount of initial resistance as students at The University who enrolled with assumptions and expectations based on earlier versions of the course confronted the new format. In addition, we expected that Twine would encounter some resistance as a consequence of racism. Both of these expectations were met. The first few times we taught the course, a record number of students dropped it in the first week when its international, multicultural, and antiracist focus became clear to them.[5] Interestingly, we estimate that proportionally fewer men than women dropped the course; we seemed to retain almost all of the men initially enrolled. We have no way of estimating the degree to which racism played a role in student's decisions to drop the course.

While we were prepared for this kind of initial response, we had assumed that once the course enrollment stabilized, and we were left with a relatively "self-selected" group of students, the resistance would lessen at least to some degree. (Because of our earlier experiences in women studies we were well aware, however, of the many and varied difficulties of teaching women studies. Thus, we did not expect our course to be free from such problems.) We were not prepared, however, for the continued and mounting resistance that we experienced, primarily from U.S. White women. The *explicit* complaints were twofold. The course was claimed to be "too hard," and the material was claimed to be "biased" and "irrelevant" to the students' lives. Students leveled the following kinds of complaints: the course requires too much reading; the lectures are too complicated; the lectures are "biased"; requiring students to know the names of central characters or theorists in films shown in class is unfair; the tests are too difficult; the concepts are too difficult; and so on.

In response to student complaints about the degree of difficulty of the course, we undertook an informal comparison to similar courses at The University. As a result of the interdisciplinary character of the Women Studies Department and of our teaching teams, we had access to a relatively large body of information to suggest that, while demanding and challenging, Introduction to Women Studies was not significantly more time-consuming than the most challenging introductory courses in several other departments in the humanities, social sciences, sciences, and mathematics. This led us to conclude that complaints of this sort arose, in large measure, as a result of students' expectations of women studies and its instructors. This conclusion was also supported by students' explicit statements to that effect.

The claims that the course was "biased" were more difficult to address, in part because they were typically expressed more obliquely. Our first task in responding to this sort of complaint was to ascertain more clearly what was meant by the claim of bias. At times, student's remarks were explicitly racist and homophobic, expressing racist and homophobic attitudes generally and racism toward Twine in particular. During discussion sections, for example, many U.S. White women would complain to Brokes that they were tired of learning about "those people" and that "she [Twine] is obsessed with racism." There seemed to be a conscious attempt on the part of some White students to appeal to Brokes' Whiteness (and presumed heterosexuality) in an attempt to elicit affirmation of their own racism toward Twine and to "divide" the teaching team. Brokes' refusal to acquiesce in either of these strategies created more dissatisfaction on the part of many students. In general, many White students were not prepared to encounter a unified inter-racial teaching team. More subtly, many U.S. White women complained that they were offended by the course material, which discussed lesbianism, sex, and sex work, including coerced prostitution, and that their own experiences were not recognized or "validated" in the course. "I took a women studies course because I wanted to learn about myself as a woman, but this course does not help me to live my life," was a common sort of complaint.

Most of the resistance to Twine was expressed within the discussion sections in the presence of the teaching assistants and in written comments on course evaluations. (One remark on a course evaluation form for Twine's course: "fire the black bitch.") While some of this resistance did come from men, some of the strongest *supporters* of the course were men, perhaps because they did not enter the course with the expectation that their identities as male and/or White would be affirmed. This held true for both U.S. White men as well as non-U.S. and non-White men. Two men wrote extremely strong, unsolicited letters in support of Twine and the course to the chair of the Women Studies Department, for example.

In an attempt to address this resistance, we introduced into the course three documents that we call "Ten Myths about Women Studies," "A Survival Guide for Introduction to Women Studies," and a "Truth in Advertising Statement" (samples are provided in the Appendixes). "Ten Myths about Women Studies" lists some of the common stereotypes about women studies courses that we encountered among our students at The University. The "Survival Guide for Introduction to Women Studies" had a dual purpose. It was intended, on one hand, to provide students with some useful strategies for improving their study skills in general and for satisfying the demands of our course in particular. It also provided students with some of the information that we gathered from their peers and from our own experiences with the course over the first two years. In this way we clarified what the students could expect if they chose to remain enrolled in the course.[6] Finally, the "Truth in Advertising Statement" highlighted the potentially offensive material to be covered in the course (for socially and politically conservative students) and again clarified the course expectations. The "Ten Myths" and "Survival Guide" were appended to a detailed syllabus, and both were read aloud during the first lecture period of the course. During the first discussion section meeting, students were asked to complete and return the "Truth in Advertising Statement." The teaching assistants were asked to emphasize the difficulty of the course and the potentially controversial and challenging nature of the course content. These materials were relatively effective in increasing students' awareness of their responsibilities in the course, and these appendixes and the growing reputation of the course decreased the resistance of White students to Twine during the second year that she taught it.

When, later in our collaboration, Brokes (still a graduate student) became principal instructor of the course, we were confident that our previous two years of experience had provided us with a good understanding of the kinds of resistance Brokes would encounter.[7] Since her syllabus remained faithful to the international, multicultural, and antiracist conception of the course and used virtually all of the same materials employed by Twine, we anticipated that due to White privilege she might even enjoy relatively less resistance from White students. We were wrong. We had not understood that an actively antiracist White instructor could generate as much, if not more, anger and resistance from White students seeking affirmation, both intellectual and personal, and a reflection of themselves from a young, White feminist scholar.

Though still coming almost exclusively from U.S. White women of middle-class and working-class backgrounds, the resistance Brokes encountered was much more formal, open, and intensely public than that encountered by Twine. It was articulated in the form of overt personal attacks on Brokes in lecture and discussion sections. In addition, within the first two weeks of the course seven students complained directly to The University's president that Introduction to Women Studies was "racist against White people" and that the instructor had asked students to sign an ideological statement—the "Truth in Advertising Statement." It was quickly concluded that these charges were entirely unfounded but not before Brokes was called upon to meet with the vice provost, the dean, the chair of Women Studies, and Twine to address the accusations. At this meeting, throughout which Twine and the chair provided unstinting support to Brokes, the allegedly offending documents were deemed by the administration to be creative teaching tools, and their use was explicitly encouraged.

We have several theories to account for the fact that more aggressive, public hostility was directed at Brokes, while Twine encountered more indirect forms of hostility. First, White students expected Brokes, as a White instructor, to be more sympathetic toward them and to not directly challenge their White privilege. They did not have these expectations of Twine. Second, since Twine was a tenure-track faculty member with a degree from a "brand-name" university (U. C. Berkeley), the students found it difficult to challenge Twine's classroom methods because they could be attributed to her training at a respected institution. In other words, Twine had credentials (academic, cultural, institutional) that provided students with a prima facie explanation of her innovations.[8] In

contrast, Brokes, at that time lacking certain academic and institutional credentials, was regarded as more "accountable" to students' demands. Because she
was a graduate student completing her training at "their" university, Brokes
was perceived as much more vulnerable and easy to punish/discipline than
Twine. Third, Brokes, in contrast to Twine, who concluded the course with a
consideration of White privilege, both *began* and ended the course by challenging students to think about their racial location and privileges.[9] Brokes, thus,
"betrayed" White students seeking affirmation and comfort at the outset of the
course. Finally, the White students may have feared being accused of racism if
they directly attacked Twine, while they did not have this fear with respect to
Brokes.

In attempting to explain the resistance from White U.S. women that we both
experienced, however, we are inclined to point out our commonalities as well
as our differences. For somewhat different reasons each of us chooses in some
contexts to reject a pedagogical model that favors a certain kind of "caretaking"
and certain forms of unconditional validation of students. Fighting against both
the racist stereotype of U.S. Black[10] scholars as "less qualified" and the stereotype of the interdisciplinary study of feminism and women's lives as peripheral
and intellectually disreputable, Twine seeks to incite a certain intellectual passion in students born of their appreciation for the rigors of academia. Brokes
shares this vision and these concerns but also believes that in some classroom
contexts an overtly "caretaking" pedagogical model tends to privilege White
students unduly, especially when it is employed by a White instructor. Thus,
we seek both to challenge our students in unconventional ways and to challenge
certain kinds of stereotypes of feminist studies and women's studies, without
denigrating alternative pedagogies or fields of inquiry. As the foregoing discussion makes clear, however, there are significant risks attached to this strategy.
The kinds of risks taken by White and non-White instructors in employing such
strategies are significantly different.

Feminists have given comparatively little attention to the forms of White
racism that White antiracist instructors encounter when they challenge White
supremacy in the classroom. We believe that it is crucial for White antiracist
instructors not only to be prepared to experience such White racism and resistance but also to develop appropriate and effective strategies to deal with it. In
light of her experiences, Brokes believes that it is particularly important for
antiracist White instructors to make the antiracist thrust of their courses clear at
the outset by drawing explicit attention, perhaps on the first day of class, to the
fact that White supremacy will be consistently challenged. Drawing attention to
some of the specific ways in which one has benefited personally from White
supremacy can be a particularly effective strategy in making clear what challenging racism involves. Brokes also thinks that if antiracist pedagogy is to be
effective, all members of a teaching team must be committed to an antiracist
stance. In large lecture courses, White graduate teaching assistants play a crucial
role in ensuring that antiracism is consistently reinforced.

Both of us regard the role played by antiracist White instructors in the academy as an essential and ineliminable component of the fight against racism. By challenging the racial hierarchies that benefit them, antiracist Whites are in a unique position, especially vis-à-vis other Whites, to legitimate an antiracist stance. We encourage all antiracist Whites to be aware of the risks attached to this use of White privilege and to employ antiracist pedagogy actively and consistently, nonetheless.

SOME CONCLUDING REFLECTIONS

The preceding discussion focuses exclusively on the resistance and challenges that we encountered during our collaboration. We think that it is also important, however, to point out the degree to which many students have benefited from our course. Overall, the course received high ratings in comparison to many other introductory courses, and each of us received letters from students, both during and after the course, attesting to their appreciation of us and of the course content. Indeed, many students communicated to us in various ways their extreme satisfaction with the course. We were especially pleased that many of our non-White and non-U.S. students expressed support for, and appreciation of, the course.

We have each profited immensely, both intellectually and personally, from our collaboration. We both believe that the benefits of teaching Introduction to Women Studies from an international, multicultural perspective and with an explicitly antiracist focus far outweigh the risks and challenges. We also recognize that both the difficulties we encountered and the strategies we employed in response to those difficulties reflect commitments that not all of those in the field of feminist studies and/or women studies share. We hope, however, that our experiences as feminist antiracist instructors are useful to everyone who shares our commitment to the fields of feminist studies and women studies.

APPENDIX A: TEN MYTHS ABOUT WOMEN STUDIES

The following are, in our experience, some of the common and mistaken assumptions that students have about Women Studies courses in particular and humanities, social science, and interdisciplinary courses in general:

1. Women Studies courses are *and should be* easier than courses like chemistry, math and engineering; they require *and should require* the investment of less study-time.

2. The conceptual material presented in courses like Women Studies is less difficult to understand and easier to learn than the concepts in courses like calculus or chemistry.

3. Grades in Women Studies are *and should be* generally higher than those in mathematics or the sciences.

4. Any student who shows up, reads all the material, turns in all the assignments will pass a Women Studies course.

5. Unlike chemistry, math, engineering, Women Studies is a *soft* subject in which one's own opinion is just as valid as anything one reads or hears in texts, lectures, or films.

6. The details don't matter in Women Studies; only the general concepts or themes are important. Students are not *and ought not be* held responsible for highly detailed information presented in such courses.

7. Women Studies courses are solely concerned with *gender*—race, class, sexual orientation, national origin, ethnicity, immigrant status, and physical ability are only tangentially or secondarily related to issues of gender and gender inequity.

8. Women Studies courses in particular and the discipline of Women Studies in general are antimale and involve the vilification of both men and masculinity.

9. In Women Studies courses students primarily discuss either their own feelings, experiences, attitudes and beliefs or their personal reactions to materials presented in the course.

10. Women Studies courses are *and should be* places in which students are always affirmed and rarely challenged.

APPENDIX B: A SURVIVAL GUIDE FOR INTRODUCTION TO WOMEN STUDIES

Part I

The following is an appropriate analogy that ought to guide the way you think about this course: *Introduction to Women Studies is to many interdisciplinary courses what Organic Chemistry is to many introductory courses in the physical sciences.* On the preceding page we listed several myths about Women Studies. If you are inclined to believe that any of them are true, and if you undertake this course under the assumption that any of them are true, then your expectations will almost certainly not be met by this course, and you should consider enrolling in another course. If you do decide to remain enrolled in this course, there are a number of things that you can do to help ensure that you *PASS* (roughly, with a grade of 1.0 or better) this course:

1. You must attend lecture and discussion section every day (except Tuesday).

2. You must read each reading-assignment thoroughly, carefully, and critically. This involves the following:

   a. outlining the article

   b. taking notes on what you have read

   c. paying attention to the specific facts and details covered in each article

   d. being able to recapitulate the main lines of argument adduced in the article

   e. mastering the study questions provided for each article

3. You must treat the films that we will see in class as texts. This means that you should:

   a. watch each film carefully and critically

   b. take notes on what you have seen/heard

   c. pay attention to specific facts and details covered in each film—this includes knowing the names of characters and commentators who appear in the films

   d. be able to recapitulate the main lines of argument, the main themes and concepts, covered in the film.

4. You must listen carefully and critically to each lecture whether presented by the instructor or a guest speaker.

5. You must complete each of the assignments on time, and, of course, your assignments must be of a sufficiently high quality and must demonstrate that you have, in fact, satisfied conditions #1, #2, #3, and #4.

6. Satisfaction of conditions of 1–5 above is insufficient to *guarantee* a passing grade in Introduction to Women Studies though, of course, doing so will make it vastly more likely that you will pass the course.

Part II

The following are some practical strategies for satisfying the above conditions:

1. You should definitely be in a STUDY GROUP. Get together with two or three other people in the course and meet with them at least once or twice a week. Practice a strategy of DIVISION OF LABOR when learning and reviewing the course material; for example, while watching a film, one person can keep track of the names of the participants in the film, while another can concentrate on extracting the main themes or arguments. You can then pool this information in study group meetings. A similar strategy can be pursued with respect to the readings, *although each student should read and take notes on each article him- or herself.*

2. You should expect to invest at least three hours of study time outside of class for every hour that you spend in class. This is a general university guideline for undergraduate courses, and at various times, e.g., before exams or when assignments are due, you will probably exceed this amount.

3. Do not fall behind.

4. Come to office hours. Both the instructor and TAs have office hours (times at which they are guaranteed to be available to assist you should you need it). Take advantage of this resource.

5. You should have a binder in which you keep all notes, handouts and the syllabus. You might want to keep a log of the basic themes of the course and the specific details relevant to each theme. You can use the discussion questions provided by the instructor to assist you in this project.

Part III

Some things that you should expect from this course, based on two consec-
utive years' worth of experience with this course, are the following:

1. Roughly 50% of students will, in all probability, fail the first test.
2. The *average* final grade assigned in this course is roughly 2.8–3.0.
3. Students who have completed this course report that they have gained the following:
   a. a sense of what it means to take a course that has a specifically and self-consciously
      multicultural and anti-racist approach
   b. a better understanding of the trends and content of current Women Studies schol-
      arship
   c. an improved ability to digest and understand complex conceptual materials
   d. an appreciation of the differences among women on the basis of race, class, sexual
      orientation, nationality and place of origin, etc.
   e. a sense of themselves as multiply-located individuals: individuals with a specific
      race, class, gender, sexual orientation, nationality, place of origin, etc.
   f. and (in part on the basis of [d]), a sense of themselves as agents in a web of complex
      social and political structures
   g. an improved set of study skills
   h. a feeling of pride and accomplishment
4. Students have also found this course both intellectually and emotionally frustrating,
   challenging, and difficult. If you are not prepared for this, then, in all probability,
   your expectations will not be met by this course, and you should consider enrolling
   in a different course.
5. Many students, especially White middle class heterosexual women, find that this
   course challenges them in ways that they did not expect to be challenged. In general,
   such students are not affirmed in this class; neither, of course, are they denigrated.
   But having one's attention drawn to the ways in which one's identity as White, and/or
   middle class and/or heterosexual enables one, though unfairly, to avoid questioning
   certain facts about the social arrangement of power and privilege is not always comfortable. If you are not prepared for this, then your expectations will, in all probability,
   not be met by this course, and you should consider enrolling in a different course.

We are firmly committed to this course. We believe it offers you a unique
opportunity to, among other things, learn important intellectual material, challenge yourself both intellectually and politically, develop and improve your analytical skills and your study skills, and develop a familiarity with a conceptual
framework that will enable you to pursue more detailed work in one or another
of the areas to which you will be introduced in this course. We are delighted
to have you as a participant in this course and will do everything we can *within*

the constraints articulated above and in the syllabus to help you be successful in this course. But we want you to approach this experience with your eyes wide open and with a clear understanding of what you are undertaking in enrolling in the class.

APPENDIX C: TRUTH IN ADVERTISING STATEMENT

This course asks you to think critically about issues in your own life. It requires you to re-think assumptions that you may have about female and male gender roles and norms and your role in perpetuating these norms. *This course does not ask you to change your behaviors, values, or way of living*, but it does ask you to think critically about what may be taken-for-granted assumptions about the world. If you are not willing to think about such controversial issues as gender equality, abortion, motherhood, prostitution, sexuality, and racism, you should consider enrolling in a different course. You will also be required to read about women who are engaged in a range of work situations including the sex industry. In order to fulfill the requirements of this course, you must be interested in reading about these topics and in discussing issues raised by these topics in discussion section. Keep the above in mind as you carefully review the following questions before making your decision about whether to enroll in or remain in this class.

1. Are you looking for an easy course that will require a minimum of reading, writing, and thinking?
2. Are you offended by material and discussions that address the issues of race and racism, sexuality, lesbianism, reproductive rights, abortion, or prostitution?
3. Do you think sexual autonomy and lesbian identity are inappropriate topics for a course and not of theoretical interest or relevance to your life?
4. Do you regard courses that require a high level of dedication and a large investment of time to be too burdensome to undertake?

I, _____, have carefully read the syllabus, the ''Ten Myths about Women Studies,'' ''The Survival Guide for Introduction to Women Studies,'' and the above statements and have made the decision to voluntarily enroll in this course with full knowledge of its expectations and requirements. I understand the content of the course readings, and by signing this statement I agree to complete all of the readings as assigned and to come to discussion sections prepared to think critically about the issues raised by the course readings, films, and lectures. I also agree to read the ''Ground Rules for Discussion'' and to be respectful of my peers.

_____

Signature

The completion of all or any part of this document is *entirely voluntary*. This document will remain in the sole possession of the instructor for this course. The document and its contents will remain confidential.

NOTES

1. Official 1995 statistics of The University.

2. No official data was collected on class composition; this information is based on our own observations and estimations over the three-year period. Official student enrollment data collected by the Department of Women Studies at The University about the racial/ethnic composition of students who participate in the Women Studies Program supports our estimations, however.

3. Because of the high student demand for this introductory course, multiple versions of it were often taught by different instructors, so student expectations of the course content were often based on which "version" of the course (and which syllabus) their friends had previously encountered. This was particularly true for students who were members of sororities or fraternities that kept files of course syllabi, exams, and other information for their members.

4. While the Women Studies Department expresses a formal commitment to issues of race, racism, and antiracism in its curriculum, this was not typical in departments outside Women Studies, so the students often had no experience with courses that were simultaneously multicultural, antiracist, and feminist in orientation.

5. A significant number of students also added the course during the first week.

6. The resistance diminished over time to Twine's version of the course because more students who were interested in antiracism and international feminisms began to enroll on the basis of "recommendations" from their friends. Their expectations were more realistic, and they did not exhibit the same degree of hostility, homophobia, or overt racism in the discussion sections or on student evaluations.

7. Brokes was asked by Women Studies to serve as the principal instructor of this course when Twine was granted a release from teaching for one term.

8. Twine received very high ratings on her course evaluations in the category of "student's confidence in instructor's knowledge of subject matter," which testifies to their acceptance of her credentials despite the dissatisfaction of some students with the "difficulty" of the course.

9. Twine always invited a White scholar to present the lecture on White racial privilege.

10. Brown-skinned American Indian scholars of African descent are virtually invisible in U.S. research universities, so it is unlikely that any student perceived Twine as of American Indian heritage. Thus, Twine was racially abused and discriminated against by students as a U.S. Black, which is how she self-identifies politically.

SUGGESTED READINGS

Bauer, D. with K. Rhoades. 1996. The meaning and metaphors of student resistance. *Antifeminism in the academy*, ed. V. Clark, S. N. Garner, M. Higgonet, and K. H. Katrack, 95–113. New York and London: Routledge.

Fox O'Barr, J., et al. 1994. Just an experiment for my women's studies class: Female students and the culture of gender. *Feminism in action: Building institutions and community through women's studies.* Chapel Hill: University of North Carolina.

Gaard, G. 1996. Anti-lesbian intellectual harassment in the academy. *Antifeminism in the academy*, ed. V. Clark, S. N. Garner, M. Higgonet, and K. H. Katrack, 115–140. New York and London: Routledge.

Maher, F. A. and M. K. Thompson Tetreault. 1994. *The feminist classroom.* New York: Basic Books. (See Chapter 5 on authority.)

.

11

Feminism in the Field of Local Knowledge: Decolonizing Subjectivities in Hawai'i

Kathleen O. Kane, University of Hawai'i, Mānoa

> In teaching women, we have two choices:
> to lend weight to the forces that indoctrinate women to passivity,
> self depreciation and a sense of powerlessness,
> in which case the issue of "taking women students seriously" is a moot
>   one;
> or to consider what we have to work against, as well as with,
> in ourselves, in our students, in the content of the curriculum,
> in the structure of the institution, in the society at large.
>
> Adrienne Rich (1979)

HISTORY RESIDES IN THE BELLY OF THE PRESENT

I begin by situating myself and locating the historical underpinnings of student expectations and experiences at the University of Hawai'i at Mānoa (UH) within the social, historical, and institutional context of postcolonialism in the Pacific. The University of Hawai'i at Mānoa is the principal campus of a state university with more than 20,000 undergraduate through doctoral-level students. Two-thirds are undergraduates, 54.6%, are women, and the median age is twenty-six years. The Women's Studies Program has five courses that meet the general education core requirements, and Introduction to Women's Studies, WS 151, is taught during, semester (sixteen weeks), day classes in fifty minutes on Monday, Wednesday, Friday or seventy-five minutes, Tuesday, Thursday; summer session term (six weeks) in seventy-five minutes, daily or equivalent hours on Tuesday, Wednesday, Thursday; Outreach College term (ten weeks) in two two-hour weekly classes, or one four-hour weekly class during evenings or Saturday. Because Introduction to Women's Studies is often taught as a writing-intensive (WI) course, class size is limited to twenty students, with a non-WI course averaging about twenty-five to thirty students.

I write and think from within the position I occupy as a white, or haole,[1] feminist working on a campus in which 69.6%[2] of the tenured and tenure-track faculty but only 21.8% of the students are also haole (University of Hawai'i Equal Employment Opportunity and Affirmative Action Office [UH EEOAA] 1993–1995).[3] Further, first-time students by geographic location are over-whelmingly from Hawai'i public and private schools (a combined 92.9%) (UH EEOAA 1994–1995) and therefore are representative of a stunning range of Asian and Pacific ethnic local diversity.[4] Class and economic status are not specifically articulated in these statistics,[5] but configurations of ethnicity and class have been extensively and historically determined through the plantation system of labor and immigration. That history inhabits the present through the great numbers of students at Mānoa and, indeed, across the UH campus system on all islands, whose knowledge of the plantation derives directly from the life experience of their grandparents. The era of the plantation in Hawai'i has passed, but its intersecting social constructs of ethnicity, gender, and class remain and are present in the classrooms at Mānoa.

Anthropologist Elvi Whittaker (1986, 192) writes that ''a portrait of Hawaii is a portrait of Western consciousness . . . its way of life a reflection of an imag-ination and a history conceived and fostered thousands of miles away.'' The history of this place is a history of colonial exploitation and domination. It is also a history of resistance and community building through social and familial alliances ''as members of an extensive and untangled net which represents se-curity and coherence'' (Hopkins 1992, 4). This history contributes to a deep local knowledge that permeates local social practice, not hidden from sight but in full and lively articulation. The question that drives my work is, Given the historical context of Hawai'i, is it possible for feminist theory and pedagogy to interact with local knowledge in ways that my entries and those of the very large numbers of non-local[6] teachers into the classroom can become continually reiterated resistances to the reenactment of colonization? Can feminist pedagogy and theory engage with local knowledge to become co-constitutive and illumi-native rather than competing over claims for truth? If so, how? From what vantage point? If not, why not?

I theorize the historical as situated in the belly of the present, not as a period of time, but as space that historical practices of dominance continue to colonize.[7] All who come to teach in Hawai'i arrive on an island chain that defines the relations between people (and therefore, relations of knowledge) as circular or weblike, reciprocal, and in continual return—rather than on a landmass that extends in straight lines and ever outward and away. All who come to these islands have much to learn. Neither our entry into Hawai'i nor entry into the classroom can be that of the open, inquisitive traveler challenged to read the landscape of land, language, bodies, food, and the imaginary in the conventional terms of encounters with difference. Such a practice names the student and her culture and ethnicity as the foreign object requiring decoding—the student is made to become foreign in her own land.

> If you are new to Hawai'i from the continental U.S.,
> you are whether you know it or not, in the process of becoming haole.
> What this means is not just being white, but becoming aware of it . . .
> look around you . . .
> you may see a mixture of races or a predominance of one or another.
> Which are you . . . the exception or the rule?
> Perhaps you might go further to ask yourself why.
> Because in fact, you are and are not the norm.
> Demographically, that is in sheer numbers, you are not.
> In almost every other way you are.
> How did this come to be? At what cost and who paid?
>
>   Louise Fuji (Kubo) (Kane 1992)

The most significant failure in the project of decolonization of pedagogy in the classroom may well be the effort to produce in a teacher an "openness" to the cultural dimensions of the local student without the accompanying or preceding political critique that demands that the teacher sets such "open" gaze upon themselves as re/enactor of the historical structures and practices of colonization. Situated at the heart of what we imagine to be the relation of each teacher to each student is the history of at least four dimensions of social constructs: those that produce the institutionalization of the categories of both teacher and student; those that produce the colonized and the colonizer in multiple domains in Hawai'i (here social practices of plantation, military, and tourism conspire with education); the teacher's self-awareness, or lack, as situated as historically produced actor/reenactor; and the diverse ethnic identities of a large majority of local students as they are connected in patterns of animated coherence with one another.[8] For most faculty and students, education here is not an extension or articulation of the intersections of one's own culture, race, ethnicity, gender, and class. It is imperative that liberatory teaching emerge from, and be accountable back to (rather than merely include), a deep knowledge and experience of significant social and historical constructs such as culture, gender, race, ethnicity, class, and sexuality. Such teaching *is* good teaching (Anderson 1996) and demands simultaneous engagement of the pedagogical and the political.

With these conditions as the backdrop for the women's studies introductory classroom, I reflect on moments and locations inside which our teaching practices *do* have the power to change our world(s), our students, and ourselves.

Politically, the classroom is the stage for the human drama of teaching and learning as empowerment, on which we as teachers define our commitments to liberatory learning for students and ourselves. In that space, teacher and student join in a rigorous and willful desire to labor in the field of knowledge (hooks 1994a) together, in re/cognition of how that field has been historically constituted and how one's place in it has been inscribed and becomes re/enacted. Pedagogically, the classroom is the space where we work our way toward the ever-present potentialities in every course, knowing they can never be replicated again. Politically and pedagogically, education ceases to be the road through the sacred grove (Aisenberg and Harrington 1984) and becomes the articulation of that which is to be attained.

EMBODIED KNOWLEDGE[9] AND HOMO NARRANS[10]

> The story depends upon every one of us to come into being.
> It needs us all,
> needs our remembering, understanding, and creating
> what we have together
> to keep on coming into being.
>
> Trinh T. Minh-ha (1989)

Of all the provinces of the feminist teacher, the most compelling is that of creating opportunities for the transformation of the aggressively overscripted terrain called reality, in expanding and diversifying experience and knowledge by engaging the intellect in conversation with embodied knowledge. The practices of speaking and listening, writing and reading one another, reside at the heart of feminist thought. They are actions that enable us to bring one another and ourselves into being through narrativization. Commitment to these practices takes its written form on the first day when we sit down together to consider a syllabus that functions not as a contract but as a map. Students new to women's studies pore over the new syllabus like travelers poring over yet undiscovered areas. It is important to them that primary landmarks be present and clear and that they have the ability to anticipate some of the open areas, tributaries, and smaller roads. Yet, the itinerary is not fixed but left open so that students' already existing knowledge and concerns can determine the best departure points and routes or make side trips or diversions possible. Syllabus-as-map produces very new and immediate assumptions about ownership of knowledge and of the course, assumptions coherent with reciprocal and transformative politics and pedagogy. By our figuring the terrain of teaching and learning as that for co-travelers—one who has traversed it before and others who have yet to do so—the dimensions and proportions of the course expand for all.

Both textually and contextually, such a syllabus communicates collaboration and reciprocity as inherent in this course; in this sense ''introductory'' takes on a radical meaning. The syllabus narrative functions as my first gift of writing to students whose writings I soon will be holding in my hands. They experience the writing as great risk, because it reveals so much about their competencies and their tenuous confidence in their own inner transformations. I offer to them that which compels me, revealing what makes me want to be there—because within a very short time, the course will be expecting them to begin to locate their own deep reasons for being there. At the heart of the syllabus-as-map and the discussion extending from it is an ethos of reciprocity that promises students that by their ability to make meanings from the inside of the course, they will do well in the course and be deeply engaged by it and, perhaps most astonishing to them, that the course will be deeply engaged *by them*.

The institution arms me so well, particularly as a haole teacher in the class-room in Hawai'i, that it is imperative that I dis/arm myself on the same terms that this kind of course will expect of them as students. Intersections of insti-tutionalized sexism and racism leave me with a great deal more authority and legitimacy in the classroom than female colleagues of color, particularly when teaching thematics of gender, race, ethnicity, class, sexuality, culture, and co-lonialism. Politically and pedagogically, I have that much more to relinquish in order to empower students, and I have the privilege of doing it without suffering from loss of legitimacy. It is not with ease that this is accomplished, and there are risks. I assert only that it must be faced and that it must be done. The syllabus is a written commitment to students at the outset that I will disclose power and knowledge in the same way that the course will be requesting of them through their work. I reflect on it as the initial, but only one, in a series of practices through which I act from within the knowledge that my privilege is not *ever* finally set to rest. The privilege that I have is so embedded that at any moment it can appear fully armed. The challenge is continually and consciously to con-front this privilege as a problem to be solved through every device made avail-able to me by the institutional imperatives.[11]

"TALKING STORY" AND THE MENSTRUAL HUT

For so many first-time students to women's studies, it is only inside the women's studies classroom that their new utterances signify meaning and legit-imacy. Even there, there are tremendous hurdles for students.

> Did you know how loud haoles are in public?
> Perhaps you have noticed how quiet some of your local students are.
> If my "good manners" have taught me to be quiet in public,
> to not impose my noise on others,
> I have to jump my rudeness hurdle each time I speak in class.
>
> Because I am so hungry for learning,
> I do it anyway,
> swallowing first my culture each time before I open my mouth.

It doesn't taste good and it is tiring.
How much easier to let the haoles in class do it,
because that is, in part, what haoles are.

Louise Fuji (Kubo) (Kane 1992)

If a local student must jump a rudeness hurdle in order to speak in class, in any class, the costs of jumping that hurdle in their first women's studies can be greater yet, particularly when she must swallow her culture each time before opening her mouth. For a haole student, this is not required—on the contrary, it is to live up to our culture when the cue is given by the teacher to do so. These behaviors reflect very deep cultural and social values about appropriate and respectful behavior, in relationship to both a teacher and other students, and signal radical differences between a culture in which the production of knowledge is constructed as relational and affiliative and a culture in which it is constructed as independent and competitive. A significant difference between the life of a local student and that of the haole teacher is a student's deep sense of community that extends throughout the islands. In a seminar for faculty and teaching assistants (TAs) entitled "Women in the Classroom,"[12] an undergraduate student[13] in women's studies spoke about what it means for her to speak in public.

Every time I say something political,
I get phone calls from ten different relatives—
"Was that you, was that you?
Shame! Shame!"[14]

Allison Yap (Kane 1992)

Intricate and cohesive family, community, and school bonds of coherence and knowledge extend throughout the islands. A feminist teacher from another geographic/cultural context is not likely to recognize the ways in which the classroom is aligned with extensive social cohesiveness. In other words, from the perspective of local students, the classroom is not private space but a public one. What Allison Yap describes is only partly captured by having what she says travel home ahead of her; rather, it infers something that lies at the heart of local island culture. It is not just Allison Yap who stands there when she speaks. Her family and community ties are part of who she is as she stands. She is connected in a complex, untangled web, and in part, this is how she knows who she is. It does not necessarily mean she will not or cannot speak, but it does mean that the bond between herself and others accompanies her into the classroom and into the act of speaking.[15] To not know with whom one is sitting is to not know whether one is going to be willing to speak or not, because the context and the risk are not only individual but relational to others outside the classroom, in an immediate sense.[16]

To not spend crucial class time together in an exchange in which we locate ourselves in relation to one another through a series of significant local referents is to delay, or entirely forgo, the opportunity for the space to establish itself according to the terms of those occupying it. This is a slightly structured form of *talking story* with one another:

> Talking story has a special meaning
> to those who make their home in Hawai'i.
> While its roots lie in ancient Hawaiian traditions
> which preserved family and social histories
> by passing down orally from generation to generation,
> talk story plays an important part
> in the everyday lives of people today.
>   Eloise Buker (Women's Support Group 1982)

"Talk story" is essential in knowing about one another, the world, and what things mean. It is both a method of knowing and a way of taking pleasure in knowing. The same sense of island community that creates and is dependent on the tradition and practice of talk story also produces students who have strong social skills for taking part in the kind of verbal interaction that takes as its *precondition* trust and respect for the island community inside which the classroom takes and re/makes its meanings. For the vast majority of students, the classroom is not separate from the community—but for the haole teacher, her own alienation from the community compels her to imagine that the classroom is a distinct and separate space.

For the feminist teacher not to grasp this is to dismiss significant local knowledge and insight and to fail to allow the formation of an environment that accounts for what *will* compel students to participate. This is not about establishing trust. I am convinced that the discourse of trust and efforts to establish it in the classroom context function to avoid thinking deeply about why trust is an issue at all. The discourse of trust is a way of putting the burden on students who have no structural power in terms of the institutional power that inhabits everything about the classroom, to respond to the request (or demand) for trust placed on them by a teacher, who walks into the classroom institutionally armed. Since the same institutional power is situated in the same set of arrangements in a women's studies course as a course in chemistry, even when we attempt to alter those structures through liberatory practices, institutionalized power is ever at hand. We who teach students introductory courses in women's studies are particularly challenged to not impose trust as a demand upon students. It is not up to us to declare that our courses are different from other courses in respect to power and authority. The decision about that will be made by each and every student as the students work their way through their first encounter with women's studies and will occur every time we teach these courses. Whether we succeed in contributing to the creation of a space in which the subversion of power is more than a gratuitous assertion made by those who have it—the achievement of this rests in the experience of the student. So, while we may work toward it in our structures and our practices, it is not in our hands to "provide" it. It is not ours to give. It resides in the space that we facilitate in opening. Once open, it resides in the cultural practices that we honor there. It is very difficult for haoles in Hawai'i to fully honor talk story as a source of knowledge as well as an expression of pleasure in knowledge. When it is tolerated as a way for students to feel comfortable in the classroom, the teacher will be appreciated for her or his openness, but the full expressive power of the practice is truncated.

> Alright, the menstrual hut is where
> tribesmen sent their menstruating women
> because they were "unclean," for god's sakes,
> and they'd go in these little huts,
> and there'd be a lot of women in there,
> and they'd talk, you know,
> sing a few songs, tell a little gossip,
> give a low back massage now and again
> I say: BRING BACK THE HUT!
>
> Kate Clinton (Pershing 1991)

During the first week of an introductory course, I often ask students what menstrual huts were, according to conventional notions. This is a small challenge for men in the class, as they have not yet had to think much about themselves in relation to menstrual huts, but it does switch them into appreciating their fortunate position of being on the inside of something and about to learn from it. First, eyes open wide, and then women begin to come up with the same picture with which Kate Clinton begins her joke. But something wonderful begins to happen when I ask them to imagine that we in the room are in that menstrual hut and ask them to say what it is that they think we'll be doing with all that time. Big eyes become big smiles, and the first answer is, "*Talk story!*"

From there, we begin to reconstruct what menstrual huts might have been from the perspective of the inside, from those who were there, and how that is us, because we are inside something, and we are really there, too. I speak with them about the conversation of feminism, which has been going on for 5,000 years of patriarchy, and of how we will all find our places in that conversation. I speak to them about how there are so many questions and contending views within feminism, that it will not be productive in this course to attempt to move outside feminism and question its legitimacy—because there is so much to talk and even argue about, from within it. We all begin to initiate ourselves into the informed notion that there are many feminisms and that we all have quite a journey ahead of us. But the metaphoric menstrual hut also signifies, because the students themselves named it, a place where local island culture, through both the idea and practice of talk story, will make possible a different kind of space than in other classes, one in which the fluid expression of embodied knowledge will join the intellect, and the role of teacher will join that of student.

HOW DID YOU LEARN TO TEACH?[17]

I learn to teach from students.[18] As a student, I learned about teaching from teachers who listened to students and, in so doing, made it possible for me to see the influence of myself and others on the processes of dealing with serious and intense social issues. I felt enlivened and empowered by the joyful, dangerous challenging of the most deeply, dearly held assumptions. I felt capable of residing within the inner space of ''the place of ecstacy—pleasure and danger'' (hooks, 1994a) and participating with others who were doing the same. All that liveliness! It was the life of the mind in complex and joyful union with lived experience, with no sense of delineation between life and reflection upon life.

> The desire [of] the other for the other,
> whole and entire . . .
> because living means wanting everything that is,
> everything that lives, and wanting it alive.
>
>   Hélène Cixous (1976)

Can education cease to be the grave through the sacred grove of academia and become instead the articulation of what is to be attained? Institutional practices obscure the real work of teaching and learning, obstructing our arrivals at a more profound desire and demand upon ourselves as teachers and as students, for movement, for liveliness within one's self-understanding as teacher—this is, simply put, a desire for life. If factory production provides the temporal structure, masculine curriculum[19] provides the epistemological structure, banking practices (Freire 1970) provide the pedagogical structure, and prisons (Foucault 1979) provide the spatial structures in what is called education, it becomes a very serious and difficult endeavor to re/create within those structures[20] the deep knowledge of why we, as women, teach and why we, as women, love learning in spite of the vast colonization of the terrain of the spirit, the intellect, and the imaginary by the economics of credentialing and social ordering. But within us resides the power to imagine, if not remember, the negations of the conditions of our existence.[21] Within us also resides the power to push the radical boundaries of the vision of liberatory feminist education beyond the point at which ''the lure of teaching for many women is the desire to re-invoke the transformational experience, their own experience of growth and change, for others . . . women invoking change in others'' (Aisenberg and Harrington 1984). We have the power to push beyond this notion, which, for all the life it brings to the work of teaching and to the work of learning, retains the teacher and the role-of-teacher at the center.

> [M]any students still seek to enter feminist classrooms
> because they continue to believe that there,
> more than any other place in the academy,

they will have an opportunity to experience
education as the practice of freedom.

bell hooks (1994a)

As a teacher, when I go beyond the re/invocation of my own experience as a
student and listen to and hear students, I grasp the politics of the classroom as
a true site of feminist vision or feminism failed.

My goal is to impart why, with all the institutionalization and colonization,
we as women and as feminists bother at all, and that when we do bother, it is
not due to masochism or a desire to replicate ourselves as mothers in the patriarchal bloodline mode, which assumes that the same blood, skin, color, culture
flow from us to our students, who look and act like us. It is one kind of birthing
and mothering, but it is not one that is conducive to freedom, neither for ourselves as teacher nor for our students; and it is not conducive to the role white
women can possibly play as "teachers" to students whose blood, skin, color,
and culture flow very differently than our own and whose voices need *space*,
not *birthing,* from us.

NOTES

1. Historically, "haole" meant "foreigner" and has evolved to mean white folks.
In Hawaiian language, "ha" is the vital breath of life, and "ole" means without. "Without breath" may refer to the fact that foreign missionaries did not greet Hawaiians in
the Hawaiian way of chanting, or literally exchanging breath, but instead with handshakes
(Lu 1998). "Haole" signifies not only skin but also sets of practices. For the purposes
of this chapter on issues of teaching and learning, it is useful to retain the indicator
"foreign," to keep lively the notion that as a newly arrived teacher from India is foreign,
so, too, is one from Boston. Distinctions made between haoles (teachers or students)
born here or living here for long periods of time and haoles newly arrived from the
continental United States are, within the context of the classroom, for the most part
irrelevant.

2. Also, distinction is not statistically made between faculty who are Asian/Pacific
from Japan and Asian/Pacific from Hawai'i. See UH EEOAA 1994–1995.

3. It is significant that 71.4% of all tenure/tenure-track faculty at Mānoa are male,
and 28.6% are female. See UH EEOAA 1994–1995.

4. Asian/Pacific 76.4% (Japanese 25.8%, Chinese 12.3%, Filipino 9.2%, Hawaiian
7.0%, Korean 3.4%, East Indian, Mixed, and Other Asian/Pacific 18.7%); Caucasian
21.8%, Hispanic 1.0%, African American .8%. See UH EEOAA 1994–1995.

5. However, some indication of economic status is revealed in the average hours
worked per week by graduating seniors: 34.8% work sixteen to twenty hours a week;
28.3% work twenty-one to thirty-five hours, and 10.3% work thirty-six hours+. See UH
EEOAA 1994–1995. These numbers underrepresent the work schedules of students in
my classes.

6. Haole from the continental United States or foreign from other countries.

7. The previous statistics are strong indicators that a spatial notion of history, rather
than a temporal one, is the only one that can facilitate this discussion.

8. Many thanks to Phyllis Turnbull for her editorial assistance throughout and for her thoughts on the best way possible to speak about local students' connections with one another.

9. Grumet (1988, 4) references, but does not quote, Merleau-Ponty (1962): ''the knowledge of the body-subject, reminding it that it is through our bodies that we live in the world. He called it knowledge in the hands and knowledge in the feet. But it is also knowledge in the womb.'' Grumet also references, but does not quote, C. Froula (1984): ''Eve's transgression is the claim of direct experience, rather than the mediated knowledge that imputes invisibility to authority.'' In ''Grandma's Story,'' Trinh (1989) locates knowledge as emerging from the belly.

10. It is not our ability to stand upright that makes us human; rather, Meyerhoff (1978) defines being human as having the ability, the necessity even, to tell a story—hence, Homo narrans.

11. No implication that the master's tools can be used to dismantle the master's house is meant here. I insist that this is a continual process, functioning within a constrained institutional context in which reiterated resistance is required.

12. Conducted at the Center for Teaching Excellence, University of Hawai'i Mānoa. fall 1991.

13. Now an adviser of students at University of Hawai'i College of Arts and Sciences.

14. ''Shame is a basis of social control in local culture; it is felt on behalf of other members of the family, group race. . . . With shame, if no one knows, it doesn't count. Compare this with middle-class white American guilt, which is an internalized sense of right and wrong ('guilty conscience'); even if no one else knows, the guilty party does and suffers'' (Hopkins 1992).

15. Working-class women in the academy experience a sense of connectedness to community and family through matrices of race/class/gender/culture, which sit in excruciating juxtaposition to the demands from within the structures of the academy to ally themselves instead as a part of an intellectual ''community.'' See Tokarczyk and Fay (1993).

16. I do not imply that the existential alienation common to feminist and postcolonial critique is not significant or real—only that it does not take its register with such specificity as in island-bound cultures.

17. Question posed by J. Cooper as a writing exercise in workshop for faculty on keeping teaching journals, Center for Teaching Excellence, UH Mānoa, 1991.

18. Some of those who have made it possible for me over the last fifteen years to learn something about teaching appear in this chapter. It has been in their presence and others like them that I have come to know what in me can be of use to others here—and what is not. But, as with any acknowledgment of gratitude, when I get it wrong, it is not their fault—it is mine.

19. ''Masculine epistemology . . . is oriented toward a subject/object dyad in which subject and object are not mutually constituting but ordered in terms of cause and effect, activity and passivity'' (Grumet 1988).

20. Audre Lorde (1984a), ever present and in contribution to our teaching, here helps us retain our understanding that the master's tools cannot be used to dismantle the master's house.

21. Grumet (1988) references Sartre (1966).

SUGGESTED READINGS

Pratt, M. B. 1984. Identity: Skin, blood, heart. *Yours in struggle: Three feminist perspectives on anti-Semitism and racism*, 11–63. New York: Long Haul.

Rohrer, J. 1997. Haole girl: Identity and white privilege in Hawai'i. *Social process in Hawai'i: Sites, identities, and voices*, ed. J. Chinen, K. O. Kane, I. M. Yoshinaga, 38: 138–161. Honolulu: University of Hawai'i.

Whittaker, E. 1986. *The mainland Haole: The white experience in Hawaii*. New York: Columbia University Press.

Part IV

APPLYING STRATEGIES

12

Cybergrrrl Education and Virtual Feminism: Using the Internet to Teach Introductory Women's Studies

Martha McCaughey, Virginia Tech, and Carol J. Burger, Virginia Tech

FOOTBALL DROVE US TO CYBERSPACE

The Virginia Tech football team's victory at the 1995 Sugar Bowl caused an unanticipated number of students to enter the fall 1996 class, swelling the enrollments of introductory-level courses across the campus. To meet the challenge presented by this flood of new students, this Research I, land-grant state university located in southwestern Virginia devoted millions of dollars to the development of on-line learning techniques. The university hoped this would reduce class size by creating some virtual classrooms through the new Internet technologies. As beneficiaries of a grant from this fund, the Women's Studies Program at Virginia Tech commenced its "cybercore" project.

We developed Web pages on commonly taught topics of the introductory course. The grant funded a Web-wise graduate student who developed the initial set of Web sites with materials provided by the instructors. Additional funds paid for the software that enabled several introductory women's studies instructors to modify existing sites ourselves and to create new sites. The fund provided stipends for other instructors, who do not necessarily teach the introductory course, to develop on-line learning modules in their areas of expertise. After one year, we had created eleven modules, all accessible from the main directory page *http://www.cis.vt.edu/was/wsmodules/moduledirectory.html* (see Figure 12.1). These modules contain general topic information, on-line readings, links to well-developed Web sites maintained by others, discussion questions,

Figure 12.1
On-line Learning Modules

VIRGINIA POLYTECHNIC INSTITUTE AND STATE UNIVERSITY

VA Tech Women's Studies

Directory of On-line
Learning Modules

please note: a tiny portion of this material is password-protected, for use by current Tech WS students only

Cybergrrrl Webguide: An introduction to the Internet itself

Service Learning

Women and Science

Lesbigay Module

Gender & Sports

WebWomen: A Women's Studies Sampler

Global Women

Girls Online

Sexual Violence & Self Defense

Gender & the Media

Women and Childbirth: Historical Perspective

Feminism and Spirituality: The Revival of the Goddess

and private chat rooms. The modules are assigned as homework or as a substitute for in-class time and then linked to regular classroom lectures and discussions. As such, these modules allow for a Web-enhanced course, not an entirely on-line course.

The original, institutional goal of the university's cybercore project was to reduce class size and maintain a high standard of educational excellence without hiring more instructors. Hence, our introductory classes increased in size from twenty-five students per class to fifty. The introductory class remained a three-credit-hour course that met for three hours per week for a semester. Our cyber-core introductory students met with us in the classroom less often, but they met with us in smaller groups because, while they were in the classroom, some of their classmates were meeting in a computer lab to do an on-line assignment. The university's project also involves tracking these Web-footed students and assessing the impact the Web-enhanced courses have on learning. We were particularly interested in how cyberspace altered, blunted, or enhanced the feminist message and atmosphere of our introductory courses.

We found that this innovative teaching practice in the introductory women's studies courses had a number of unanticipated feminist benefits. This chapter outlines the details of this teaching strategy and the feminist lessons that this taught our students and us. It also provides a discussion of the course's structure and offers practical organizational strategies and sample assignments using the Web, Web site addresses for those wishing to incorporate the Internet in their introductory women's courses and suggested readings. Since our grant allowed us to gather and create a sophisticated package of on-line learning modules, those wishing to enhance their introductory women's studies courses with the Internet need not invest the time or money that we did. Much of the groundwork has been done, and those wishing to develop on-line learning modules or a classroom Web page can take advantage of the materials we have already compiled and published on the Web. Although we used Macintosh computers and a variety of Web page-making software (e.g., Netscape Composer, BBEdit, and Claris Home Page), students and instructors with PCs can just as easily take advantage of what we have created and put on the World Wide Web.

VIRTUAL FEMINISM, OR, WHY WE LIKE THE WEB

We have long known that students often resist the feminist message of the introductory women's studies course. Few students sign up for introductory class knowing the history of women's studies or even that women's studies is connected with feminism. Instead, expecting a "you've come a long way, baby" type of history course, many students remain upset and resistant throughout the semester. Some students attempt to disqualify their instructor as "strange," "angry," "bitchy," or "lesbian" and then dismiss the basic women's studies critique on those grounds. Using the Internet in teaching women's studies allowed a broader range of feminist voices to reach the student. Through the Web's feminist pages, students experienced a chorus of feminisms. Using the Internet allowed students to explore feminist issues in the privacy of their own computer terminals. Students who were uncomfortable talking about homosexuality in class, for instance, could access any link they liked in our "lesbigay module." Students could explore new ideas in a safe (cyber)space. They could also interact with fellow students in the on-line chat rooms. One result was greater comfort with the material, increased in-class participation, and a decreased tendency to dismiss defensively the issues raised by the instructors in class. For instance, one student wrote:

Before taking this class, I always associated any group or organization with the word "feminist" in it as male bashing and only concerned with putting down men to make women look better. I hate to admit that, but the word "feminist" used to scare me. I didn't want people to think I was some kind of a "male hater." However, after researching and reading on the Internet for this class, I have learned differently. I have learned that being a feminist isn't about hating men. It's about women fighting for the right to be respected for the things they want to be respected for, not for what men say women should be respected for. I checked out the Feminist Majority home page and learned about some of the things that this organization does to help raise consciousness about women's issues. They have opened foundations to educate about women's issues, they have helped to increase the number of women running for political offices, helped pass bills such as the Violence Against Women Act. These were things that I was totally unaware that feminist organizations did.

As this comment makes clear, using the Internet to teach an introductory course can help put students at ease, making them less resistant to the education we offer and to the material presented in class and in the readings.

Furthermore, we were able to use the Internet to teach some practical feminist lessons we would normally have tried to teach in the classroom. For instance, we encouraged students to think about why technologies such as the Internet are associated with, and more often used by, males. We discussed computer resistance and gender in computer-mediated communication. The following student's remark, made in a module chat room after reading an on-line article, exemplifies one such feminist lesson learned about computers:

I just finished reading the [on-line] article on women and technology and computers. . . . I began to think about my own experiences with computers growing up. My sister and I were never allowed to get near my dad's computer. My mom always said that it was my dad's and that we weren't allowed to touch it!! I don't remember this ever making me mad, it was just an understanding to me that our "family computer" was only my dad's. I think this began to really affect me when I came to college and realized that computer literacy was an essential and that I didn't know the first thing about computers!!

As the student's remark illustrates, having students use the Internet in our course sparked the consciousness-raising typical of a successful introductory class.

Another student was hesitant to stay in the Web-enhanced introductory class because the year before she had taken a workshop offered by university computer personnel, who are not always sensitive to the needs of women. She fled the workshop in tears after being yelled at by a frustrated male instructor and had not used any Internet technology since. The introductory course provides a context and a forum to explore the very frustrations and anxieties that might make some female students hesitant to use the technology. Students like this became excited by the feminist analysis of their experience and felt empowered by mastering the new technology from which they had felt alienated.

The first assignment of the Web-enhanced course is designed to familiarize students with the Internet itself and does so in a way that connects feminist analysis to this new communications medium, furthering our aim of empowering female students and encouraging their active involvement in feminist issues. By studying the "Cybergrrrl Webguide" module first, students learn about the Internet and visit Web sites about women, minorities, and technology. The module begins by introducing students to the Internet, explaining what e-mail is, what a Web site address is, why a URL looks the way it does, and ends with a series of articles and links to Web sites about women and minority groups that use the Internet to organize politically or identify positively with the technology. We provide discussion questions to help get student conversation going in the chat room, which is a password-protected conversation space on the Web where the students discuss what they have learned (see Figure 12.2). By politicizing the use of the Internet by women and minorities, the on-line assignment was itself a feminist lesson and participatory experience.

On-line learning also helps empower female students by creating a greater diversity of opportunities to raise questions, state opinions, share stories, and offer analyses. Lucretia McCulley and Patricia Patterson studied the effects of on-line learning in the context of their Women and Power in American Politics course. They found that on-line learning facilitated female students' "coming to voice" because "electronic communication reduces students' own preoccupation with physical appearance and self-presentation, as typified by the following student comment: 'Electronic mail eliminates the need for concern about one's appearance and voice' '' (McCulley and Patterson 1995: 5). Their students also "proposed that electronic mail offers a kinder, less intimidating environment for less aggressive students to network not only with each other, but with politically engaged others at the grassroots" (McCulley and Patterson 1996: 5).

CYBERGRRRL EDUCATION

Teaching with the Internet in an introductory women's studies course offers many opportunities to present the issues we would normally cover in other ways. For example, to discuss how gender inequality operates at the level of everyday personal interaction (for example, that men interrupt women in conversation more often than vice versa), we assigned our students to read an on-line article about gender differences in on-line communication (for example, men typically post longer messages to on-line discussion lists [Herring 1994]). To discuss the kinds of activism surrounding the issue of gender violence, we asked students to find and discuss three groups engaged in the fight to end gender violence.

On-line learning modules helped overcome two common problems with the

Figure 12.2
On-line Student Chat Room

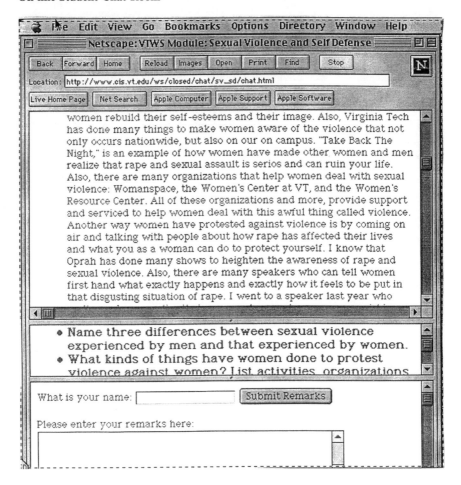

introductory course: instructor turnover and the breadth of the introductory course. Like many women's studies programs, we must "borrow" a variety of instructors from other departments, making for a huge number of instructors teaching our introductory course, with a diversity of specialties, and with the expectation that they will cover a broad set of materials and issues. Many of us find it difficult to cover the overwhelmingly wide range of scholarship presented in the introductory course as effectively as we can cover the scholarship in our own areas of expertise. The on-line modules, created by various instructors, contain information and innovative research in specific areas of women's studies—for example, global women's issues or gender and sports—allowing us to teach the introductory course in the most effective possible way. The on-line modules help broaden the teaching of introductory instructors, who at Virginia Tech are mostly white women, and allow students, who are also overwhelmingly white women, access to the views of women with a diversity of backgrounds and perspectives. Furthermore, because the modules contain so much information, students can pursue self-directed study in specific areas of interest, join international e-mail discussion groups (listservs), and find out how they can become involved in specific types of political action.

A primary learning goal of the introductory course is for students to interpret and understand reality in a different way. Learning involves comprehending the world by reinterpreting knowledge. Using the Web, we discovered, can facilitate this kind of learning. In emphasizing the interpretation of social reality in new/feminist ways, the introductory women's studies classroom is personal and internal, as opposed to a learning that is external, something done by the teacher and memorized by the learner (Ramsden 1992). It may be that this type of learning is best encouraged through on-line modules.

The on-line module assignments provide students in crisis access to help and support. Some students need to seek help after learning about sensitive topics such as eating disorders, sexual assault, or hate crimes. Each on-line module includes links to local resources available to students in need of more information, counseling, medical attention, or support groups. Many such local resources (how to get HIV testing, for example) have their own Web sites, so it is quite convenient to simply add a link to those sites.

The Web-enhanced introductory course allows us to discuss current events more effectively. Not only can new links be added to a given on-line module in seconds, but information from current news sources can be posted instantly so that students can grapple with that information. For example, when a feminist statement was made about a recent news story on schoolboys who shot schoolgirls, students could access it on the course news page. Similarly, when students raise a question about an unanticipated topic, the instructor can post information on this topic to the course Web site sooner than they might be able to print, photocopy, and distribute such information.

INSTRUCTIONAL STRATEGIES FOR WEB-ENHANCED COURSES

Initially, some students experienced anxiety about what was required of them. This is understandable, because so much of the learning in a Web-enhanced course is self-directed, and each on-line module has far too many screens of information, articles, and links for a student to study in a few hours. The following student's remark, made at midsemester, reveals the anxiety about the instructor's expectations and evaluation criteria that the freedom of self-directed learning on the Web can produce:

On-line learning is alright, but I do not know if I prefer it over the classroom because I do not exactly know if what I am doing on the web by myself is absolutely correct. I am a bit worried about the material that I am going to be tested on in a few weeks because we all search some different links, but then we sometimes search the same links. I do not know how the test will be or be like, but I feel like I have been doing the work that has been demanded, but at the same time I feel like it will be hard for me to pass this course because I feel like everything is in the air and not defined well. That is just how I feel; I think it is an interesting class, and the Internet adds a new dimension to the class that a lecture class could not provide.

Thus, instructors using on-line modules must either assign very specific on-line readings and links or allow students flexibility while explaining clearly how students' knowledge will be evaluated and/or tested. Giving students some specific discussion questions to answer after exploring a module (either in a chat room or on paper to submit for a grade) can help provide the structure many students seek. Students can also be asked to write a paper or do a project on one particular topic area that a module covers. (When grading such assignments, it was quite obvious which students explored the module and which did not.) Students can also be given exam questions based on overall Web assignments (for example, ''Discuss three main ways women's birthing experiences have changed over the last century'').

Teachers have long known that good assignments can wind up providing them with more teaching material. This course provides such opportunities by, for instance, having students search the Web for on-line resources in specific topic areas. Students often find sites their instructor was unaware of and can write reviews of the sites. These new sites can be added to the on-line modules as links. Students can also be assigned to create, in groups, a Web site on a particular topic. This can motivate students to do their best work because their work will have a wide public audience. A final, related benefit of the Web-enhanced women's studies course is its increased opportunities for students to interact with one another and share their work. For example, one assignment involved students' finding images from popular magazines that either reinforce or challenge gender norms. Instead of students' turning these in to the instructor only, we scanned the images and put them onto a password-protected Web page, so that students could see what their classmates found. Instructors can also post students' work to the course home page so that they can read each other's work (though it is important to forewarn the students about this and ensure that such pages are password-protected).

So that students do not feel alienated from their instructor, it is important for instructors to clarify that they are still available to students and even require students to visit during office hours at least once. If the Web-enhanced introductory course provides access to in-depth information about feminist issues, it also means that some students will require attention when struggling with difficult concepts and controversial issues. In such cases, the class chat room is inappropriate, and students need to be reminded that their instructor still gives individual attention during old-fashioned office hours.

In order to teach a Web-enhanced introductory course, students must have access to computers with Internet connections that are fast enough to support the Web pages. Because of limited connection spread, it is a good idea to keep graphics simple on any Web pages you create for student use. We advise against putting students on a class listserv because, if working from home computers, their computers might not be able to support the many e-mail messages they would receive while on listservs for more than one course. Some universities have more computer resources for students than others. Students should have technical support available in the computer labs in which they are assigned to work or a teaching assistant who is familiar with the technology. This helps reduce student anxiety and allows them to ask questions if a Web site is not working. Finally, it is helpful to establish a backup plan with students in case the technology fails. For instance, if an assignment is due at 5:00 P.M. over e-mail, but e-mail goes down at 4:00 P.M., students should know in advance if they are to submit a hard copy, or if they are to wait and submit their assignment once e-mail is operational again.

Instructors should know how to create Web pages. New software programs now allow you to do this quite easily (with the feel of a word-processing program), without knowing HTML (hypertext markup language). Anyone with Netscape Communicator has the option to use Netscape Composer, software for building Web pages. Software such as Claris Home Page (for Mac or PC operating systems) is available to purchase as well. Instructors can develop their own class home page on which to add links to local resources, information, and current events, in addition to linking to the resources of other programs such as our on-line learning modules. After creating a Web page, instructors must find out how to publish it on the World Wide Web. We suggest contacting the person in charge of the Web server in one's department or institution. That person should be able to explain how to go about putting a Web page on the university's server and how much space is available. This person will also know whether or not the university provides students with space for Web pages. Those desiring to use a chat room will need to create their own, since ours is password-protected, for use by our currently enrolled students only. Instructors would also do well to consult their librarian for information about fair use and copyright laws. (See suggested readings about fair use and other issues in Web-based teaching.) Finally, instructors may wish to give students guidelines for "netiquette." (We recommend Don E. Descy's guidelines at *http://w3.ag.uiuc.edu: 80/AIM/Discovery/Net/email/netiquette.html.*)

CONCLUSION

The use of on-line modules in an introductory women's studies course or other social sciences/humanities courses has not been universally accepted by the instructors or students of such classes. We found that the Internet can be used as a positive—and feminist—pedagogical tool by allowing private exploration of intimidating topics, increasing students' access to opportunities for activism and to local crisis resources, and expanding the instructors' repertoire of material. The start-up time investment for instructors has shrunk dramatically because of the Web resources compiled and made available by others (see next section). We suggest that women's studies courses, especially those with larger than desired enrollments, would benefit from the inclusion of on-line learning modules, Web-based assignments, and chat rooms. Of course, how women's studies instructors will incorporate on-line materials into their courses can and should vary widely. Some instructors might choose to give one on-line assignment all semester, for instance, while others may wish to use the Web as a regular part of the class.

Whether or not Web work could substitute for in-class learning, as in distance-learning courses, is another question entirely. Our experiment has shown the feminist benefits of a Web-enhanced women's studies class, not an on-line course. Our courses still involve in-class lectures, discussions, and student presentations. Web-based assignments remain only a portion of our total assignments and of students' overall course grade. As such, cybergrrrl education takes advantage of virtual feminism for an empowering, consciousness-raising course in the best tradition of introductory women's studies teaching.

SUGGESTED WEB RESOURCES

Editor's note: Every effort has been made to provide current Internet information. However, readers are advised that Internet and e-mail addresses are subject to change.

Directory of Online Learning Modules for Introductory Women's Studies, Virginia Tech. This page is the directory linking browsers to all the on-line modules: *http://www.cis.vt.edu/was/wsmodules/moduledirectory.html*

Directory of Gender-Related Internet Resources for Academic Research, a collection of links compiled by Helen Fallon as part of a thesis for the master's degree in women's studies at University College, Dublin, Ireland: *http://www.dcu.ie/staff/hfallon/thesis.htm*

Gender Studies Resource Page, compiled by Madelyn Detloff while in the Department of English and in women's studies at the University of California, Santa Barbara. Includes many links to queer sites as well as feminist sites: *http://www.rain.org/~detloff/chloe.html*

Selected Women and Gender Resources on the World Wide Web, a comprehensive site for women's studies resources from the University of Wisconsin System Women's Studies Librarian's Office: *http://www.library.wisc.edu/libraries/WomensStudies/others.htm*

Diversity Web, a site that links colleges and universities that are working to engage the diversity of U.S. society in educational mission, campus climate, curriculum focus, and connections with the larger society. Cosponsored by American Association of Colleges and Universities (AAC&U) and the University of Maryland, College Park, this site includes resources for people interested in curriculum change: *http://www.inform.umd.edu/DiversityWeb/*

Voice of the Shuttle: Gender Studies Page, a site based at the University of California, Santa Barbara, with links to issues and readings in the humanities, cultural studies, and feminist theory: *http://humanitas.ucsb.edu/cgi-bin/mfs/01/gender.html*

Library Resources on Women's Studies. A site based on Northern Arizona University's library holdings. Issued by the National Clearinghouse for Academic Advising *http://www.nau.edu/~wst/access/biglist.html*

Free thirty-day trial version of Claris Home Page (for either Mac or PC users): *http://www.claris.com*

SUGGESTED READINGS

Brooks, D. W. 1997 *Web-teaching: A guide to designing interactive teaching for the World Wide Web.* New York: Plenum.

Crews, K. D. 1993. *Copyright, fair use, and the challenge for universities: Promoting the progress of higher education,* imprint, xiv, 247; 23 cm. Chicago: University of Chicago Press, xiv, 247: 23 cm.

Gilbert, L and C. Kile. 1996. *Surfer grrls: Look Ethel! An Internet guide for us!* Seattle: Seal.

Korenman, J. 1997 *Internet resources for women: Using electronic media in curriculum transformation.* Baltimore: National Center for Curriculum Transformation.

Lindemeyer, R. B. 1997. *Fair use: Guidelines for educational multimedia.* Produced by Centers in Cooperation with the PBS/Adult Learning Satellite Service, WETA-COM, Inc. and Iowa Public Television Consortium of College and University Media.

Spender, D. 1996. *Nattering on the Net: Women, power and cyberspace.* North Melbourne, Australia: Spinifex.

13

Webbed Women: Information Technology in the Introduction to Women's Studies Classroom

Maria Pramaggiore, North Carolina State University, with Beth Hardin, SAS Institute

In "Facing the 1990s: Problems and Possibilities for Women's Studies," Joanna De Groot and Mary Maynard (1993) place several issues on the women's studies agenda, including diversity, the challenges of postmodernist theory, and the ambivalent relation between women's studies and gender studies. In 1993, before the World Wide Web became a household phrase, DeGroot and Maynard could not have anticipated that information technologies might pose problems or offer possibilities for feminist education in and beyond the university classroom. In the late 1990s, however, university teachers are learning that we must come to terms with the educational uses and abuses of the Internet and related information technologies.

At North Carolina State University (NCSU), where I, Maria Pramaggiore, teach, some administrators view information technologies as cost-effective delivery systems for disseminating information, reflecting widely held beliefs that these technologies are a panacea for public education. In the College of Humanities and Social Sciences (CHASS), where our Women's Studies Program is located, many faculty members perceive these technologies as a threat to traditional classroom instruction, to the structure of the professoriate, and to public education. Those of us who teach women's studies must become involved in this discussion; feminist theorists of technology, as Donna Haraway suggests (1991: 21), must find ways to analyze, respond to, and intervene in the "politics of technoscience" as it unfolds in education at every level.

This chapter charts the development and implementation of an Introduction to Women's Studies course at North Carolina State University that incorporated new information and communication technologies in support of specific feminist pedagogical goals. I taught one section of the course in the fall of 1995 and a second section in the fall of 1997. Introduction to Women's Studies is a particularly appropriate location from which to explore whether or not information technologies can support and enhance the feminist classroom. First, the feminist pedagogical emphasis on a student-centered, nonhierarchical learning environment resonates with claims made about the benefits of using technology in the classroom or as a virtual classroom. Theorists and practitioners have argued that information technologies intrinsically promote collaborative, decentralized, democratic learning modes (Paxton 1996; Spender 1995). Moreover, in an introductory women's studies course, students approach technology in the context of a proactive feminist analysis. Lisbet Van Zoonen's (1992: 23–24) perspective is particularly useful; she stresses that information technologies are a "product of social relations [that reflect] patriarchal ideas and values" but also argues that users change the social meaning and practices surrounding the technologies.

I planned and taught this course with the assistance of Beth Hardin, a master's student in technical communication. In 1997, Melinda Brown, an information technology specialist in the NCSU libraries, assisted us. I should emphasize that this course was never conceived of as an on-line courses. I intended to use the technologies—a listserv and World Wide Web page—to supplement, rather than to supplant, the traditional classroom and the important experiences of group work and face-to-face discussion.

It should also be noted that no university funding was available to support planning the course or constructing the Web page. After our pilot semester in 1995, NCSU launched Project 25, which offered professors release time and technical support on a competitive basis to integrate information technology into existing courses or to design new on-line courses. A preliminary assessment of Project 25 indicates that faculty believe the university community underestimates the investment of time instructors must make in using information technology as a pedagogical tool.[1]

Negotiating institutional constraints and the contentious terrain of feminist perspectives on technology, Beth and I integrated technology into the course in a way that combines feminist critique with empowered intervention. In her thesis, Beth describes this as an "empowered feminist approach" to using technology (Hardin 1998: 6).

VIRTUAL AND INSTITUTIONAL REALITIES: THE NCSU ENVIRONMENT

North Carolina State University is a Research I land-grant institution, chartered in 1887. Currently, the university serves more than 27,000 students; its three largest colleges are Engineering (1,335 graduates in 1997), Agriculture and Life Sciences (873), and Humanities and Social Sciences (807). In terms of majors, the most "male" college is Engineering, which has a 20/80 female-to-male ratio; by contrast, the most "female" college measured by majors is CHASS, with a 55/45 female-to-male ratio.

The Women's Studies Program is housed in the CHASS. Women's studies offers a university-wide minor as well as internship and study-abroad opportunities. In existence since the early 1990s, the small, but growing, program has suffered from a lack of institutional commitment and resources, partly stemming from its location in CHASS at a technological university. Recently, women's studies has garnered more institutional support and recognition by developing links to science and engineering colleges.

The introductory course, a requirement for the minor, is limited to an enrollment of twenty-five students, which is quite remarkable for such a large institution.[2] In fall 1995, twenty-three students enrolled in the course; in fall 1997, nineteen students enrolled. The composition of both classes was overwhelmingly female, white, and heterosexual. In 1995, two male students took the course: one Asian American man and one African American man. Two African American women were enrolled that semester; the other nineteen women were white. In 1997, sixteen white women, one African American woman, one Asian American woman, and one Latina were enrolled. In 1995, two self-identified bisexual women took the course; in 1997, no students identified their sexuality as anything other than heterosexual. (The course enrollment approximated the racial composition of NCSU in recent years: in 1997, 10% of students were African American, and 80% were white.) At 90% and 100% in 1995 and 1997, respectively, women were vastly overrepresented relative to the university population, which was 41% female in 1997. Finally, the distribution of student majors was surprisingly broad. We had anticipated that most students would have declared majors in CHASS, the institutional home of women's studies. Instead, only 20% of students in 1995 and 36% of students in 1997 were humanities or social sciences majors.

SYNTHESIS: A COMPUTER-ASSISTED FEMINIST PEDAGOGY

Our mode of integrating technology into the course was influenced by current feminist critiques of information technologies. Emily Jessup (1997) summarizes a number of studies conducted in the late 1980s that argue for the existence of a technological "gender gap." This gap manifests itself in elementary school and continues throughout primary and secondary education. Some studies observe that girls use computers less frequently than boys, that girls use computers for different purposes than men, and that women have less confidence about using computers than boys do (Gerver 1997). Ongoing research suggests that women play a small role in the design and production of information technologies and are in the minority of Internet users. Many women Internet users have

argued that masculine styles of interaction dominate on-line culture (Cherny and
Weise 1996; Spender 1995); some claim these practices deter women who do
have access to, and interest in, the technology.

Other views of women and information technology stress the growing presence of women on the Web. For example, some users have estimated that
women's Web sites on the Internet increased from 5% to 34% of all sites between 1992 and 1996 (Wakeford 1997: 61). Furthermore, women have created
"alternative spaces in computing culture" that go unrecognized, especially if
they are feminist in content (Wakeford 1997: 53). In *SurferGrrrls*, Laurel Gilbert
and Crystal Kile address the gender gap, the deterrents to women's development
and use of information technology, and the subversive and emancipatory possibilities the Internet offers to women. They acknowledge the statistical evidence
that implies men dominate the Web; for example, in May 1996, men made up
66% of Internet users (Gilbert and Kile 1996: 3). Gilbert and Kile (4) also point
out that statistics cannot provide information about how women use the Internet
to empower themselves:

We wrote *SurferGrrrls* to show the world once and for all that women are a kicking,
amazing, important part of Internet culture, not anomalies. We wrote it because women
are using the Internet in personally and economically empowering ways, and their examples can inspire other women. And we wrote this book because even though women
and girls from many walks of life are doing extremely fun, fabulous and useful stuff on
the Internet, this myth still persists that the Net is a "guy thing" or a "geek thing" or
a "white thing" or something only for the affluent, the businessman, or those interested
in the alt.sex newsgroup hierarchy.

Gilbert and Kile (4) point out that women's participation can change the dominant practices of, and metaphors that surround, on-line culture:

Finally, so much of the way we think about the Internet has been determined by "manly"
metaphors (the frontier, the highway) and by cyberpunk (we dig it, but it's not really a
female-friendly vision in a lot of ways), that we decided it was time to take a look at
the visions suggested by women's spaces on the Net, our participation in on-line culture
and the sites and creations women offer to the developing Net at large.

These analyses, which include both feminist critique of the culture of technology and calls for intervention in social practices, guided the design of our
course. Beth and I were not persuaded by arguments that technology is inherently antithetical to the concerns and learning styles of women, a perspective
characterized as the "radical" feminist viewpoint (Van Zoonen 1992). Neither
were we convinced that women merely need to develop technological skills in
order to participate in the public sphere, a stance characterized as the "liberal"
feminist viewpoint. We wanted to make current technological practices available
to students caught in a technological gender gap at NCSU, where women students are underrepresented in the colleges that train students to use technology

(engineering and the sciences). We were also committed to exploring information and communications technologies as gendered cultural practices.

We planned to use information technologies—the course listserv and World Wide Web page—to support and enhance the following feminist pedagogical goals: (1) decenter the traditional authority structure of the classroom, (2) encourage learner-centered learning, (3) empower students with technological skills and an understanding of technology as a gendered social process, and (4) expose students to the varied and abundant Web resources by and about women. The next section outlines the way we integrated information technologies into the course in support of these goals and what our students told us about their experiences on surveys distributed at midterm and the end of the semester.

IN THE VIRTUAL TRENCHES: TEACHING WITH TECHNOLOGY

Teaching with technology meant not only familiarizing students with the technology, which we accomplished in three in-class training sessions, but also constructing a course-specific Web page and assignments that would take advantage of the features of the technology. Beth constructed a Web site where students could read the syllabus, follow links to related Web sites (organized according to syllabus topics), e-mail Beth or me, and e-mail the course listserv. We might have simply provided Web training and allowed students to use existing resources on the Web, but we felt that a course Web page would increase the sense of community in the class and provide ease of access to all course technology. We established a closed listserv so that only students enrolled in the class could participate. This feature allows the list managers to forward external messages in the context of course material and to prevent disruptive flames or junk e-mail from reaching class members.

Further information (including the course syllabus) is available on our Web page at *http://www2.ncsu.edu/unity/lockers/class/hss200/ws.html*.

Decenter Authority

The model of teaching forwarded by those who celebrate new information technologies and one often hailed in feminist pedagogy is that of the instructor as facilitator. Dale Spender (1995: 115) writes that in the age of electronic information, ''[t]he relationship between teachers and students will enter a new phase: one where cooperation rather than hierarchy sets the terms.'' We employed the course listserv to achieve this goal. Students were required to use the listserv on three occasions: to post their peer reviews of a short paper, to respond to a film, and to post an interview and Web site to the listserv. The first assignment asked students to read another student's paper (identified only by ID number) and to summarize and provide constructive and critical feedback to the class listserv. The evaluator's comments were available to the entire class, although only the paper's author knew her or his paper was being reviewed.

Students received points on this assignment according to how thoroughly they critiqued the paper. They could earn as many points for their peer evaluation as they did for the paper itself, which meant that their role as evaluators was as important as their performance as writers.

This exercise was meant to encourage students to think of their own interpretive, writing, and evaluative processes in relation to those of their peers. Sharing the reviews with the class was intended to promote a sense of a community of learners, each of whom bore a responsibility as both writer and critic. The group's access to all the peer reviews allowed students to learn from one another as a group and might call into question the monopoly of the teacher as a single authoritative source.

The third assignment (the second is discussed later) asked students to locate a Web site related to body image issues, to interview a person outside the course while visiting that site, and to summarize the comments in a post to the listserv. I reminded them to post the interviewee's comments anonymously and to inform the interviewee that her or his comments would be shared with the class. This assignment allowed students to pursue their own interests within the broad subject area of the course and to act as a facilitator for the class by presenting the observations and ideas arrived at by their collaboration with the interviewee.

Finally, students were frequently encouraged to use the listserv to extend discussion of course topics and to communicate with one another about topics such as events on campus. In this way, the instructor could be seen more as a facilitator than authority figure, and student concerns could be placed in the foreground. I adopted a noninterventionist stance; occasionally, I forwarded Web sites relating to student comments and questions, and Beth provided technical assistance. In end-of-semester surveys from both semesters, a majority of students (29/33) answered yes to the question, "Was the listserv a different experience than the classroom because discussion was not led by the professor?" Open-ended responses indicated that it was easier for students to express themselves on the listserv, that students felt that more open criticism occurred on the listserv (for better and worse), that it was easier to "talk" to other students than to the professor, that students could talk about how they really felt, that the listserv provided a sense of freedom (and possibly of being out of control), and that they found discussions begun by peers were easier to join.

In 1995, students experienced the ways in which new technologies can be used to express antifeminist sentiments and to silence women. Early in the term, after a heated outburst in class discussion, a male student submitted a flame to the listserv, posted in all capital letters (a format that was specifically mentioned as inappropriate in our training materials). The student challenged the class to respond to propositions such as "women's place is in the home" and signed the message in a suggestive and threatening manner. "[NAME], so you know whose name to scream." I responded to the post on the listserv, suggesting that class members' time might be better spent addressing the concerns of the course rather than answering immature and inflammatory formulations. The student in question persisted in his confrontational behavior, e-mailing students individually to berate them for their "stupid" contributions to class discussion. While this student's disruption drew attention and resources away from legitimate topics—and intimidated some women students—it also provided students with first-hand evidence on the gender dynamics of communication. In 1995, 17/19 students answered yes to a question asking if the listserv allowed the discussion of things that would not have been discussed in class. Open-ended comments suggested this outcome was not always positive. Several students wrote that those who sent misogynist messages would not have felt free to make those comments in class. Others felt the list allowed discussion of matters "too controversial" for the classroom. By contrast, in 1997, most students wrote that most matters discussed on the listserv could have been and often were discussed in class.

The 1995 experience supports the contention that confrontational styles of interaction may intimidate some women. However, a number of women students posted assertive and thoughtful responses that analyzed the incident according to models of gendered power relations. In-class training can provide students with an understanding of netiquette but cannot avert instances such as this one, where a student deliberately flouts the rules. Under these circumstances, repeated offenses would have resulted in his elimination from the listserv just as repeated classroom disturbances might result in ejecting a student from the classroom. The situation highlighted the dilemma facing many feminist teachers who attempt to democratize their classrooms only to find a single vocal student or small group usurping authority. It also raises questions concerning the proper regulation of communication technologies, on campus and off, particularly when First Amendment rights often are invoked to protect inappropriate communication and harassment. In pedagogical terms, the experience has forced me to rethink whether it is necessary (or desirable or even possible) to relinquish authority to promote student-centered learning. Creating a learning community in which all students are able to participate is not synonymous with an opinionated free-for-all; information technologies are no "better" than the traditional classroom at fostering such an environment and may, in fact, offer disruptive students easier access to individuals and the class as a whole.

While eschewing a role as moderator except in rare instances such as the flame, I wanted the listserv to be a "safer" space to explore personal responses to course material. The second listserv assignment addressed the goals of de-centering authority and encouraging learner-centered learning while attempting to create such a space. It asked students to post a response to the film *The Accused* (Kaplan 1988) taking into account our class reading and discussion of sexual terrorism and sexual harassment. We anticipated that the responses might be personal as well as analytical and that the listserv might permit such an approach, and this happened. Students had profound reactions to the film and became aware of issues raised in the assigned readings in a personal way, for example, concerns about campus safety. In surveys from 1995 and 1997, a majority of students felt that the dynamics of the listserv discussion affected their thinking about the reading (20/33); several commented specifically on this assignment.

Overall, the listserv did provide an alternative forum in which the instructor was not the sole authority figure and in which students perceived a greater ability to express themselves. The listserv experience varied according to the students in the course; in the class without deliberately confrontational students, more students perceived the listserv as an extension of classroom discussion rather than as an alternative forum. For example, two students in 1997 wrote that "we were allowed to speak our opinions in class" and that class discussions were "open." Nevertheless, another student in that class indicated it was "awesome" to hear "your peers speaking out." In 1995, there was a greater volume of listserv messages not devoted to assignments than in 1997; however, in both semesters students felt the listserv created a sense of community. It may be the case that well-designed assignments using the listserv can promote community just as well as a listserv used for ongoing discussions.

Encourage Learner-Centered Learning

Although the Web page reflected the concerns of the instructors, it eventually incorporated the interests of the students in the course. The first Internet assignment asked students to find a Web site related to women's history. We visited those sites together in class, and each student introduced the class to her area of interest within women's history. Those sites were then linked to the Web page. Over the course of each semester, the links the students provided mapped out the issues of academic and personal interest and, in a sense, the personality of that group. Students were required to contribute to the Web page in the first Internet assignment, to inform students of Web sites of interest in their third (body image) listserv assignment, and to use at least one Web site as a reference for their final paper.

By expanding the Web page, students were able to investigate women's resources and current topics on the Web with a great deal more flexibility than any textbook or syllabus could offer. We hoped that providing students with a tool to pursue their own interests might make them feel that the course addressed their individual concerns and interests as well as those of the instructors. Obviously, the listserv and Web page also gave students access to the course materials and instructors outside class time and office hours, which may have an empowering effect on students as they take more responsibility for their own learning. One student in 1997 mentioned that using the Web page and the listserv permitted her to think more deliberately about the assignments.

Responses to the Web page were overwhelmingly positive. Most students in both semesters responded that the Web page gave them a different sense of women's studies (29/35). They wrote that there were more contemporary issues on the Web than in the text and a great deal of information circulating on the

Web, and that they were exposed to a much broader range of issues relating to women than they expected before the course. The Web page also provided what one student called "an interactive link between class and 'real life.' " A significant minority of students (12/25) suggested that we encourage students to use the Web more—by requiring students to bring in a URL each month and scheduling more in-class time using the Web.

The Web page did help students feel that they had the opportunity to explore areas of interest to them that diverged from course content and schedule. The body image assignment synthesized students' use of the technology in an important way for learner-centered learning. Students selected the Web site, chose an interviewee, and composed a summary for a community of peers already established in class and on the listserv throughout the semester. Here, they were able to demonstrate the extent to which they could integrate their own personal experiences and perspectives with academic research and make it available for group consideration and discussion.

Empower Students with Technological Skills and an Understanding of Technology as a Gendered Social Process

At the beginning of each semester, I set aside several class meetings for in-class training, and Beth and Melinda were available at scheduled out-of-class lab sessions to offer assistance. In 1995, most students had never used their university computer accounts. By 1997, all of the students had at least logged onto their account once before taking the course. Despite students' increasing facility and familiarity with information technology, the training sessions were useful because they encouraged skilled and recalcitrant students alike to explore the Web page thoroughly and to learn from their peers. Students felt more proficient with computers as a result of taking the course: in both semesters, students used computers more outside class (25/34) and felt positive about using technology in the classroom (27/32) as a result of taking this course. One student wrote of "a higher degree of confidence to go in and look for any subject I choose."

In 1995 and 1997, I taught Marge Piercy's (1991) feminist science fiction novel *He, She and It*, which presents a feminist protagonist as an information technology expert. By 1997, I felt that more of the course's critical content should expose students to feminist perspectives on gender and technology. I added readings from *SurferGrrrls* (Gilbert and Kile 1996) throughout that semester. The book helped students grasp the technology (with Glossary and Frequently Asked Question sections) and also showed students that the Internet is a space that women can explore and construct (the book includes lists of Web sites about women and/or created by women). Students in both 1995 and 1997 indicated that they felt technology was an important tool for women to learn; in 1997 students were more likely to mention that they appreciated learning about "women and technology."

Expose Students to the Varied and Abundant Resources on Women and Gender on the Web

We were convinced that exploring the Web would provide students with the means to find a vast array of women's resources, from university archives to personal Web pages. Surveys indicated that the Web and the listserv did validate the importance of women's studies because students were exposed to feminist analyses beyond the confines of our classroom and our university. I felt this exposure was critical at a university with a chilly campus climate. Students wrote that they experienced a great degree of diversity, creative avenues of expression, and a greater awareness of society as a result of the Web page.

CONCLUSION

Several general comments that students made cannot be characterized according to the four goals. They include a greater sense of access to the instructor, a feeling of greater student interaction (though this was not defined as peer interaction or interaction with instructor), and a sense of "bonding" that made this course a more personal experience than others. Clearly, these goals might be achieved in the traditional classroom and may not be attributable to the use of information technologies. It was useful to learn, however, that integrating these technologies in the classroom did not produce any obvious impediments to student–teacher interaction and the personal bond created among students in the course.

In this project, Beth and I attempted to use information technology to enact a feminist pedagogy that critiques gendered social relations and provides a means of intervening in them. Like Terry and Calvert (1997: 9), we felt that

[t]o refuse such an engagement [with technology] is perhaps not merely to forego the strategic opportunity to transform or even invent radically different technologies for feminist and progressive projects; crucial decision-making about our futures requires this critical engagement.

Clearly, the relationship of women to technology and the gendering of our emerging technoculture must be further theorized and evaluated in education, the workplace, the home, and cyberspace, among other real and virtual locations.

NOTES

Editors' note: Every effort has been made to provide current Internet information. However, readers are advised that Internet and e-mail addresses are subject to change.

   1. The assessment is located at *http://courses.ncsu.edu/info/f97_assessment.html*.

   2. The Women's Studies Program has never turned students away from the course. The small enrollment reflects the program's lack of resources for recruiting, bureau-

cratic impediments to publicizing our courses, and a somewhat ''chilly'' institutional climate for women.

SUGGESTED READING

Damarin, S. K. 1992. Women and information technology: Framing some issues for education. *Feminist Teacher* 6.2: 16–20.

Gurak, L. J. and N. L. Bayer. 1994. Making gender visible: Extending feminist critiques of technology to technical communication. *Technical Communication Quarterly* 3.3: 257–270.

Kramerae, C. and H. J. Taylor. 1997. Women and men on electronic networks: A conversation or a monologue? *Literacy, technology and society: Confronting the issues*, ed. G Hawisher and C. Selfe, 348–358. Upper Saddle River, NJ: Prentice-Hall.

14

Reading *Glamour* Magazine:
The Production of "Woman"

Stacy Wolf, George Washington University

A stereotype of feminism repeated so frequently as to be absurd is that feminism takes all of the fun out of life. Not only are feminists humorless and dour, the story goes, but feminist teachers force their students to disdain popular culture and to label all television and film racist, sexist, and horrible. In fact, students in feminist classes do often confess that the course has made it "hard to go to the movies anymore," but the admission of the effects of feminism is invariably accompanied by the exhilaration that comes with the power to critique.

The image of the old-time, no-fun feminist (often imaged as a lesbian-feminist) has been recently countered by the "do-me" feminist, the unapologetic capitalist, materialist, individualist. Fueled by an ideology of liberal feminism, this perspective privileges individual autonomy and choice over social structures. Even literary scholar Elaine Showalter (1997: 80) confessed in an article for *Vogue* that she loves to shop and wear lipstick.

But more students (and more of us) live in contradictions. As feminist teachers and feminist students we function complexly in relation to popular culture, at once consuming it and critiquing it. If we can afford it, we long for the "retail therapy" of shopping, even as we are aware of being constantly addressed by culture precisely because it wants us to believe that shopping will make us feel better.

In teaching women's studies, especially to students on an introductory level, I think it is important to embrace the contradictions. Significantly, I am not arguing for absolute relativism but rather for a contested, contradictory engagement with culture. In this chapter, I describe and, at times, enact through lecture notes my use of *Glamour* magazine as the first text of an introductory-level women's studies class. Reading *Glamour* models a contradictory critical praxis (that is, pleasurable consumption and critical rejection) and reiterates the significance of understanding identities as socially, economically, and politically structured, rather than simply individually devised.

WOMEN'S STUDIES 101 AT UNIVERSITY OF WISCONSIN-MADISON

For three semesters, I taught a 120-student lecture course, The Meanings of "Woman" in Western Culture, at the University of Wisconsin–Madison, a large, midwestern state university located in a politically progressive city. Students' familiarity with, and interest in, feminism varied tremendously. The one-semester course (taught every semester) was one of three introductory-level women's studies classes; another introduced women's studies issues in the social sciences, and a third in the sciences. Women's studies majors were required to take either the humanities or the social science introductory course and the science introductory course. The course I taught also fulfilled a university "minority" requirement and so attracted a range of students, from freshmen to seniors (most were sophomores), from English majors to math majors. Most were as-yet-undeclared humanities or social science majors. Most, but certainly not all, of the students were women, and several were "out" lesbians, and, like all of the University of Wisconsin (UW), most of the students were white and middle-class. Much of the class seemed sympathetic to a feminist perspective, although almost always phrased as, "I'm not a feminist, but . . ."

Students met with a teaching assistant in twenty-student, fifty-minute discussion sections once a week to discuss the reading, but in my two, fifty-minute lectures each week, I worked to create a direct rapport with the students and to regularly disrupt the authoritative structure of the lecture by having students do in-class writings, answer questions, engage in discussion, and present their own analyses of a representation of "woman." I taught the course with an emphasis on rigorous, poststructuralist-oriented, theoretical analyses of representations and created assignments to enable students to practice cultural criticism at everyday sites—from television to their other classes (by analyzing the ideology of course syllabi), and from theater to consumer culture. Of every text, we asked, What is "woman" made to mean here? How are those meanings constructed? What is significant about those meanings?

Students tended to be surprised that, in a women's studies course, they were "allowed" to read *Glamour* magazine and, even more, to enjoy it. I think this "surprise" unsettled their assumptions about feminism and a feminist critique.

INTRODUCING THE TOOLS: THEORIES OF REPRESENTATION

To methodologically and ideologically frame our reading of *Glamour*, I first introduced some key analytical concepts of representation. Assumptions of the course, I explained, include:

1. Representations are in many forms—theater, film, fiction, television, advertising, and so on. Representations are not only about art or forms that frame or mark representations as such. They are all around us.
2. Representations are constructions.
3. All representations are ideological, whether or not they have an explicitly "political" message. Put another way, representations are ideologically mediated constructions. Every image serves someone. There are no neutral images.
4. Representations both shape reality and are shaped by reality, but representations are not the same thing as reality. Representation is not reflection. Representation cannot be proven to directly affect reality. We try to complicate a simplistic reflective or effects model.[1]
5. Representations matter. Therefore, it is not useful to assert that "we are reading too much into this."

I defined the terms "naturalization" (images are constructed to make certain elements of gender seem natural) and "mystification" (the means by which representations are constructed to reinforce the illusion of the natural) to set up how our reading of *Glamour* is aimed to denaturalize and to demystify the magazine's representations. For example, when we look at *Glamour*, we can focus on demystifying its production by looking closely at the choices the editors, writers, photographers, and layout people made in putting it together. We can think about the juxtaposition of certain images with certain words to think about how the magazine wants us to respond. But then we can look at it from a slightly different angle and think about why we are supposed to respond in certain ways. Why do certain images of beauty seem "natural"? Why does it seem "natural" that wealth, art, and beauty are connected? Why does it seem "normal" to want to be thin and young?

The terms "mystification" and "naturalization" are slightly different ways of looking at the same process, and they require the same kind of extreme self-consciousness about cultural products. Learning to denaturalize and demystify is hard because it requires that we look at assumptions that are often hard to see. With everything we read and see and hear, we try to keep asking ourselves, What are the underlying assumptions here?

JOHN BERGER'S *WAYS OF SEEING*

We read John Berger's *Ways of Seeing* (1972) concurrently with *Glamour*, and his text supplied some of the vocabulary of our critique, for example:

1. the male gaze[2]

2. the assumption of a male address

3. women's self-surveillance and split consciousness: "This unequal relationship [that painters and owners of European art were usually men and the objects of art were women] is still so deeply embedded in our culture that it still structures the consciousness [that is, ideology] of many women. They do to themselves what men do to them. They survey, like men, their own femininity" (Berger 1972: 63). (I asked, Does this statement resonate for you? How? Or how not?)

4. the same activity is differently interpreted depending on whether a man or a woman performs it. "Men act and women appear," Berger (1972: 47) writes and critiques. Men are seen as (active) subjects and woman as (passive) objects.

5. female narcissism

6. Berger (1972: 64) invites the reader to transform the nude pictures (in the text) of women into men. He writes, "Then notice the violence which that transformation does. Not to the image, but to the assumptions of a likely viewer." (I asked, What does he mean by this?)

We discussed, Is Berger's notion of women's self-surveillance applicable in the context of a magazine that presumes a female audience? Is there a female gaze? What is it? Do you see signs of it in *Glamour*? Or is the male gaze so naturalized in our viewing conventions that even women look at women from a heterosexual male point of view?

WOMEN'S MAGAZINES, PROS AND CONS

Women's magazines, like many representational texts, are extremely contradictory and deliver mixed messages. Each and every page, each and every word and image in *Glamour* constructs what "woman" means. The text raises a fundamental question of structure versus agency: Do we use these magazines, or do they use us? How?

There are a number of positive aspects to women's magazines:

1. They constitute an important element of women's mass culture. Women's magazines form an imaginary community that ties women together, particularly women who spend much time alone, at home, and/or with children. Historically, when more women stayed at home, magazines provided a way of feeling connected. (A related exercise might ask students to describe the particular "community" implied by this or another magazine and the values a given magazine creates.)

2. *Glamour* provides a variety of images of women and increasingly diverse images. Many of the images are empowering. (A related exercise might ask students to compare representations of women across magazines to delineate the intended reader or the ideological work of the magazine.)

3. *Glamour* provides useful information about health, money, and politics. It frequently

shows women how to become empowered at work, in relationships, and in relation to oneself and one's physical and emotional well-being.

4. *Glamour* provides a woman-to-woman exchange and a sense of community. For example, the letters to the editor and advice letters in several columns on clothes, sex and health, and money create a sense of community for many readers. The voice of the reader, phrased in questions, allows other readers to feel justified in their questions. The tone of the answers is one of a sister, good friend, or caring mentor.

But *Glamour* should also be seen for its nonempowering practices and politics:

1. Because they depend on advertisers, women's magazines are falsely autonomous in their fashion and makeup advice. In fact, early in the production of *Ms. Magazine*, then-editor Gloria Steinem lost a major cosmetics account because the women on the cover were not wearing enough makeup (Wolf 1991: 81).

2. Women readers of *Glamour* are produced first and foremost as consumers in the magazine. The reader's key identity is one who buys.

3. Women's magazines have long practiced airbrushing of models to eliminate imperfections on the skin or to make eyes a different color, but now, more and more magazines are using computer-altered images—morphing. The women who are set up as role models for appearance, then, are not and cannot be real women at all. They are only social and technological constructions. It is a painful irony that the bodies and faces against which women judge our appearance are technologically created.

4. The address in women's magazines tends to be in the interrogative or imperative mode—the question or the command (Williamson 1980: 56). Judith Williamson describes the frequent, searching question in which the reader is led to find her "true nature." The question, Williamson points out, is often followed by the pep-talk imperative, which emphasizes that she can change it (her hair, her body, her life, herself, anything) if she works hard enough. Williamson argues that women's magazines sell because they fuel this unending search for a new self and that the new self comes about primarily through sexuality (Williamson 1980: 55–61). Naomi Wolf has a harsher critique. She says that the tone is condescending and heckling and that the rhetoric of almost-threats would never be found in men's magazines (Wolf 1991: 69–77).

5. The magazine tends to reduce all problems to the individual and her psychology. *Glamour* does not emphasize the social construction of identity but implies that, as a woman, whatever you are—in mind or spirit but especially in body—you can change it or deal with it. The message of self-empowerment overvalues the power of the individual. This message can be empowering but also tends to blame the victims of dominant ideology. It uses an ideology of individualism, which is extremely difficult to notice because it is so pervasive and naturalized in our culture. In actuality, social relations structure many of the "ways we are." Change often is not just a question of trying harder or wearing different clothes. Faludi (1991: 70–72) argues that women's magazines facilitate a form of psychic isolation by urging women to try harder to fix themselves and solve their own problems by themselves.

6. *Glamour* features, relatively speaking, very few women of color, and it completely

erases lesbians and working-class women, except for the occasional article about a sister or friend who is a lesbian (Inness 1997). There is very little, if any, attention paid to older women. What it means to be a woman, according to *Glamour*, is probably white and definitely heterosexual and young and at least middle-class.

QUESTIONS FOR *GLAMOUR*

I distributed the following list of questions, which formed the basis for our discussion for the second day of the *Glamour* unit.

Ways of Reading, or Questions for *Glamour* as a Cultural Text

Context: Experiential Questions to Help You Be a Bit More Self-Conscious About Your Reading (Habits)

Do you usually read *Glamour*? If so, how does having to read it for a class change your relationship to it? Or does it? If you do not usually read it, how did you feel about buying it or reading it? If you do not usually read it, why not? What magazines do you read? What are the stereotypes you have of the people who do read *Glamour* (if you have them)?

Where did you sit to read or to look at it? At a desk or table? In a soft chair? In bed? Did you look at it alone or with someone? How did your attitude toward this assignment compare to your "normal" assignments? Did you sit with the magazine and this list of questions at the same time, or did you look at the magazine first and then look at the questions?

How did you read *Glamour* or look at it? Did you read it cover to cover? Did you start in the back? Did you skim through and find what interested you to come back to? Did you eventually read all of it?

Do you have any desire to save this magazine? Why or why not?

What Does this Text Say about the Meanings of Woman?

Text: Look Closely at the Cover, Advertisements, Articles, Regular Features, Photographs

According to *Glamour*, what does it mean to be a woman? You may have a number of contradictory answers to this question. For example, do the ads and the articles construct Woman in the same way?

According to *Glamour*, what should women care about? think about? What should they want to buy? have? eat? wear?

How does the magazine work rhetorically? How does it persuade you to have certain desires? How would you read the pictures if there were no words?

Think about address. Who is *Glamour*'s presumed audience? How can you tell? Who is the "you" of the text and images? How would you describe the authorial voice? Is it different in different articles or ads? Who is excluded from this magazine? What kinds of women do you not see pictured or addressed here? Do you think it matters? Why or why not?

How does *Glamour* establish, show, or clarify gender difference(s)? How does it position women in relation to men? What does being a woman have to do with men, according to *Glamour*?

Try to look at the magazine from different points of view. Try to consider your various identity locations (gender, race, class, sexual orientation, ethnicity, age, dis/ability). Do certain locations let you enjoy *Glamour* more than others? Also try to consider what this text looks like from positions other than your own.

What does *Glamour* naturalize? What assumptions about women or Woman are unquestioned? What, in the context of this magazine, is "glamour"? What is "beauty"? What is "beautiful"? What are these ideals defined against?

How did reading Berger influence your reading of *Glamour*? Do you see any examples here of what he talks about?

A note about reading. All reading is active. Looking at pictures and making meaning of them is reading, too. Even the simplest description is (already) interpretation. Try to be aware of how your reading is active. Are you a resistant reader? A conforming reader? What kinds of things do you look for?

STUDENTS' RESPONSES

Using the preceding questions as a guide, students read *Glamour* with a vengeance. They practice semiotic analyses of advertisements, close readings of articles, and explorations of address—who is included and excluded, who is positioned as central and marginal, what is rendered "normal" and "natural." The exercise is fun; it also relies on a variety of critical skills of reading and analyzing language and images. The students practice ideological critique as they see *Glamour*'s hegemonic meanings and its interpellative practices. Significantly, from the beginning of the course, the exercise encourages students to have an active relationship to cultural texts. They invariably pepper the magazine with Post-Its and use markers to underline passages; in short, they use the text.

Each time I have used this exercise, many students are angered by their new awareness of *Glamour*'s inclusions, exclusions, assumptions, and values. For many students, this exercise reinforces and pinpoints an exclusion they already felt but perhaps had not clearly articulated. For others, the project clarifies why they find *Glamour* pleasurable and useful. Many of the students learned to read from an identity location outside their own. Some students are furious (at me) for having spent money on the magazine and time analyzing what they see as a conservative, materialistic, antifeminist text. Other students find a feminist perspective of which they were previously unaware.

When we discuss *Glamour* in class, I do not encourage a conclusive summary of *Glamour*'s positive or negative value, and I insist that each comment, whether in praise or in critique, be supported by textual evidence of image or word. In the end, we are left with more questions than answers, with ambivalence and anger and sometimes pleasure. The pleasure may very well be one of an expanded repertoire of critical skills, of a newfound sense of power to deconstruct dominant ideology.

I have found that reading *Glamour* is consistently successful, as it allows (and, in fact, requires) students to take pleasure in the magazine while critiquing it. This assignment models the complexity of feminist praxis—a project of pleasure and pain, of the personal and the political—and stresses the need for complex, contradictory, deeply engaged analyses of multigenred texts.

NOTES

1. Both Naomi Wolf (1991) and Susan Faludi (1991) argue that both advertising and the fashion industry try to shape women's desires and that they do so with more or less success, depending on the time period. Faludi describes how the media shapes what we believe, and she asserts that it does not at all reflect what people believe. My notion of the relationship between "truth" and the "media" is slightly more nuanced and positively inflected toward the media.

2. Suzanna Walters (1995:50–66, 86–115) summarizes and historicizes theories of the male gaze and questions their usefulness from a more recent, cultural studies perspective. Berger's (1972) account, while somewhat dated, is a concise introduction to the issues of the male gaze.

SUGGESTED READINGS

Coward, R. 1985. *Female desires: How they are sought, bought and packaged.* New York: Grove Weidenfeld.

Doner, K. 1993. Women's magazines: Slouching towards feminism. *Social Policy* 23: 37–43.

Gaines, J. and C. Herzog, eds, 1990. *Fabrications: Costume and the female body.* New York: Routledge.

McCracken, E. 1993. *Decoding women's magazines from "Mademoiselle" to "Ms."* New York: St. Martin's.

Williamson, J. 1978. *Decoding advertisements: Ideology and meaning in advertising.* New York: Marion Boyars.

Willis, S. 1991. *A primer for daily life.* New York: Routledge.

15

"MY FATHER'S WASP": Spelling the Dimensions of Difference

Helen M. Bannan, University of Wisconsin, Oshkosh

Teaching students to understand how society construes differences among people to confer privilege and justify discrimination is one of the most important and challenging tasks in introductory women's studies classes. Many of us approach the topic through two classic articles by Audre Lorde and Peggy McIntosh that together define the interlocking nature of various systems of oppression and explain how individuals' unconscious responses perpetuate the status quo. In "Age, Race, Class, and Sex: Women Redefining Difference," Lorde (1984b:116) powerfully delineates the complex interaction of characteristics that form the core of the "mythical norm":

In america, this norm is usually defined as white, thin, male, young, heterosexual, christian, and financially secure. It is with this mythical norm that the trappings of power reside within this society. Those of us who stand outside that power often identify one way in which we are different, and we assume that to be the primary cause of all oppression, forgetting other distortions around difference, some of which we ourselves may be practicing.

In "White Privilege and Male Privilege," McIntosh (1998) brilliantly clarifies how these multiple, "forgotten" distortions are acted out, as those deemed "normal" assume the rewards of that status: privilege, "an invisible package of unearned assets" (94).

Despite the cogent analysis in these essays, student resistance to any admission of privilege often dampens discussion of these essential concepts. For the past fifteen years, in introductory classes enrolling from fifteen to fifty students, at three different large, public universities in three different regions, I have used an acronym that clarifies how several of the most critical categories of difference intersect and how this intersection shapes both group experiences and individual identities. I spell out Lorde's "mythical norm," with a few additions:

Male
Young adult

Financially secure (middle-class or above)
Attractive
Thin and tall
Healthy
Eastern-Establishment
Right-handed
'Straight (as in heterosexual orientation)

White
Anglo (used linguistically: speaker of standard English)
Saxon (referring to ethnicity)
Protestant

Students in my women's studies senior seminar at the University of New Mexico (UNM) in the 1980s helped me develop this acronym from my initially much shorter version; subsequent students at Florida Atlantic University (FAU) and West Virginia University (WVU) helped me refine it. In the 1980s, the majority of New Mexico's population belonged to "minority" groups, and students at UNM were particularly aware of how ethnic and cultural differences shaped their experience of gender. Yet they suggested adding other categories of distinction, highlighting region, appearance, and handedness. By broadening its inclusiveness, virtually all of us could see ourselves, at least at some point in our lives, as both privileged and deviant, which seemed to alleviate some of the guilt-induced resistance and denial that discussion of privilege often evokes.

In my syllabus for the introductory course, I schedule this session at the end of the first month—early, because it is so important, but not too early, so that students are somewhat accustomed to me and to each other. Since the acronym encompasses so much, its presentation works best in a three-hour, once-a-week class, but I have often spread the discussion over two sessions in a seventy-five-minute, twice-weekly format and even given miniversions in fifty-minute classes. I ground the discussion by assigning the Lorde (1984b) and McIntosh (1998) essays that inspired it.

After students respond briefly to the key concepts of these articles, I write the acronym on the blackboard, noting that this is one way to spell "mythical norm." I briefly identify the category of privilege that each letter represents in our culture. Then we all take a few moments to "spell ourselves" according to this alphabet, writing privately in our notebooks. I emphasize that if, as we discuss individual items, anyone wishes to self-disclose, that is welcomed, but no one should feel required to do so.

At this point, using a concrete example of an individual's complex identity establishes clarity. I generally "spell myself" on the blackboard, but my lack of hesitation is symptomatic of heterosexual privilege. A gay, lesbian, or bisexual instructor not comfortable with coming out to the class can use other examples—self-disclosure should be optional for everyone in the class! Sucheng Chan's (1989) autobiographical piece, "You're Short, Besides!"—which explodes stereotypes of Asian-Americans and women with disabilities—is a very effective choice. For most of us, life's complexity makes "spelling" ourselves simply or in pronounceable words nearly impossible. My particular constellation of letters (Female; Middle-aged; Working-class background/now financially secure; Plain-looking; Average weight/tall; Healthy but asthmatic; Northeastern origin, but not Establishment, with varied regions of residence; Right-handed; Straight, but strongly women-identified; White; Anglo; Irish-German; Catholic) emphasizes the fact of shifting identities over the life course and comes up with gobbledygook: FMWPAHNRSWAIC. As we go through this, I encourage students to join in spontaneously, ask questions, compare responses, and so on.

Then we go through the acronym again, slowly, our analysis emphasizing interactions between categories. First we focus on the dimensions of difference used as the first letter in each "word" of the acronym; these are the most significant stratification systems conferring power in contemporary America: Male (gender), Financially secure (class), Straight (sexual orientation), and White (race). We begin examining one way these major categories interact by analyzing how racist stereotypes differ by gender. I usually ask the students to name some stereotypes of white, black, and Hispanic men and women, and we then compare these, highlighting the double jeopardy experienced by women of color who are forced to cope simultaneously with racism and sexism. Employment and income statistics of women from different racial/ethnic groups prove that these distinctions continue to have very real effects (Amott and Matthaei 1996).

Class intersects with gender in many other ways, since a woman's class status is generally ascribed to her, through males in her family, rather than earned by her individually. I begin here by asking how secure most women are financially and inquiring about the basis of that security. The tenuous grasp that middle-class homemakers have on their class position is indicated by their 73% post-divorce impoverishment relative to their ex-husbands' 42% rise in living standards (Weitzman 1985:339; Grella 1990). Working-class women of all racial and ethnic backgrounds have never been able to assume that they will be provided for, regardless of their marital status. If they are providing for themselves, in the segmented labor market of poorly paid "women's jobs" or even more poorly paid "minority women's jobs," financial security is a dream. It is important to note here that statistics do not determine individual lives; college students aspiring to middle-class status resent the assumption that as women of color they are destined for domestic, factory, or clerical jobs.

Combining discussions of class and race proved effective for me both in southeast Florida and in New Mexico, where my students' racial backgrounds reflected the diverse demography of these states, and in West Virginia, where nearly all of my students were white. In all three universities, most of my students were working-class in origin and viscerally understood the attitudinal as well as economic aspects of class. Seeing both similarities and differences among themselves and between themselves and myriad "others" somehow helped the students feel validated and willing to stretch to understand other perspectives.

Ideologies of equality and self-made success soften the effects of classism, but homophobia has no such mitigating mythology. Lesbianism directly challenges the basic cultural belief that the heterosexual romantic love plot should define women's lives and challenges the conservative backgrounds of many college students. Here I begin by asking students to calculate the costs lesbians incur by rejecting heterosexual marriage: losing not only "normalcy" but the ascribed status and extra income of a husband, as well as benefits like health insurance that employers regularly provide for spouses. Since women earn, at latest count, seventy-six cents to the male dollar (Feminist News 1998), the joint income of a couple composed of two women statistically will be less than a male and female pair, making financial security more difficult to achieve. Awareness of homophobia makes many lesbians hesitate to be "out" at work, fearing employment discrimination or harassment (Friskopp and Silverstein 1995; Levine and Leonard 1984).

Highlighting how lesbians experience class issues emphasizes that they, too, have whole lives, not just sex lives, which seems to surprise students with little experience of people with different sexual orientations. Noting further how lesbians of color may experience different varieties of sexism and homophobia within their own cultural groups, and that homosexual men of their own or other groups face different forms of discrimination, again breaks down dichotomous thinking, one of the key goals of this exercise.

To get beyond us versus them, we need to accept our myriad differences without presuming hierarchy: to see and reject the privileges, the unearned advantages we have been taught to assume unconsciously. Considering dimensions of difference less formally sanctioned as determinants of deviance in our culture seems to enhance my students' ability to understand the workings of privilege within interlocking systems of oppression. The following analysis summarizes key points toward which I guide discussion; the exercise evokes somewhat different responses each time, due to the unique personality of each class section.

Several of the letters in "MY FATHER'S WASP" refer to outward appearances:

Young, Attractive, Thin, and Tall. I begin here by asking students to name the ideal age in contemporary America. My introductory students, who have ranged from seventeen to over seventy, invariably choose the mid-twenties. My youngest students report that as teens, they feel they are not taken seriously as people but are denigrated as "kids." My older students state that they began to hear negative comments about their age in their thirties, with incidents of being patronized or rendered invisible increasing as they age. Since female life expectancy is longer than male, women predominate in the elderly portion of every ethnic group, and the problems of aging are multiplied as they are tied to class and race. Statistics demonstrate this with appalling clarity: African American and Hispanic elderly women are twice as likely as their white counterparts, and five times as likely as elderly white men, to fall below the poverty line (Hardy and Hazelrigg 1995).

For women particularly, age is connected to prescriptions demanding their Attractiveness, a definition we deconstruct, emphasizing how its elements intersect with other categories of difference. The assumption that to be feminine a woman must be beautiful and that to be beautiful she must be Thin, preferably be Tall, and at least appear to be Young makes women extremely conscious of how they look, and, as oppression is internalized, most of us become extremely critical of our own bodies. Homophobic mythology "explaining" lesbianism as a refuge for unattractive women oppresses both straight and gay women by reaffirming a sex-object definition of women's worth, denying all women respect and legitimacy of sexual choice. In a culture that demands female beauty and then narrowly defines it in terms of light skin, distinctively bland (and white-identified) facial features, and thin body type, women are oppressed more than men by "looksism," and women of color more than white women. Those women privileged by their appearance cannot feel secure in their status, since every advancing year and additional calorie threatens their status, a dubious advantage because those women considered particularly attractive may have to struggle to be taken seriously on any other basis than their looks. Thus, claiming the privileges of attractiveness is both temporary and costly to women (Freedman 1986; Brownmiller 1984; Wolf 1991). Standards of attractiveness, especially those involving height, do affect men, but older, white, middle-class men are often considered distinguished, with their greater power and money compensating for their aging faces and bodies.

Two attributes in the acronym have to do with abilities: Healthy and Right-handed. We begin here in our classroom, naming the privileges we assume each meeting: being able to read, climb stairs, hear, take notes comfortably on a standard desk, and so on. Some of these differences may be invisible until a specific challenge arises. We chose Healthy to designate the privilege of having a body free from major constraints to its physical and mental functioning, after a struggle: we did not want to categorize as "unhealthy" all those who would be so labeled if one accepted the assumption that difference from any norm necessarily implies the opposite. However, one of the purposes of this entire exercise is, as Robin Lakoff (1989: 374) has written, to help move us "past one undiscussed, but highly toxic disability—dichotomization. Humanity as a whole takes comfort from polarizations, . . . forgetting that all these properties function as continua, not dichotomies." People without disabilities are privileged and probably are not conscious that the concept "handicap," too, is a social construction, elaborating upon a physical or mental problem by adding to it, metaphorically, both stairs and stares: building physical obstacles to active participation by those with limitations and responding to disabled people with distancing and pity, based on stereotypes about their helplessness and dependence.

Gender, class, race, sexual orientation, and age all intersect with disability and chronic illness. Given the beauty imperative for women, women with obvious disabilities have an especially strong challenge to achieve self-esteem and a positive body image, including appreciation of their sexuality. Women with disabilities are generally assumed to be dependent, and rehabilitation programs predominantly geared toward helping men reflect such discriminatory attitudes. The intersection of race, class, and disability has financial consequences for women of color: black women with disabilities earn twenty-two cents to the dollar earned by white men without disabilities (Asch and Fine 1988). Since the age group with the highest percentage of disabled and chronically ill members is the elderly, and since this group is predominantly female, younger women need to understand that the privileges of health that they enjoy may, like beauty, be only temporary.

Except for those lucky few ambidextrous people, handedness is less subject to change, and obstacles are constantly confronted by left-handed people in this Right-handed world. The accumulation of small daily discomforts, while not disabling, creates a consciousness of distinction significant enough that several of my left-handed students urged me to add handedness to the acronym as a dimension of difference. As a righty, I had underestimated the persistent difficulties that lefties experience, a classic example of the numbing effects of privilege.

Other attributes in the acronym concern geographic and cultural origins: Eastern Establishment and Anglo-Saxon. My students in New Mexico and West Virginia considered substituting coastal, but, despite the prominence of the urban and academic centers on the West Coast, we decided that the Boston through Washington corridor is still the center of power in this nation, and the concept of region is experienced as closely tied to class. For instance, my Florida students insisted upon adding "Establishment" to Eastern, since they felt geographically Eastern but far removed from the "Establishment" elite who vacation in Palm Beach, geographically a few miles, but socially and politically light-years away from FAU.

Collegians in West Virginia and New Mexico were convinced that this elite group views those who live far from the centers of power as provincial: if people were *really* bright, motivated, talented, and so on, they would not still be in (fill in the blank). Regional stereotypes, sometimes tinged with ethnic prejudices targeting an area's dominant groups, persist and often form the basis of humor and media misrepresentations that romanticize or ridicule cultural distinctions. Redneck jokes (which generally have class, as well as regional, dimensions) are acceptable in some places where other varieties of ethnocentric humor are not. Regions with particularly distinct histories and self-conscious identities include stereotypical images of women as part of their sense of regional uniqueness: Appalachian "hillbillies," western "sunbonnet saints," and southern "steel magnolias" populate old and new regional mythologies. Also, the typical picture illustrating each of these stereotypes has a white face, erasing the experiences of regional women of color.

Anglo, in terms of English-language dominance, is clearly still a privileged characteristic that intersects with gender in ways that oppress women who are not native speakers of English. My Chicana and Indian students in New Mexico and my Latina and Haitian students in Florida insisted that Anglo sexist attitudes still defined a woman who spoke English with an accent as more sexually accessible. Language is clearly a critically important aspect of culture, and women as cultural conservators and family educators may have a particularly close tie to their "mother tongues" and resist linguistic assimilation on the basis of cultural pride. In recent years, the term "Anglo" has become more widely used outside the Southwest as a contrast to Hispanic, underlining the cultural and ethnic connotations of Anglo-Saxon, still the dominant cultural tradition in the United States.

Stereotypes remain with us, and ethnicity retains its power as an important dimension of difference, although sometimes overlooked or patronizingly romanticized. As ethnocentrism intersects with sexism, racism, and classism, women of various groups become saddled with gendered ethnic stereotypes, often involving their particular styles of motherhood and their deviation from Miss America norms of beauty. Visions of ethnic women popularized in mass media are often riddled with class bias and misogyny, sugarcoated with nostalgia about Mama's cooking and the tough-but-sweet "girls" of the old neighborhood. Lesbians are made invisible, as ethnic women are defined by such stereotypes only in terms of family roles and relationships to men.

Ethnic differences also intersect with racial ones in ways that privileged groups often ignore. Few white Americans are content to describe their own ethnic roots in continental terms, as Euro-Americans, yet parallel terminology generally is used for African-Americans, Native Americans, and Asian-Americans. Within these labels are hidden many cultural differences based on varying tribal, national, and ethnic origins. The differences among Navajo and Lakota, Korean and Vietnamese, Haitian and Barbadian, Cuban and Chicana are at least as significant as are those among European "hyphenated Americans" (Irish-, Polish-, Italian-, Norwegian-, etc.). None of these differences should be dismissed as inconsequential. Increasing rates of racial/ethnic intermarriage in the late twentieth century have complicated these designations even more, as individuals insist on honoring all of their heritages.

The final attribute in this alphabet of normalcy is **P**rotestant. Religion's power as a dimension of difference, particularly among academic "secular humanists," may seem to be waning. Yet, the recent rise of the self-defined Moral Majority revealed the potent force of Protestant righteousness, even if subsequent evangelical scandals sapped this particular Samson's strength. As my conscious choice of that metaphor indicates, biblical imagery remains part of standard American discourse. My students in all parts of the country have reported that justification of homophobia based on religious teachings is still prevalent, and anti-Semitism and anti-Catholicism, tied to our xenophobic past, have unfortunately not yet disappeared. Religious prejudice is often tied to ethnic discrimination and also to classism, since fundamentalist faiths are perceived as lower-class and are not generally as well respected as mainline denominations.

The intersection of gender with religion is important as well, since most religious practitioners, if not clergy, are female (Lindsey 1990; Weiss 1991: 147–149). The image of the nun as an avenging angel of repression, evident in many popular novels and plays, contrasts with older images emphasizing piety and dedication. Some feminists seek to express their spirituality in newly rediscovered goddess traditions, while others choose to work to reform patriarchal religion from within their congregations. Lesbians of differing religious backgrounds have become more visible and vocal in claiming their own expressions of spirituality, taking pride in identities their religions have traditionally condemned.

As the old song goes, "Put them all together, they spell"—not mother and not, in fact, most of us. Students are often shocked when they realize that "MY FATHER'S WASP" actually spells "self" for so few of them. Using this acronym helps students understand that the differences among us represent a full spectrum of shades rather than a strict black/white dichotomy. Graphing the intersections of so many variations demonstrates that we are both more alike and more different from each other than is usually assumed. By challenging all students to see themselves both as insiders and as outsiders, to claim both their privilege and their difference, and to incorporate their own experience into the acronym, this unconventional spelling lesson involves students in their own learning, consistent with principles of feminist pedagogy. Since each group of students elaborates upon the acronym differently, I am reminded each semester of the multivariant reality that women's studies must consciously embrace and continuously champion. As I write this, I am packing to move to Wisconsin, where I expect my midwestern students to show me further variations.

SUGGESTED READINGS

Amott, T. and J. Matthaei. 1996. *Race, gender and work*. 2nd ed. Boston: South End.
Friskopp, A. and S. Silverstein. 1995. *Straight jobs, gay lives*. New York: Scribner.
Lorde, A. 1984. *Sister outsider*. Freedom, CA: Crossing.

16

Encouraging Feminism: Teaching *The Handmaid's Tale* in the Introductory Women's Studies Classroom

Lisa M. Logan, University of Central Florida

> The uniqueness of Women's Studies has been and remains its refusal to accept sterile divisions between academy and community, between the growth of the mind and the health of the body, between intellect and passion, between the individual and society.
>
> National Women's Studies Association Constitution

> Each thing is really valid and really there. It is through a field of such valid objects that I must pick my way.
>
> *The Handmaid's Tale*

> Context is all.
>
> *The Handmaid's Tale*

Feminism. The reactions to, and definitions of, this word are at once the most rewarding and the most traumatic for both the students I have taught in the Introduction to Women's Studies course and for me. For two semesters and at two different state institutions, I have wondered what to do about student resistance to, and intimidation by, the word "feminism." What follows is a discussion of how Margaret Atwood's (1985) *The Handmaid's Tale* helped students and me as their teacher to figure out what to do about our highly personal and emotional relationships to feminism—the word, the concept, and the practice.[1]

Although some of my colleagues embrace Atwood's dystopian novel as one of their all-time favorite feminist reads, a number of them dismiss it as a "sell-out."[2] In the classroom, however, the book enabled us to negotiate differences through the safety of fiction, to make sense of the course and each other, and to understand practically the efficacy of feminisms.

First let me clarify both institutional context and my own position. This chapter uses my classroom experiences at the Stark Campus of Kent State University (KSU), a 2,000-student regional satellite in Canton, Ohio—and the University of Central Florida (UCF), Orlando, a relatively new but rapidly growing member of Florida's state university system that serves 28,000 students. While these institutions might seem incompatible for this discussion, the two have much in common. Canton's bland, rust-belt, middling conservatism has only recently given way to the bland, strip-mall, middle-class consumerism that also typifies, physically and mentally, Orlando's Disney-inspired landscape. Both state institutions offer students geographic and economic accessibility to a college education, and many of these students are the first to earn bachelor's degrees in their families. Women's studies at Kent State and the University of Central Florida both have program rather than departmental status, offer minors rather than majors, and were in their formative stages (less than five years) when I taught in them. Each time, the introductory women's studies course enrolled twenty women and one man. Because of these institutional similarities, this chapter purposefully conflates the two classrooms when my experiences there are uniform and clarifies explicitly when a case is true only for one institution.

While I position myself as an East Coast, abstract-thinking, white, middle-class, heterosexual, academic feminist, specializing in early American women's captivity literatures, I do not require that my students identify as feminist. Nevertheless, the titles of the course textbooks I used, Jo Freeman's (1995) *Women: A Feminist Perspective* and Sheila Ruth's (1998) *Issues in Feminism* raise the issue conspicuously on the first day of class. Further, during initial class discussions, a small percentage of women in each class of twenty-one (three Cantonites and five Orlandians) immediately identified themselves as "feminist," which intimidated many of those who enrolled "just out of curiosity" or to meet an elective or diversity course requirement.

Added to these differences are other circumstances that make the introductory women's studies classroom feel, like feminism itself, unsafe or at least unsettling—and to some extent it should be.[3] The class confronts powerful and personal issues and experiences related to sexuality, gender, race, and patriarchal authority, issues and experiences that resonate differently for each of us, depending on our backgrounds, belief systems, and cultural situatedness. We admit personal genres of response. such as narrative experience and the journal, sometimes mixing these with formal academic discourse. Outside our known disciplines, methods of critical inquiry and criteria for evaluation shift even as I refuse authoritarianism. Friends, boyfriends, parents, employers, colleagues, and deans may disapprove, discourage, or at least question the merits of our course of study.

Given its marginal position in these institutions and their curricula and that faculty and students are all in this "new place" together, the introductory women's studies classroom might be easily idealized as the antidote to Atwood's dystopian Gilead—a safe, utopian community based on shared strangeness in a strange land. The reality, however, is more like the handmaid's world than we at first realize: consensus is often a chimera, achieved not through community but through the silencing of differences. Many students craved the safety of consensus; they wanted to feel that they were understood, that there were no hard feelings. At the same time, however, they could not ignore the differences that emerged with each class day. At KSU, all students identified, at least publicly, as white and heterosexual; the slightly more diverse UCF class enrolled two women of color and one woman who came out as a lesbian late in the semester. In each class, several students identified as devout Christians, while several others openly dismissed religion. Racism, classism, and homophobia bubbled beneath polite surfaces. Students tried to follow the careful discussion guidelines I distributed, which ask that we speak respectfully but also as ourselves, and they often managed conflicting positions by prefacing their comments with explicit, polite, and sometimes unnecessary qualifiers. But at other times, especially around issues of sexuality, politics, and religion, students manifested open hostility or defensiveness. Whether friendly or hostile, however, students demanded from me and their textbooks a definitive "feminist" solution to the conflicts at hand. Despite my repeated suggestion that, like Adrienne Rich's (1980) "lesbian continuum," there exists a feminist continuum on which we might position ourselves, they pressed their demanding questions. What is an exact definition of "feminism"? What is *the* "feminist" position on sexual orientation? marriage? religion? abortion?

In Atwood's fictional, yet chillingly familiar, Gilead, we found distance enough to explore safely the differences among ourselves and our relationships to feminism. In Gilead we could recognize and confront patriarchal authority and religious extremism without taking it personally. We could care about, and sympathize with, women as various as Offred, whom students saw as "an ordinary woman"; her mother, a militant feminist; and Moira, a gay activist, each of whom acts out her own politics and choices. Like Atwood's Offred, we "pick[ed our] way" through a frightening world; through the double lens of feminist theory and Offred's testimony, we rethought pornography, rape, motherhood, romantic love, sexuality, medicine, law, politics, history, socialization, religion, academia, patriarchy, and feminism itself. Atwood's broad critique of patriarchal institutions *and feminism* appealed to many different disciplinary perspectives and experiences. Like Offred, whose relationship with her mother is complicated by disparate feminist politics, many students feared and misunderstood their feminist foremothers, whom they mythologized as bra-burning crusaders doomed to lives of loneliness. As the semester wore on, and students grew in their knowledge of women's studies, they found themselves having to pick their way through a familiar world grown unfamiliar, much as Offred moves through a university town without a university, relearning the buildings and objects in a new context. Atwood's portrayal of defamiliarization mirrors students' reactions to viewing their world through the lens of feminist theory and practice. As one student exclaimed, "I'm twenty-three years old and I'm about to graduate, and I have to rethink everything I've ever known." The novel's chilling strangeness served as a vehicle through and against which students began to define their own feminist politics and take stands—they began to admit the diversity of feminism.

The Handmaid's Tale, as many students put it, synthesized a whole semester of women's studies, and so I assigned it toward the end of the course (see Appendix A). We read it in conversation with feminist critiques of knowledge, heterosexual love and marriage, medicine, religion, politics, law, language, and so on. By the time we read Atwood's novel, students could apprehend the feminist questions it raises and, from interdisciplinary and feminist perspectives, could respond through their own experiences as women and men in patriarchal institutions.

For example, when we discussed feminism and medicine, we examined the institutionalization of medical knowledge and how this knowledge has focused on women's reproductive organs and controlled the choices women have available to them. Students had a difficult time viewing the "science" of medicine as politicized and patriarchal. One premed student was especially resistant to alternative forms of health care until she read of Offred's visit to the doctor. She wrote that Atwood's book compares to today's patriarchal

institution of medicine. . . . The visit to the doctor [is] characteristic of the visit that many women experience. The doctor is male [and] dominate[s] her. She [is] a nameless, faceless piece of meat on the table . . . in her most vulnerable position . . . fear discourages us from asking questions or from taking an active role in our health care.

This student wondered about the efficacy of Offred's diet, lack of exercise, and clothing and saw Atwood's book as a "call to action." She argued that women need to "tak[e] responsibility" for medical knowledge about their bodies to make informed choices about health care.

One of the toughest aspects of the course was also the most rewarding for many of us when we went back to it through *The Handmaid's Tale*. Because religion and spirituality are so personal and so powerful and because the nature of the introductory course allows us to spend only a day or two on that unit, the reading assignment was rather unstructured. I asked students to read through the collections *Womanspirit Rising* (Christ and Plaskow 1979) and *Weaving the Visions* (Plaskow and Christ 1989) and to become "experts" on one or two essays that struck them. The result was a rather tense, but careful and sensitive, discussion that respected differences and acknowledged that religions are often hierarchical institutions that have historically reinforced gender roles, legitimated women's oppression, controlled women's bodies, and excluded women from positions of power.

This discussion laid a foundation for Atwood's scathing critique of religious fundamentalism. Students, including committed Christians, objected strongly to the biblically based roles available to women in Gilead *and* to the rote recital of Scripture. Two Sunday school teachers wondered aloud about their responsibilities to teach young boys and girls about women. Many students wondered how they could reconcile their Christian faiths with a feminist position. One student, commenting on the relationship between Offred and Moira, admitted to a conflict between her religion's teachings about sexuality and her best friend's recent coming out as a lesbian.

Ultimately, students steered the discussion to the differences between spirituality and patriarchal religion. Disturbed by the lack of true spiritual feeling in the book, one student argued that Offred's recital of the Latinate inscription left by her predecessor, "nolite te bastardes carborundorum" (don't let the bastards grind you down), is a sort of self-defined prayer. While some might find this reading of Offred too hopeful, it emphasizes women's responsibility for their own spirituality and acknowledges alternatives to patriarchal structures. She wrote,

[Atwood] questions the hierarchical system, without ever having Offred give up her beliefs or spirituality. This demonstrates the ability for women to maintain a religious life, without having to accept the sexism that often accompanies traditional religious institutions. This allows for women readers to be the masters of their destinies. Too often when faced with resistance by a powerful and respected body, women back away.... Atwood offers an alternative: find religion, God, spirituality within yourself.... To follow blindly what a social institution prescribes for you is letting the bastards grind you down. To Atwood, religion is social and surface label. True spirituality and a connection to your maker comes solely from yourself.

Another student, inspired by Audre Lorde's (1984a) "The Uses of the Erotic," suggested that real spirituality comes from a connection to one's physical body. The religious fundamentalism represented in Atwood's book "train[s] us to fear our desires and cravings, causing distortion, misnaming, and lack of responsibility." She viewed the book as a feminist call to value the body equally with the spirit. Given Atwood's devastating critique, many students' religious conservatism, and my own past experience with discussions of religion, I expected defensiveness; instead, when the problems were embedded in narrative fiction, students responded honestly and as feminist thinkers capable of respecting differences.

When we turned to politics, we discussed how Atwood's book illustrates that "the personal is political," an idea most students had never considered.[4] As

Cynthia Burack (1988–1989) has observed, students are accustomed to seeing politics and the law as something "out there." That gender politics enter our lives, bodies, behaviors, interactions, and language was a completely new and difficult idea. From a political perspective, Offred seemed familiar to students. She resists political responsibility, literally refusing to involve herself in "the Resistance." What is more, her resistance to resistance is accompanied by immersion in romance.[5] As one student knowingly put it, there seems to be a conflict for women in patriarchal culture between "getting a man" and having political views. If one is "taken care of," she wrote, one "doesn't need political or legal rights." Offred's apolitical stance and hunger for companionship speak to students' real dilemmas—specifically, to what extent do women's relationships interfere with their political identities? How can one act on feminist principles *and* love a man?

Earlier in the semester when we discussed the impact of patriarchal marriage on women's lives, students acknowledged the problems but insisted that their marriages would be/were different. Two students tried to argue that women in patriarchal cultures should simply boycott marriage, but few others agreed. The passage in *The Handmaid's Tale* when Luke wants to make love with June/Offred after she has just been stripped of job, money, and independence brought us back to that earlier discussion of marriage. Offred remembers that "some balance" had "shifted" and that "[w]e are not each other's, anymore. Instead, I am his" (236). This passage really brought home for students—in chilling ways, they admitted—the intersections between romance and power.

Atwood's last chapter, in which academics view Offred, with whom we have come to sympathize, merely as a vehicle through which they can understand the Gileadean power structure, encouraged us to question academic hierarchies and boundaries. Students were deeply troubled by the historians' interest in the Gileadean empire rather than Offred's personal history and were incensed at the following comment that illustrates just how far academic inquiry can miss the point: "She could have told us much about the workings of the Gileadean empire, had she had the instincts of a reporter or a spy. What would we not give, now, for even twenty pages or so of print-out from Waterford's private computer!" (393).

Using this chapter, we discussed the penultimate course assignment, a personal essay based on an interview with a role model, whom students had to consider through the lenses of their own experiences and feminist theory. For Offred, the point of composing her narrative is to assert a self that has been erased and to preserve hope that someone is out there to hear. Atwood uses Offred's personal voice to make a political point. I, too, want students to make this connection practically, to combine their personal and academic voices and their experiential and theoretical thinking. For Atwood's Offred and students in introductory women's studies classes, the risk lies in speaking personally, without the neutral shield of public discourse. What is gained is an assertion of self that does not rely solely on, nor hide behind, academic language.

This assignment led to discussions in class and in student essays about that persistent question of the course, What counts as feminism? This question is problematized by Atwood's book, in which the concerns are clearly feminist, but the actions of the heroine are more ambiguous. Students used the book and their personal essays about their role models to interrogate definitions of feminism and feminist action, and they frequently decided, like Offred, that "context [was] all."

Several students interviewed their mothers, who often refused the label "feminist." One explored her mother's decision to stay in a bad marriage against her own recent decision to bear a child without its father's support:

My mom resembles the position Offred is in. Both women do not *have* to be there, but their alternative is not very promising either. Offred could face a life cleaning up toxic waste and starving to death. [By leaving a bad marriage] Mom could face a possibly violent husband and practically starve trying to take care of two kids on her own with no job.

In this student's opinion, the failure to resist can be a form of personal heroism, a practical necessity. Another student worked toward a definition of feminism through her mother's example:

I have always seen her as living a woman-identified life, basing her choices on her own needs and desires. As she spoke to me about the shaping experiences in her life, I more fully understood how so many of her choices . . . have been based on a relationship between sex and class. She has made her own way as a single mother in a culture without adequate support systems that human beings, and, more specifically, women deserve and require. . . . The way she has lived her life has perhaps been the most important factor in the development of my own feminist consciousness. As her daughter, and as a woman, I have seen in her life what is at stake in the decisions of an unmarried woman, a single mother, and an economically depressed citizen.

Her writing really highlights the distance between academic theory and personal experience and suggests that the latter has shaped this daughter. She concludes, "For my mother, feminism is not a lofty or intellectualized set of ideologies, but a set of personal questions that a strong woman must ask herself as she learns to make her way through single motherhood." Later, this student asked the class if this sentence described what Offred does, making her way through Gilead based on questions and decisions that enable her daily survival.

Another student interviewed her grandmother, whom she characterized as a tough, realistic woman who refused to reassure her granddaughter that "everything would be all right." She wrote,

I have, with this class, begun a journey and . . . I must devote myself to [its] completion. . . . What I am searching for may change throughout my life, but I must remain committed to the process of questioning how I feel, what my position is, and how I can better society. I am presently searching for a way to reconcile my homophobic attitudes and my religious beliefs with the goals and beliefs of feminism.

This project was an important first step in figuring out who she was, her "feelings, attitudes, and ambitions" and her "position in society." Her words acknowledge that practicing feminist politics is hard and can destabilize or put at risk what we have been taught.

Using *The Handmaid's Tale* as a synthesizing text is not without problems. Specifically, because Offred's references to the racism and classism in Gilead are more implicit than explicit, I needed to direct students' attention to the differences among women. One African American woman heard resonances of slavery throughout the text, especially when Offred points out that "forgiveness too is power. To beg for it is a power, and to withhold or bestow it is a power, perhaps the greatest" (174). This student told the class that the relationships of "mistrust, exploitation, and betrayal" among women in Gilead paralleled the problems in the feminist movement pointed out by Audre Lorde (1984a) in *Sister Outsider*. In this respect, she said, the book became a part of her, "a mirror to me."

Atwood's text worked as a mirror for most of my students. For this reason, the final exam (see Appendix B) asked them to choose a passage, analyze the way the language works, how that passage is thematically important to the book as a whole, and, most importantly, how that passage bears on an issue discussed in the course. The range of questions inspired by the book is suggested in the following list of topics that students chose in addition to those discussed earlier:

women's socialization

female eroticism as constructed by the male gaze

relationship between knowledge and power

censorship and human rights

women's biology as destiny

structures of power (private/domestic vs. public/institutional)

silence

violence against women

While their responses to the book were diverse and personal to them—no two students have chosen the same passage yet—they have told me that *The Handmaid's Tale* is what "brought the course together" for them. Our collective immersion in a fictional world gave us a kind of commonality from which to do what Offred begins to do—"to make distinctions," to "get it clear" in our own minds. That is what I want for them—to find their own way among feminisms.

APPENDIX A: ATWOOD: GENERAL QUESTIONS FOR THE WHOLE BOOK

- What kind of heroine is Offred? (if she is one at all)
- What is Atwood's critique of the Right and patriarchal institutions?
- What is her critique of the Left and feminism?
- What does she say about binary thinking?
- What "warning," if any, is she offering?
- What does the book say about our ability to understand/read/write history?
- How does Atwood's depiction of the three men in Offred's life comment on relationships between men and women?

APPENDIX B: FINAL EXAM QUESTION

Directions: Choose a short passage from *The Handmaid's Tale* and in 500 words (two typed, double-spaced pages), explain the importance of the passage on the following three levels:

1. Language use: How does this passage use language to convey information about a character, theme, or issue? Explain how this passage uses particular words to get readers thinking in specific ways.

2. Relationship to the book as a whole: How does this passage connect with important themes or issues raised throughout the book? Discuss the ways that this passage connects with other parts of the book and asks readers to think about particular themes, e.g., religion, marriage, medicine, politics, etc. *Be careful to focus narrowly enough on one issue, but you can explain how that one issue works in complicated ways.*

3. Relationship of the passage/book to an issue studied in class: How does this passage and issue in the book speak to a discussion we've had during the semester about a particular issue facing women under patriarchy? For example, how does the passage you chose and the way it figures in the book address the problem of women in patriarchal marriage, religion, medical or educational institutions, etc. or of identifying as feminist in a patriarchal culture? *Again, focus on only one issue and show how Atwood's book talks back to or raises questions about this issue.*

What I'm Looking For/Evaluation

I'll be assessing your ideas and your sound and thorough knowledge of Atwood's book and the issues raised by it, as well as by the course materials. You don't have much time/space, so get to your point quickly and without a lot of extra words or information. The most successful final exams will focus narrowly on their quote and use that quote to discuss other, deeper levels.

NOTES

I wish to thank my women's studies students and colleagues at Kent State University, Stark Campus, and University of Central Florida, whose work has taught me so much. I am grateful to my colleague Nina Manasan Greenberg for helping me to clarify my thinking throughout the drafting of this manuscript.

1. While Atwood's novel is widely taught in universities, the recently published *Approaches to Teaching Atwood's "The Handmaid's Tale" and Other Works* includes no essays on how the book might be used in the women's studies classroom. See Wilson, Friedman, and Hengen (1996).

2. For lively discussions of the relationships among Atwood's feminism, cultural feminism, and *The Handmaid's Tale*, see McCarthy (1986); Ehrenreich (1986); Greene (1986); LeBihan (1991); Reesman (1991).

3. My assumptions about what is at stake in safety are, in large part, derived from Martin and Mohanty's (1986) consideration of home as a metaphorical category. They maintain that feminist analyses and politics of safe space must acknowledge the ways that safety is constituted, that is, by inclusion *and* exclusion.

4. Here Burack's (1988–1989) work was really helpful in guiding me.

5. Miner (1991) discusses the dangers of the love plot to women.

SUGGESTED READINGS

Register, C. 1979. Brief, a-mazing movements: Dealing with despair in the women's studies classroom. *Women's Studies Quarterly* 7 (Fall): 161–165.

Wilson, S. R., T. B. Friedman, and S. Hengen, eds. 1996. *Approaches to teaching Atwood's "The Handmaid's Tale" and other works*. New York: Modern Language Association.

17

The Outrageous Act as Gender Busting: An Experiential Challenge to Gender Roles

Sandra D. Shattuck, University of Arizona,
Judith McDaniel, University of Arizona, and
Judy Nolte Temple, University of Arizona

I listen, and I forget. I see, and I remember. I do, and I understand.[1]

OUTRAGEOUS EVERYWHERE

In the 1970s, civil rights demonstrations, antiwar actions, and consciousness-raising proved to a cohort of women that the personal was the political. Acts considered commonplace today were then perceived as outrageous and outraging: keeping one's own surname after marriage, openly choosing to love another woman, wearing pants to the office. Perhaps because women's studies faculty of a certain age have viscerally felt what it means to resist and redefine gender restrictions, it is discouraging to encounter students who think it has always been this way: women are welcomed to participate in intercollegiate sports, half of the students in law schools are females, and women can have credit cards in their own names. Some of us who recall the heady effects of rebellion when outrageousness seemed to be everywhere decided to share this feeling with our students who had not had an activist experience. The outrageous act or gender-busting assignment that three faculty members at the University of Arizona Women's Studies Department use in introductory classes asks students to feel the gender scripts operating with more subtlety today by engaging in the act of stepping ever so slightly over the boundaries that still constrict our lives and our imaginations.

The origins of this action assignment, which has been used primarily in women's studies and sociology classes, are neither simple nor readily available. Indeed, we have found only one published account of a similar exercise for the introductory women's studies course (O'Barr, LaRocque, and Peskowitz 1994). Our outrageous act or gender busting is called the "feminist action project" or "liberating act" at Rutgers, the "gender-role violation exercise" at Duke, and "breaching experiments" by a sociologist working in the early 1960s.[2] Fixing an exact name for this particular exercise is as difficult as naming a precise moment when the exercise was conceived.

For Judy Temple, the first instructor to teach the outrageous act at the University of Arizona, the idea began with a personal response to a proposal by Charlotte Bunch, who spoke at a 1988 summer workshop sponsored by the Southwest Institute for Research on Women (SIROW), called "Teaching Women's Studies from an International Perspective."[3] The goal of the workshop was the integration of international materials by and about women into the core women's studies curriculum. Bunch suggested to workshop participants that they examine the gender texts of their own culture by spending a day carrying around a book clearly marked as lesbian. She predicted that people would stare, move away from the carrier, or make bigoted comments. The purpose of her assignment was to show how including "foreign" materials in the ethnocentric classroom could broaden our perceptions of worldwide gender systems and also clarify our critical thinking about those systems operating almost invisibly within our own cultures. Temple had also given much thought to the comments of workshop speaker Abena Busia, who observed that only when we are taken out of our own comfortable context do we learn by experience. Busia noted that a fish does not know or feel what water is until it is taken out of its life source, and she urged that we have our students *feel* in order to learn deeply.

Temple had read Gloria Steinem's (1983) collection *Outrageous Acts and Everyday Rebellions* and took part of its title as the intent of the assignment. In her original conception, Temple asked students to think of an "outrageous act" that would elicit gender policing, to perform this act, to describe their own feelings about being outrageous, to recount the reactions of others, and to analyze the gendered scenario they had provoked. This short, three-page writing assignment soon became the most discomforting—and successful—learning experience in the class, for many students held notions that once upon a time there may have been sexism and inequality, but in these enlightened times, men could willfully be full-time fathers, women could enter any profession they sought on equal terms, and all marriages would be egalitarian. The water in which these students skillfully maneuvered appeared remarkably unclouded.

EVOLUTION OF AN ACT

Judy Temple, Sandra Shattuck, and Judith McDaniel all teach women's studies at the University of Arizona, a land-grant public institution with approximately 34,000 students, who are predominantly "white, non-hispanic" (68.8%).[4] The combined total of students grouped under other ethnicities makes up 22.7% of the population while 8.5% represents "non-resident Alien" and "unknown." General education courses that include diversity components are part of the curricular requirement for students in the College of Liberal Arts. Women's studies courses, including Introduction to Women's Studies (WS100) and Women in Western Culture (WS200), are selected by some students as being the path of least resistance. As one student remarked, "I didn't want to learn about foreigners or that *etha, ethna*? ethnicity thing, so I chose this class because it would be about sex." Each semester the Women's Studies Department currently offers at least six sections of general education with classes ranging in size from thirty to sixty-five students. Starting in 1998, many more students, including those in the Colleges of Engineering and Agriculture, were required to take core general education classes. At the same time that the student population taking general education courses was doubled, the diversity requirement was cut in half—a move that women's studies and area studies at the University of Arizona vigorously opposed. Women's studies majors are also required to take the two general education course offerings (WS100 and WS200). Thus, the classroom mix can include beginning students taking lower-division course work, resistant students often taking the mandatory general education course in their very last semester, and several women's studies majors with substantial background in feminist theory. Approximately 15% of the students in these courses are male.

Shattuck and McDaniel both learned about the outrageous act assignment from Temple and incorporated it into their classes, where individual teaching styles began to slightly modify the exercise. Shattuck's assignment description divides the outrageous act into a preact, act, and postact, where students answer the following questions: (Preact) What is your outrageous act? What stereotype are you challenging? What is the setting of the act, and who is your audience? What are your expectations? How do you feel, and what do you learn about yourself as you plan the act?; (Act) Describe the act, reactions of the audience, and your feelings; (Postact) Did you learn anything more from your own reactions and feelings and those of the audience after you completed the act? What did you learn about yourself, others, and gender stereotypes?

McDaniel calls her assignment gender busting and asks students to choose an environment in which they are well known (family, close friends) or a setting in which they might have certain gender expectations of themselves (changing the oil in the car, caring for a younger sibling). Students then act in a way that is contrary to others' or their own gender expectations. In addition to the criteria listed in Shattuck's assignment description, McDaniel asks students to refer to class readings and discussions to answer the question, What does your experience have to do with gender as a social construct?

Initially, Temple found markedly different student reactions to the assignment. Many male students planned acts that would require them to perform "femi-

nine'' or ''gay'' acts, such as wearing nail polish to the grocery store or shopping for their undergarments in the women's lingerie department. In contrast,
some feminist students found it difficult to imagine an action more outrageous
than what they had already achieved—being a women's studies major, or giving
up custody of their children in order to return to college. More traditional female
students thought it would be outrageous to see how quickly they could lure a
male driver off the road to assist them with their disabled car. The impulse was
to discomfort someone else, rather than bring the outrage onto the performers
themselves. The refined criteria, therefore, prohibited students from performing
acts that would reinforce gender stereotypes or homophobia: helpless female,
clerk embarrassed by transvestite shopper. Students also proposed doing acts
with accomplices so that they would have partners in pain. Since we internalize
gender individually, the assignment required that students act alone and not tell
others that this was ''just an exercise'' until the scenario had run its course.
Student anxiety over conceiving of an act and imagining its consequences increased and indicated that learning, however unsettling, was taking place. Students' comfortable waters were becoming turbulent.

Thus, negotiation became the centerpiece of the assignment and led to productive class discussions of how all of us are constantly performing gender and
negotiating within a surprisingly narrow system of acceptable acts. Each class
closed with an individual's proposal of his or her act and Temple's response.
Instead of closing notebooks and leaning toward the classroom exit, students
listened, sympathized with their peers' pleas for minimal outrageousness, and
learned.

ALREADY OUTRAGEOUS

The students who have the most difficulty with this assignment grew up in
homes with already transformed gender expectations. ''I can do anything I
want,'' wails a student (usually a woman), ''so how can I do this assignment?''
These women already live the outrageous acts that many of their more traditional
peers propose (inviting a boyfriend on a date and paying for everything, changing a major from English to engineering). For these students, the challenge lies
in uncovering societal standards rather than confronting their own or their families' expectations.

One young woman who had been raised to repair her own car and to pursue
any career found the assignment impossible. McDaniel encouraged her: ''Think
about this campus environment. What is expected of a 'generic female' right
here?'' The student realized that physically strong women were not considered
feminine, and so her gender busting consisted of carrying a large box across
campus. She expected stares and offers of help from men, but ''no one paid
any attention,'' so she tried the experiment again. While the student carried her
large box, a tall, strong, male friend walked alongside her carrying nothing. The
response was quite different: ''People were outraged. He got more comments

than I could have imagined, all of the put downs.'' Gender, she concluded, does not exist in a vacuum. While this student may have been raised to carry her own load, she learned that her culture expects a man to jump in when women do ''men's work.''

Gender busting helps these already outrageous students to understand that the expanded sex-role definition they grew up with is not that of the larger world. During the assignment, these students also often remembered occasions where their own transformed gender expectations had challenged or upset others.

COMPLEXITIES OF OUTRAGEOUSNESS: EXPECTED AND UNEXPECTED

As we researched the origins and variations of this assignment, an instructor challenged us to explain why we had students do a ''false'' act when there were so many actual problems that needed solutions. She wondered if our assignment prevented students from taking ''real'' opportunities to challenge sexism on a daily basis.

We think that the students who do this exercise are doing something real. Students cannot challenge sexism if they are unable to either recognize or understand it. The ''false'' act of gender busting allows students a deeper understanding of sexism, precisely because students construct a face in order to be outrageous, rather than complicit. Most students understand that they code-switch many times during the day, using appropriate language, gesture, dress, and behavior as situations demand. As a poet and fiction writer, McDaniel frequently tells her students, ''I tell the truth about my life in my poetry, and in my fiction I tell the truth by lying.'' Fiction creates artificial situations in which readers may find out new truths about themselves or their culture. Students who create fictional selves with which to encounter the world, similarly, discover new truths about themselves and the culture in which they are immersed. Creating the fiction does not, in itself, seem to be a problem to us.

There have been, however, unintended consequences as a result of this exercise. We have each cautioned students that a woman walking alone in the dark across campus because she has always wanted to be able to do so is not the kind of outrageous act we seek. But the instructor also needs to be aware that creating a fictional self can lead the student and others into potentially dangerous territory. In one instance, a student gave her three-year-old nephew a doll at his birthday party. The nephew's father was furious, wrenched the present away from the child, and screamed at the student. One of the benefits of individual negotiation of each act, as recommended by Judy Temple, includes a discussion of how to avoid any kind of harm. While the instructor cannot anticipate every negative side effect or unintended consequence, repeated experience ensures more effective troubleshooting.

Another complexity we debated regards using an exercise that targets gender, when all of us believe in investigating the interlocking ways that heterosexism and homophobia, racism, classism, ageism, ableism, sexism, and ethnocentrism structure our society. One potential problem arises when the outrageous act is performed in a culture that is significantly different from the majority culture of the classroom. An Anglo man trying to do a gender role reversal in Mexico at the parental home of his Mexican girlfriend by clearing the dishes from the table after a Sunday meal encounters both culture and gender when his host tells him to sit down and not do women's work. When this same student tells his gender-busting exercise to the class and fellow students roll their eyes or nod their heads, as if this level of machismo were expected from unenlightened Mexican men, this is the moment for the instructor to step in and foreground students' responses. What is the eye rolling all about? Could the host's response have occurred in other cultures? If so, where would we have found this response? In fact, we discover that many Anglo students acknowledge similar events in their homes. One of the solutions to cultural complexities is to insist that students situate their gender busting within their own specific cultures.

Another student's first idea for an outrageous act was to apply at a bar as a bouncer. Sitting in her wheelchair in class, this student explained to us that she thought the bouncer idea probably would not fly, because she would be unable to isolate the reason for her expected job denial. Attending to this student's talk about how ableism and sexism intersect provides a rich pedagogical moment. In another case, a male student proposed the outrageous act of using a public women's rest room, reasoning that gender-segregated rest rooms promoted sexism the way that race-segregated rest rooms promoted racism. By pointing out that Jim Crow laws and their concomitant violence differ radically from sex-segregated bathrooms, the instructor can enter into a critical moment that attends to the ways in which racism and sexism act in concert but have specific histories and different articulations.

The outrageous act presents further complexities for lesbians and gay men, who sometimes fall into the category of those who have "been there and done that" when it comes to gender busting. They are sometimes seriously offended by the obvious homophobia of students, particularly male students, who think that all they have to do to be outrageous is to perform stereotypical, sitcom-level, gay impersonations. We use this opportunity, also, to talk about homophobia as a tool of gender stereotyping and gender enforcement.[5]

We welcome the complexities that result from this assignment. The benefit to a teacher is the opportunity to engage students in real, immediate discourse about issues that are too often distant and theoretical.

VARIATIONS ON AN ACT

Like its genesis and name, the assignment description of the outrageous act enjoys a good deal of variety on our campus and others. However, similarities include the following: (1) the ability to identify some kind of norm or stereotype; (2) a division of the assignment into before, during, and after components; (3)

an attention to one's own feelings and the reactions of others; (4) a linking of the experiential with the theoretical; (5) the requirements that the exercise must be nonviolent and legal; and, we would add, (6) a requirement that the act not harm one's self or others.

The form of the assignment is almost always an analytical paper; however, other forms of presentation are possible. For instance, Shattuck offers the possibility of filming the act. One student took this option; analysis took the form of an oral report, where the student spoke to the guidelines of the exercise after the entire class viewed his video. Other forms might include a report posted to a class listserv or the creation of a Web site based on the experience and its results.

Many of the variations on this exercise involve the before, during, and after components of the assignment. The amount of time spent on deciding on an act and the ways to prepare for the act include individual teacher–student conferences, collective class discussion, smaller group discussion, and posting ideas to a class listserv, among others. Conceptualization and hypothesis building, crucial to any writing assignment, are major components of a successful project. After the students have turned in their papers, we usually devote a full class period to informal discussion of students' experiences of doing the acts. This postact class always results in a highly energized discussion, as well as something of a bonding experience; students tell their stories, so that everyone gets to laugh or agonize at the results. In the larger classroom, an alternative to a full class discussion is smaller group discussions.

Another variation involves the timing of the assignment during the semester. Most instructors tend to require the assignment's completion during the middle or at the end of the course. By this time, students are more familiar with the various theoretical underpinnings of the course and are better able to test course materials in an experiential manner. The rationale for requiring the assignment toward the end of the course also involves the need for time to build a certain level of trust and community; the powerful emotions and experiences resulting from many students' participation in their outrageous acts can be fully shared only in an atmosphere of trust.

The feminist action project, as practiced by Johanna Foster at Rutgers, illustrates an alternative. Students must "identify a social problem impacting women/girls"; after analysis of the problem, students then choose a "legal and ethical action aimed at solving this problem." If students choose not to do the action, they have the option to research an organization "dedicated to fighting gender inequality." Foster mentions that this past year, about 80% of the class chose to complete a feminist action project. Some of these students' projects included writing letters to editors of women's magazines or to members of congress, holding meetings in dorms about sexual violence, and handing out condoms on campus while engaging peers in discussions about gender and sex.

One other variation of the outrageous act and other exercises is whether the student completes the exercise alone or with an observer or other participant.

Judy Temple insists on solo attempts, feeling that more than one participant obscures the personal nature of the gender learning. McDaniel prefers that students act alone but has occasionally approved a "twosome" project, while Shattuck will allow other participants.

A final variation we have noted is whether or not the instructor chooses to complete the exercise along with the students. As far as we know, Judy Temple stands alone in her willingness to be equally outrageous with her students. Temple's rationale is a desire to push her own boundaries and to demonstrate to students that we all can continue to grow.

OUTRAGEOUSNESS AS FEMINIST PEDAGOGY

Feminist pedagogy requires an understanding of relationships between the personal and the political, between the practical and the theoretical. Experiential exercises such as the outrageous act allow students to engage the course material in ways that link both the inside and the outside of the classroom, so that what goes on inside the university relates to what happens in students' homes, their work, their play. As a student said in a class evaluation: "The outrageous act was a good project in testing just how the stereotypes of society do affect us. We are much bolder and liberal in class, but when put to the test I believe it illustrated the power of the image of women that society has constructed."

If the personal is political, then the outrageous act asks students to act personally in order to understand politically. When a student tests a gender stereotype and finds it alive and kicking, her empirical exercise convinces her in ways no article or lecture can. Even if this student's exercise proves that a particular gender stereotype is no longer valid or has shifted, her act substantially facilitates her engagement with the course and her understanding of social structures, norms, and values. This kind of understanding can also lead the student to better identify moments where change might take place, so that the possibility of personal and political action can become actualities.

Engaging in outrageous acts often elicits strong emotions, and instructors must be prepared to engage this strength. Feminist pedagogy also insists on a methodology of learning that invites a weaving of thought and emotion. Attending to the affective results of gender busting means being able to listen well and to provide a classroom atmosphere where everyone's stories get told and heard. As one male student said of his act, "I was more scared . . . than I've been scared of anything in quite a while. I've learned that it really does take courage to question oppression and challenge sexism. I know now that some things we most take for granted require more effort and bravery than we consider."

Gender busting also offers opportunities for collaborative learning, which fulfills feminist pedagogy's mandate to focus on the process of learning rather than solely on its product. Negotiating the act with both instructor and other students, reporting on the act and discussing it in class, in small groups, or on class listservs, and peer critiquing of writing assignments all serve as ways for some kind of collective learning to take place.

McDaniel, Temple, and Shattuck have required the outrageous act of all their students in the introductory women's studies classroom, and so it is not uncommon to hear students voice their negative expectations. The following woman's comment on a final course evaluation is not an isolated one: "The first thing I learned was that it wasn't a male bashing class [happy face drawing] . . . I learned that a feminist doesn't have to hate men!" Another student made this comment: "It's nice to know a feminist is not just a 'woman activist,' for all of us are 'feminist' in some way." Although most of us feminists (particularly those of us who view teaching as a part of our activism) would agree that dislodging the terms "feminism" and "activism" from each other is both impossible and most likely undesirable, this particular student speaks for many others whose attitudes toward activism range from indifference to disdain. Because gender busting asks students to be actors, they can challenge stereotypes in a playful way that does not require them to decide whether or not they are feminist, or whether or not they wish to engage in some kind of political action. Once students engage in the play, they usually learn deeply and seriously, and this learning can lead to both transformation and action, as the following examples of outrageous acts demonstrate.

EXAMPLES OF OUTRAGEOUS ACTS/GENDER BUSTING

One student who lived in a fraternity rented a "gender inappropriate" movie (*Backstage at the Kirov*, a movie of the ballet *Swan Lake*) and watched it in the social room. Within three minutes, a frat brother walking through said, "What the hell are you watching?" Another two dozen residents made similar comments. To this student's surprise, however, one of the frat brothers sat down on the couch and watched with him. This student concluded that "there is a certain pressure to do what is expected of you because of your gender, and if you step out of that mold then you get questioned or criticized. I did think when my friend sat down next to me and began to watch that it was cool, because not only did he not criticize me for stepping outside of what would normally be expected from me, he stepped with me."

A women's studies major decided on the subtle act of simply standing in the curtained-off pornography section of a local used-book store. The first time she became a silent presence, all of the men fled the area like roaches. On her second attempt, a customer complained, and the manager asked her to leave the area, as she was making men "uncomfortable." She voiced her right to be in that area and then left with dignity.

A female student opposed the Los Angeles Country Club's no-pants dress code for women by trying to wearing slacks in its dining room. When stopped at the door with her parents, the student proclaimed to the enforcer, "This is the '90s, you know, not the 1890s.'' This student reported at semester's end that her father had received a letter from the board of directors telling him to ''control'' the women in his family.

A student told her fiancé over the phone that she would not take his name when they married. The student reported on the ensuing argument and said, ''I am seriously thinking about keeping my name. I did not tell him that simply for the sake of the project.''

A male student carried a Cabbage Patch Kid doll around campus all day. While only a few female friends asked why he was carrying the doll around, some of his male friends asked if he was queer, and others refused to be seen walking with him. When the student later joined some of his male friends for a game of pool, they ''began to molest and harass the doll for fun.'' This student concludes: ''We fear what we do not understand. And usually this fear turns into hatred, anger, and even violence.''

A middle-aged female student decided to ''outrage'' her husband and teenage daughters by writing them a heartfelt letter stating her desire to go on to graduate school. She anticipated they would protest, given the sacrifices they had already made while she earned her undergraduate degree. To her surprise, the family called a meeting in response to her letter and stated their support for her dream. She is now a graduate student in the highly competitive Anthropology Department at the University of Arizona.

NOTES

Editors' note: Every effort has been made to provide current Internet information. However, readers are advised that Internet and e-mail addresses are subject to change.

1. Akan saying quoted by Professor Abena Busia.
2. The sociologist Harold Garfinkel (1967), discusses his ''breaching experiments'' as empirical studies. Many thanks to Patricia MacCorquodale for pointing out Garfinkel's work as a possible originator for exercises like the outrageous act.
3. For an in-depth discussion of this workshop, see Judy Temple's article written under the surname Lensink (1991).
4. *UA Fact Book. http://daps.arizona.edu/daps/factbook/data.*
5. See Suzanne Pharr's (1988) excellent discussion of this issue.

SUGGESTED READINGS

Editors' note: Every effort has been made to provide current Internet information. However, readers are advised that Internet and e-mail addresses are subject to change.

Bibliography: Feminist teaching practices. http://www.massey.ac.nz/~wwwms/Teaching. html
Goodman, D. and S. Shapiro. 1997. Sexism curriculum design. *Teaching for diversity*

and social justice, ed. M. Adams, L.A. Bell, and P. Griffin, 110–140. New York: Routledge.

O'Barr, J. 1994. *Feminism in action*. Chapel Hill: University of North Carolina.

Weiler, K. 1988. *Women teaching for change: Gender, class and power*. South Hadley, MA: Bergin and Garvey.

18

Outrageous/Liberating Acts: Putting Feminism into Practice

Ann Mussey, Rutgers, The State University of New Jersey, and Amy Kesselman, State University of New York, New Paltz

> We are all organizers, and no organizer should ever end a meeting or a book or an article without ideas for practical action. After all, a movement depends on people moving. What are we going to do differently when we get up tomorrow? . . .
>
> If each person in the room promises that in the twenty-four hours beginning the very next day she or he will do at least one outrageous thing in the cause of simple justice, then I promise I will, too.
>
> Gloria Steinem, *Outrageous Acts and Everyday Rebellions* (1983)

We have been teaching the introductory women's studies course for many years in several different places. Our goals for the course go beyond the transmission of a body of disciplinary knowledge. True to the roots of women's studies in second wave feminist activism, the course creates awareness of women's oppression in its myriad forms, invites students to reexamine their own lives through feminist lenses, illuminates the ways that gender, race, and class structure power relations in public and private life, and sets the stage for students to put what they have learned into action. The liberating act assignment (see Appendix) has been a powerful tool in accomplishing all these goals.

The assignment was inspired by Gloria Steinem's collection of essays *Outrageous Acts and Everyday Rebellions* (1983). In the essay "Far from the Opposite Shore," Steinem emphasizes the necessity for a wide variety of tactics in combating both individual and institutional sexism and challenges her readers to commit "outrageous acts" both as individuals and in groups. Being outrageous, to Steinem and others who have adopted her formulation, means refusing to accommodate sexist norms, challenging prevailing patriarchal assumptions and practices, and upsetting the normal functioning of gender. In an article on gender policy in education, Catherine Marshall (1997: 73–74) argues that gender is "so naturalized and institutionalized that it is not to be questioned or challenged." She urges feminist educators to be "outrageous because of the intractability and invisibility of the problem of gender inequity." Throughout history women have advanced their causes by acting outrageously in word and deed— pushing at the boundaries of deeply ingrained beliefs about gender. The outrageous/liberating act exercise invites students to participate in this tradition.

We have been using this exercise for many years without knowing who first devised it. Mussey learned it in 1990 when she first taught the course at Rutgers, the State University of New Jersey. She then introduced the exercise to women's studies at the State University of New York (SUNY), New Paltz, in 1994, where she taught the introductory course with Kesselman. After considerable research we have discovered that the originator of the exercise was Sherry Rosen, an adjunct lecturer in the Women's Studies Program at Rutgers who devised the exercise in 1984, a year after Steinem's collection was published. Faculty continue to use the exercise at both Rutgers and SUNY, New Paltz. Teachers of the introductory course at the University of Arizona and Portland State University use variants of the assignment, suggesting that the idea of acting "outrageously" with liberatory intentions has inspired several teachers of the introductory women's studies course.

In the version that we use, the exercise asks students to perform a pro-women act, something inspired by what they have learned in the course. The acts must be "nonviolent" (not harmful either mentally or physically to themselves or others), legal, and performed during the course of the term. (Students cannot make promises that it will happen during the summer.) It can be done as an individual or a group project. The original exercise had students write a short essay analyzing the relationship of their act to the course content. However, as the assignment evolved at Rutgers, the essay was replaced by a journal entry and a brief oral presentation in which students explain their act and its significance to them. Students are graded not on the act itself but on the basis of their ability to analyze its meaning in the context of the course material.

Sometime during the course of its development at Rutgers, the name of the exercise changed from "outrageous act" to "liberating action." Although we do not know why the name was changed, the use of "liberating" is quite conscious for us now. Students in the introductory women's studies course at both Rutgers and SUNY, New Paltz, come from a range of backgrounds. In both universities, the course fulfills a general education requirement, and feminist ideas are new to most students. As a result, we encounter students who are resistant to feminism in the early stages of the course. While outrageous acts do indeed grow quite naturally out of the course material, a requirement to act "outrageously" on a syllabus can reinforce some of their worst fears about feminism. At least in the beginning, students are likely to be more receptive to the idea of performing a "liberating action."

We also believe that "liberating action" expresses the element of "consciousness-raising" so important to the course material used at New Paltz. We want students to understand the significance of social and political change and the role collective action plays in creating such change. However, many students who are just beginning to understand the workings of gender need to connect personally with the course material before engaging in political action. A "liberating action" allows students to adapt it to their own needs. Students must define "pro-women" for themselves and are given great latitude in determining their act. While some students are enthusiastic about confrontation and collective action, others choose to engage in educational activities, and still others use the exercise to apply a feminist perspective to their own lives, changing their own behavior and reshaping their relationships with others. At New Paltz, students are given the option of performing the act either as an individual or as a group project. At Rutgers, however, instructors of the introductory course have frequently defined the assignment as a group project in order to emphasize collective political action rather than individual change.

THE "LIBERATING ACTION" ASSIGNMENT IN THE CLASSROOM

Initially, many students feel mystified about what they are "supposed to do." They have become dependent on the direction of teachers as authorities, and they are uncertain when they must rely on themselves. We anticipate this problem by beginning to talk about the assignment weeks in advance of the due date. We go over the assignment, reminding them of all the parameters. Students' uncertainty about the assignment invariably leads to requests for examples, and instructors approach this in different ways. Amy gives students a few examples, usually choosing actions students have done in the past that are not easily reproducible. Ann, on the other hand, does not provide any examples of previous acts, because she believes that facing the uncertainty and the doubt is an important part of the process for some students. Depending on themselves for ideas builds self-confidence and enhances their sense of self-determination. Ann addresses the difficulties students may have with defining an act by asking them to review things they have learned from the course that were especially meaningful to them or perhaps enraged them. This generally provides enough spark to ignite their own thoughts about what would signify a "pro-women" act to them. Their resistance gives way to a recognition of countless possibilities.

"OUTRAGEOUS" RECOGNITION

As students examine their experiences for the workings of gender and the possibility of intervention, they become more conscious of the sexism in their world. They soon begin to think about alternatives to accepting, colluding, or tuning out the endless humiliations and insults they encounter. One student, for example, was riding the New York subway at rush hour during spring break when she felt a man's hand sliding up her thigh. Normally, she wrote in her journal entry, she would have moved stealthily away, avoiding calling attention to herself or to him. The train was crowded, however, and there was no room to move. Suddenly, she realized that a liberating action opportunity had presented itself. In a loud voice she yelled, "Get your fucking hand off my ass!" All eyes turned toward the groper, and other women in the car began ridiculing him mercilessly. He got off the train at the next exit, and the student felt enormously exhilarated both by her own action and by the feeling of solidarity among the women in the train.

SELF-DETERMINATION IN PERSONAL RELATIONSHIPS

Most of our students are traditional college-age students who are in the process of figuring out how they want to define themselves. They are feeling their way through an often bewildering web of sexual and emotional relationships. The assignment encourages them to incorporate feminism into this process. One student, ashamed of her body, habitually wore a coat or jacket in class. For her liberating action, she stopped wearing it and found that at first she was terrified that everyone would stare at her but soon discovered that she actually felt more self-confident.

At both Rutgers and SUNY, New Paltz, the student body is diverse. While the majority of students are white and American-born, a substantial number in each class are students of color, immigrants, and/or children of immigrants. For many, the liberating action project has been an opportunity for them to claim their right to self-determination. The changes students make in their lives sometimes collide with the cultures of their families. One student defied her parents' wishes that she become an accountant, a dependable occupation that does not require graduate education. As a dutiful Chinese daughter, she had suppressed her lifelong passion for science to obey her parents. For her liberating action, she changed her major to biology, and, armed with a stack of descriptions of careers in science that she had gotten from the career development office, she informed her parents of her change in major with such fierce determination that they agreed to support her choice. In her journal entry, she reflected on her struggle to maintain a respectful relationship with her parents while claiming the right to shape her own destiny.

The introductory women's studies course stimulates many students to redefine their relationships with friends and lovers. After hearing about the patterns of abusive control that accompany battering in relationships, several women each semester have terminated relationships with abusive boyfriends. Recognizing that their choices are affected by the peer culture in which they live, many students have sought to change that culture by making clear their own opposition to sexist behavior. One student organized a group of her friends to confront the abusive boyfriend of a close friend. Another informed a friend that she was showing up at her house with a pickup truck to help her leave her abusive partner. "You can call me in the morning to call it off," she said, "otherwise I'll be there." The move went as scheduled, and she was installed at a friend's house.

While most of the students in our introductory courses are women, there are always a few men in each class. For men, intervening in peer culture can be difficult. In his journal entry, a member of a fraternity reflected on the criticism of fraternities he had come across in his women's studies reading. After writing about his conflicted feelings, he concluded that rather than quit a fraternity that had been an important source of support for him, he wanted to use the group pressure embedded in fraternity life to challenge the sexist behavior of its members. As a leader in his fraternity, he was able to organize a workshop for his brothers devoted to creating a new norm for relating to women in which objectification, exploitation, and trivialization were not tolerated. Going around the room, each man elaborated on the meaning of "being a dick" in his relationships with women, and they all pledged to help each other avoid such behavior in the future. Another male student struggled with his attitude toward homosexuality throughout the term as the instructor talked about the relationship between the hatred of gay men and sexist ideas about women. For his liberating action, he publicly defended a gay man in his neighborhood against the ridicule of his friends. He felt proud that he was able to speak out on behalf of this gay man and pleased with his new acceptance of homosexuality.

CONFRONTATIONS WITH THE PAST AND THE PRESENT

Many of the young women in the introductory women's studies course look back in bitterness and anger at their high school experiences. Several students have written letters to principals and teachers describing the destructive implications of school practices. One student, who had been very quiet throughout the entire semester, stunned all of us by describing her journey back to the classroom of her seventh-grade math teacher. In front of the classroom, she confronted the teacher about his contemptuous treatment of female students, announced that despite his lack of encouragement in seventh grade, she had become a math/elementary education major, and told the female students in the class not to be discouraged by their teacher's lack of support. Without waiting for a response, she walked out. In another high school classroom, a student had been enraged when her health education teacher told the class that "any young lady who was smart and acted properly would not have to worry about being raped." Having been raped by her best friend a year before, the teacher's words "made me feel like a bad person." For her liberating action, she discussed the situation with several students who were still at the high school and wrote a letter to the teacher explaining the scope of sexual assault and harassment in the high school and the destructive effect of her statement. The teacher responded positively, apologized for her statement, invited further discussion, and proposed to the principal that they introduce a course focused on sex. The principal got approval from the school board and is planning to invite the student to be a guest speaker in the class.

Both Rutgers and SUNY, New Paltz, are state-supported schools, and many students receive some form of financial aid. Most students at SUNY, New Paltz, and many at Rutgers work part-time at low-wage jobs. Students have often used their liberating action projects to challenge sexual harassment and unequal pay at the workplace. These efforts are educational whether or not they are successful. Students sometimes learn that individual action is insufficient to change institutional practices, sometimes they learn the snowballing effect that their own individual resistance has on coworkers, and sometimes they organize collective action. A student who worked at a video rental store was distressed by a male coworker who kept touching her as he passed by her. When she began talking to her female coworkers, she discovered that they also were disturbed by unnecessary and intrusive touching. They all tried to avoid working with this man but were not always successful. For her liberating action, the students talked to the manager, who then talked with the other employees. The offender was fired and told that the reason was sexual harassment.

GROUP PROJECTS

When students are given the option of doing the assignment in a group, they are able to form groups around some commonality, usually an interest in performing the same action. A group of students in the course at New Paltz were members of the women's soccer team. The team had lost its coach, a strong advocate for women's soccer, and as a result it lost the use of the best soccer field and was given inferior soccer balls. The students' liberating action proceeded in several steps, teaching them the need to be persistent, assertive, and, when necessary, threatening. When several meetings with the chair of the Athletics Department got them nowhere, they mentioned that the school was in violation of Title IX. The chair did an about-face. The team got new uniforms, new soccer balls, and part-time use of the good field.

The groups at Rutgers are usually constituted by the instructor at the beginning of the term, and students work together consistently throughout the course on other projects prior to the outrageous act assignment. When students do not choose the other group members, the outrageous act teaches them both the joys and the perils of coalition politics. They must work with others often unlike themselves to define what it means to engage in a "pro-women" act. They need to figure out what concerns they share and develop a project that reflects the ideas of all group members. One group of students in Annette Igra's class at Rutgers decided to confront bigotry at the shopping mall. Four of the students were African-American women, one an African-American man, and one a white woman. Dressed as various characters (a poor, elderly African-American woman, an upscale African-American man shopping for a wedding ring, and a teenage mall rat), they went from shop to shop observing the way they were treated and reporting hostile treatment to store managers. They then constructed a rating sheet and distributed it to their classmates in time for Christmas shopping. Another group rewrote the U.S. Constitution to include groups that had been excluded and posted it around the campus asking for comments. A third group created a video of themselves enacting a bra-burning ritual in which each member spoke about the significance of her bra as she threw it into a Weber barbecue grill. Holding up her bra, one woman explained that it had been torn while she was raped, and she sewed it back together to throw it on the fire.

THE PRESENTATIONS

The presentation of student projects is a powerful experience. One instructor at Rutgers created a ceremony by darkening the room and lighting a candle, which students passed to each other as they talked about what they had done. At New Paltz we arrange a single two-hour meeting for the presentations. This allows plenty of time for twenty-five students to talk about their acts. We have also used a two-hour slot for classes up to forty students, but this is not ideal because it requires timekeeping to hear from each person. During the presentations, students describe their actions, the significance of what they did, and how their actions connect with what they learned in the course. There are often tears as students describe acts that represent personal struggles, cheers as they report triumphs. The cumulative impact is always enormously moving as we listen to the myriad ways that people put feminist ideas into practice in their personal lives, supporting and educating others and challenging inequity and exploitation. As students describe their interactions with people outside the class, it is clear that the ideas of the course are radiating outward in ever-widening circles.

Creating the right climate in the classroom during the presentations is one of the challenges of the assignment. Many students are quite nervous about their presentation because they are unused to speaking in a large group. Some will invariably try to diminish their accomplishments, so it can be helpful to begin by asking them not to preface their presentation with ''this probably won't seem very liberating, but I . . .'' Others are anxious because their act brings up strong emotions like pain or anger that make them feel vulnerable. During the presentations, students often speak openly for the first time about having been raped or sexually abused as children. For this reason, we have added the proviso to the written assignment that they choose something they will be able to share with the class. The acts that elicit spontaneous clapping, laughter, or heart-stopping silence need no intervention. The difficulty comes not from those acts that are deeply felt by the class but from those acts that do not seem to create any notable response. Probing for more details or reflection can often shake things loose. But some acts will not generate much of a response, and even though we are clear from the beginning that they are not being graded on the content of their act, a lukewarm response can often serve as a judgment itself. Asking students to hold their responses until the end is one way to address this problem, but it also eliminates the spontaneity that can be so powerful. We also find that some presentations call for more questions and that to put that conversation off to the end would kill the exchange. We continue to work on how to shape the presentation time.

We have always held the "liberating action" class toward the end of the semester. However, because the presentations create the feeling of a shared community, students have suggested that we do it earlier in the term. They feel a new sense of commitment to their classmates and to feminist action as a result of the presentations. We are considering doing the project earlier in the term or perhaps having them do two outrageous acts during the class—the first an individual project and the second a group project.

We heartily recommend this exercise for use in the introductory women's studies courses and invite teachers to adapt and reshape it. It enables students to see themselves as agents, defining and performing their act without the direction of an external authority. Second, it teaches students about making change in their worlds and often about collective political action, especially when performed as a group exercise. Many learn to think of the effects of their actions in relationship to other women and to imagine the possibilities for social change.

APPENDIX: THE LIBERATING ACTION ASSIGNMENT

In the spirit of Gloria Steinem's essays entitled *Outrageous Acts and Everyday Rebellions*, you are asked to perform a positive, "pro-women" act that represents, for you, something you would not or could not have done prior to this course. Your outrageous act cannot be harmful to yourself or others (either mentally, emotionally or physically), and it must be legal. You are encouraged to do your liberating act as group project with other students in the class. It is up to you to define what "liberating" and "pro-women" mean to you (and your group). It must be something that you do during this semester; you may not use something you did before taking this class. We strongly recommend that you plan your act before you carry it out. Because it must not harm you or others, you must carefully consider the possible outcomes of your act before the enactment. Also, select something that you are willing to share with the class.

Your two-page journal entry should describe the act, explain why it was a "liberating," "pro-women" act, reflect on the reactions your act elicited, and analyze it in terms of the course material. In addition to the journal entry, you will give a short presentation to the class explaining your liberating action.

SUGGESTED READINGS

hooks, b. 1994. *Teaching to transgress, education as the practice of freedom.* New York: Routledge.

Marshall, C. 1997. *Gender equity and schooling: Policy and practice.* New York: Garland.

Steinem, G. 1983. *Outrageous acts and everyday rebellions.* New York: Holt, Rinehart, and Winston.

Part V

CONCLUSION:
UNDOING OUR HABITS

19

When Things Fall Apart

Jane A. Rinehart, Gonzaga University

> When things fall apart and we're on the verge of we know not what, the test for each of us is to stay on that brink. . . . From this point of view, the only time we ever know what is really going on is when the rug's been pulled out and we can't find anywhere to land. We use these situations either to wake ourselves up or to put ourselves to sleep.
>
> Chodron (1997: 9)

INTRODUCTION

"Staying on the brink" is compelling for me, because I know how strongly I resist it. I am drawn to accounts of similar struggles by other teachers. Jane Tompkins (1996: 121) has written about her efforts to shift the burden of performance in the classroom from herself to her students, to experience "the thrill of being together with students in a class instead of being all alone up there in front." This led her into new ways of acting that felt both exhilarating and terrifying: "This kind of teaching seemed to require a new kind of writing, a form that would reflect the spasmodic, concentrated quality of the experience, its precariousness, the constant sense of teetering on the brink" (Tompkins 1996: 140). Like Tompkins, staying on the brink and learning to value that experience have given me a different view of what it means for a teacher to be "in control."

"Control" is a major issue in discussions of feminist education, often formulated in terms of dichotomies—a well-established habit in Western thought and practice. Some examples are characterizations of women's studies classrooms either as sites of rigid ideological indoctrination or as sites where the participants are "out of control," that is, immersed in emotional self-disclosure and the infamous male bashing. Another example is the version in which feminists and their allies (multiculturalists, leftist radicals) are "taking control" of universities. In this dichotomy, the guardians of tradition and Reason oppose the canon busters.[1] These dichotomous frames influence the perceptions of various constituencies of the university: faculty, administrators, students, trustees, and parents.[2]

One strategy for managing these difficulties is mounting a good defense, which involves consistently portraying women's studies in a positive light: "Yes, we're political, but so is everyone, and our politics are better" or "Yes, we encourage our students to bring their personal experiences and feelings into classroom discussions, but this makes for stronger and more integrated inquiry."[3] Defensive strategies are understandable and often effective. However, they preserve the original terms of attack: the assumption that people can be lined up on the different sides of a clearly marked line and that ambiguity and struggle can be avoided. This seems to surrender unnecessarily to the terms that feminist education seeks to contest.

What if, instead of trying to take control by shifting the labels given to the two sides in the dichotomies, we admitted that "the true nature of things is that you're never in control" (Chodron in hooks 1997: 98)? Such an admission goes against the grain. It is a radical undoing of habits and structures dedicated to taking control and being in control. Constructing the introductory course in women's studies as a continuing experience for both teacher and students of admitting insecurity, and facing the pain of this, holds the promise of fostering a new consciousness that does not depend on conquest and exclusion. It moves women's studies out of the zone of confrontation created by constant battles for control and toward experiences of openness, questioning, and possibilities.

I strive to be compassionate toward myself and my students in the midst of the challenges presented by feminist inquiry. I read often about creating a "safe space" for students in the classroom, but I cannot apply this concept to my own experience. We, the students and I, seem quite unsafe. We are outside the limits of our routine ways of knowing and fumbling around trying to find our way back inside. Gradually, I came to realize that instead of denying where we are, the better move is to be fully present to that place and that moment (Chodron 1991: 4). This means letting go of the idea that I could and should make everything safe for us. I have not let go of that notion once and for all, but I am not in its grip. The writings of Pema Chodron have given me support and guidance in how to live out this insight that it helps to "start where you are," rather than seeking to escape (Chodron 1994).

Both Alice Walker and bell hooks have identified themselves as students of Pema Chodron, and their practices of feminist education can be interpreted as expressions of her teaching. Both teach by opening their hearts and minds and inviting readers/listeners into relationship. Walker and hooks believe that hard questions and painful situations cannot be avoided; at the same time, each is concerned that all participants in a learning situation be respected and encouraged. In *Warrior Marks* (1993b), Walker shows that criticism can avoid arrogance and maintain connection and that one can move to the edges of the comfortable and still survive. Actually, her work is about something more than survival: a hazardous journey "guaranteed to work the heart into a bolder shape" (4). Similarly, hooks writes and teaches within a moral perspective of antiracism and antisexism that accepts discomfort—both her own and that of her students and readers. Hooks (1990: 8) acknowledges the difficulty of practicing critique in a manner that does not reproduce a dichotomous scheme: "This desire to simplify one's critical response, to contain it within a dualistic model of good and bad, accepted and rejected, is an approach to ways of knowing that a liberatory pedagogy seeks to alter."

Trungpa Rinpoche, Pema Chodron's teacher, proclaimed, "Chaos should be regarded as extremely good news" (Chodron 1997: xi). Believing this would, I think, make a positive difference for women's studies teachers and students, because it invites us to relax in the face of the disorder and disorientation that thinking about gender produces. The more familiar response is to tighten up, but that makes the work of understanding how gender has shaped our world and us more difficult. This chapter offers a characterization of Women's Studies [WOMS] 201 as an opportunity to learn *in the midst of* chaos and uncertainty. It describes Introduction to Women's Studies in terms of *giving up control* and focuses on one dimension of teaching where the temptations to exert control seem especially fierce: classroom discussions. It asks the question, How does discussion change when we practice working with, rather than against, chaos? One story, an experience of being able to let go and the surprising result, is used to show what can change when being "nailed to the present moment" (Chodron 1997: 5) is conceived as a place of teaching and learning.

This chapter is not about teaching introductory women's studies as a sitting meditation. I do not present an explicit spiritual practice in the course or encourage students to do the meditative exercises of Tibetan Buddhism as taught by Pema Chodron. Instead, what I offer here is a description of the effects of these teachings and practices on *my* consciousness and the difference this makes in how I approach the challenges of introducing students to feminist inquiry. I am sharing a basic shift of perspective that I have experienced as liberating and that I believe may hold some promise for others. I mean to be tentative rather than forceful and to avoid preaching.[4]

CONTEXT

I have been teaching sociology and women's studies in the College of Arts and Sciences at Gonzaga University, a small (about 2,000 undergraduates) Jesuit school located in the Pacific Northwest, since 1974. Many (although not all) of its students come from economically privileged backgrounds and have grown up in communities that do not have large ethnic or racial minority populations. The typical WOMS 201 class has an enrollment between thirty-five and forty students, and two-thirds or more of these are usually eighteen to twenty-two years old. Most often, the class has ten or fewer male students and a similarly small number of students of color. It is quite rare for students to self-identify as gay or bisexual during classroom discussions; I can recall only a handful that have done so. Since Gonzaga officially established its Women's Studies Program in 1991, the course has been offered on a twice-per-week schedule every fall semester, with each class lasting seventy-five minutes. The identification of the school with Christian values encourages courteous behaviors toward others. Even though I find that the students at Gonzaga are less likely than they were twenty-five years ago to grant me automatic respect as the teacher, most of them are well mannered and want to avoid conflict.[5]

Gonzaga's explicit commitments to dialogue with, and care for, others and its mission statement's identification of social justice as a key dimension of a Gonzaga education support the presence of women's studies courses in the curriculum. Nevertheless, I am teaching a subject that my students have been encouraged to suspect. They bring with them to my courses in women's studies, especially to the introductory course, many negative images of feminism. The "f-word" problem that others have written about is present in our classroom (Bauer 1990; Faludi 1991; Hogeland 1994; Neitz 1985). Still, it is not as large a problem as it would be if the students in Sex, Gender, and Society were there involuntarily. They may not wish to label themselves as feminists, but they have volunteered to explore how feminist perspectives influence our understanding of social interaction, social structures, and culture. This course is one of many that students can take to fulfill a core social science requirement, and it is an elective for sociology majors or minors. The only students required to take it are those pursuing the twenty-one-credit concentration in women's studies. So, I am not facing students who resist being "forced to learn this stuff," but this is not to say they agree with everything I say or with the views expressed in the course texts.

The traditionalism of the institution is another significant part of my context. The Western intellectual heritage, in both the religious and secular manifestations, has been shaped by a framework composed of dichotomies: true/false, reason/emotion, rational/irrational, and objective/subjective. The first side of these dichotomies is the privileged side (Flax 1990; Hekman 1990). Many of the students I teach take for granted these distinctions and their way of privileging and marginalizing. They expect that teachers will tell them what is true, that the classroom is a place for reasoned discussion rather than emotional disclosure, that it is possible to readily distinguish rational practices from their opposite, and that knowers are (and should be) separate from what they know. Contesting these premises is unnerving to some students and can elicit strong reactions. Other students have moved away from the comforts of these certainties, but often their stance is an equally questionable approach to feminist inquiry: "It is all just a matter of personal preference and opinion." Since I take the approach of "working together" to develop an interpretive consensus, both kinds of students can be disturbed. I am viewed either as failing to do academics properly (criticizing "Truth," bringing in emotion, revealing subjectivity) or as imposing my point of view on an irredeemable plurality. Struggling with these two negative perspectives is a challenge throughout every semester. My allegiance to collaborative learning methods is based on the tools this approach has given me for staying with the struggle.

COLLABORATION MEANS LETTING GO

When I first began teaching on the university level, I barely took time to catch my breath as I raced through material that seemed very important. I worried a lot about fitting everything in. By temperament and family background, I am a person who readily assumes responsibility and takes control: a conscientious perfectionist. As a neophyte college instructor, I lectured for every class period, assuming this meant I had full control of what happened in class. Of course, this was an illusion because I had no control over what students heard and remembered.

In the beginning, my work in women's studies was somewhat of an exception to this pattern of taking control. I began teaching the course that would later become WOMS 201, Sex, Gender, and Society, in 1974 as a sociology upper-division elective called Women and Society. In this course, the seams showed, creating more opportunity for student participation. We used collections of readings rather than a textbook, and there was a great deal of interaction because the material was so fresh and controversial. Several students argued with me and with each other about various feminist views; the atmosphere was lively.

As I continued to teach the course, however, I gave it more organization and played a larger role as the "transmitter of knowledge." I now had files filled with syllabi, assignments, rationales for my grading procedures, and examinations. My teaching acquired sheen; it became quite polished and competent. I was also older, and this reinforced the impression that I could be trusted to produce a worthwhile course. That was a problem. My courses became my production, with only minor roles for the students to play. When I read Finkel and Monk's (1983) article on teachers needing to overcome "the Atlas Complex," I saw myself. Although I was successful as the producer and star of my courses, I could not avoid the contradiction between urging students to become involved social analysts and activists for social change and, at the same time, keeping them distant from significant responsibility for the course. I was making everything happen while I was also criticizing a society and culture that foster a diminished concept of citizenship.

Descriptions of collaborative learning (Bouton and Garth 1983; Bruffee 1984, 1993; Gabelnick et al. 1990; Graff 1992; MacGregor 1990; Rau and Heyl 1990;

Tarule 1996; Whipple 1987) have released me from the futility of blaming students for this and given me some tools for acting differently. They contain practical strategies for designing my courses differently that integrate my intellectual perspectives on the social construction of knowledge and the need for critical interpretation of current social arrangements with concrete classroom methods. Collaborative learning gives students the responsibility for interpreting texts, evaluating various perspectives, making judgments, and articulating these in small and large groups. Even though collaborative learning strategies require a considerable amount of preparation and organization on the teacher's part, these are different from the controlling forms I had practiced earlier.

Setting the students in motion and giving them most of the responsibility for the work of any particular class day take me out of the driver's seat. I provide the map with the structured discussion work sheets. I intervene when that seems necessary to clear up minor confusion or to offer encouragement when discussion stalls in a group. I use various methods to hold students accountable for doing the necessary work before and during class. Still, it is up to the students to make things happen, and this is risky. Sometimes the "wrong" things happen, or not enough of the "right" things. Things are messy, and we do not feel very good. It is hard for me to resist making knowledge into a neater package.

I am surprised by just how hard that is. I think it should be easier (despite my personality type) because of my view that building social relationships within conversations is integral to vital intellectual, ethical, and political activity.[6] I want students to *practice* feminist social analysis, not just read about it, but this does not save me from fearing the tensions and ambiguities that inevitably arise within the relationships and conversations of Introduction to Women's Studies. Pema Chodron's writings have helped me to work with that fear: "No one ever tells us to stop running away from fear" (Chodron 1997: 4). Chodron has helped me realize that if we stop running and get to know our fears, we can learn important things.

AND LETTING GO IS DIFFICULT

I used to just dive right into the course on the first day. After a few semesters of experiencing the tidal wave of unexpressed anxieties and conflicting expectations, I realized the importance of beginning more slowly, spending time on exploring our starting points and establishing a consensus about ground rules. The importance of this commitment has been well expressed by Woodbridge (1994: 135):

In a more purely pedagogical sense, decentered teaching is hard, much harder than an old-style dictatorial lecture. If we simply abdicate sovereignty without having something in its place, the classroom will be like a country that has had a revolution, but has no democratic institutions in place. A teacher must forge such institutions, from the beginning of each course.

I have not given up entirely on lecturing, but I have learned that students will not take the role of teaching and learning partner seriously if I do it too often, especially at the beginning of the semester. My WOMS 201 students bring many hesitations and fears with them, as well as a lack of experience with collaborative learning. This is a potent brew, and facing up to that in the beginning of the semester seems necessary.

Now I set aside the first three or four class periods for this task. These classes are grouped on the syllabus as a unit labeled ''Building the Conversation.'' I do this to highlight conversation as a crucial aspect of the work we will be doing together in the course. One of the first topics we discuss is ''male bashing,'' using a short handout I have written on this topic (Appendix A). I present the charge of male bashing as a defense that many people use to blame feminists for the discomfort they feel about changes in gender-based beliefs and practices. This view is presented as a suggestion for one way of thinking about what the label ''male bashing'' accomplishes.[7] The tone of the handout is deliberately conversational. I make it clear that I have made some mistakes in responding to students who have accused feminist writers or women's studies courses of male bashing. This seems very important to me—positioning myself from the beginning of the course as someone trying to figure out how to say things better.

Most of the time, the discussion about male bashing goes well, but not all the time. One semester, it was clear from the first day that two students were going to be harshly critical of feminism. One of them, an African American student in her mid-twenties, was especially outspoken: ''Feminism is just garbage. It is all about blaming men and refusing to take responsibility for your own life.'' The other critic was a white, middle-aged man who was less vehement but also quite resistant on the ground that ''feminist social science'' was an oxymoron. He was committed to value-free inquiry, and he also believed that male bashing was an apt description of feminism.

These two students do not match my earlier description of Gonzaga's students in that both were older than the typical undergraduate at this university, one was not white, and both were more willing than most of my students to declare their disagreements with the course during class time. However, they do fit the characterization of most of my students as imbued with dichotomous approaches; neither was comfortable with an exploratory form of inquiry based on recognition of multiple pieces of truth in need of careful interpretation. The male student was committed to objective scientific knowledge with definitive answers, and the female student was just as committed to her own perspective and experience as the most important source of ''Truth.'' Coming from different places, both regarded feminist sociology with enormous suspicion and were not shy about expressing their views.

I spoke with both of these students separately outside class during the first week and suggested that they reconsider taking the course. I pointed out that agreement with the texts or lectures was not required and said that I would welcome their criticism of the theories and research we would be studying. But

I stressed that they would be expected to take the course material seriously, that they could not just dismiss it. They chose to stay in the course and to criticize it at every opportunity. We talked often during office hours about how they participated in class discussions. Often their comments were so negative that the other members of their small groups either erupted in anger or ignored them.

At the midpoint of the semester, we spent an entire class period reflecting on what was happening in the small groups, reviewing the "Guidelines for Class Participation" handout distributed at the beginning (Appendix B), and trying to come up with better ways to respond to continuing conflicts that were often polarizing and silencing. I gave the class members a list of ten points expressing my view of our difficulties (Appendix C), and we talked about it. After that, the group discussions did improve somewhat, but this class remained fragile, always on the brink of disruptive conflict.

Looking at that list today, I am struck by the effort I made to avoid denying how hard our situation was and that we would probably continue to have problems. Some of the class members thought the "solution" at this midpoint was for me to lecture every class day and allow only a brief amount of time for comments or questions. I refused this strategy because it would have meant giving up on collaboration entirely. I kept coming back to the students with ideas I borrowed from Parker Palmer (1991) about the demands of public life. Among strangers, we encounter both fear and promise. When we stay at home or try to make everywhere we go into a version of home, we are trapped within our habitual perspectives. Although this may feel safe, it is not. We cannot relax because we are always watching the door, always concentrating on getting things to go our own way. Moving into relationships with people we do not know and might not choose carries the risk that we will be unsafe. A classroom learning community always presents the possibility of fulfilling Palmer's definition of community: "that place where the person you least want to live with always lives" (Palmer 1987: 20). Learning is as much about this challenge as it is about specific texts, perhaps even more so, because this sort of experience is less and less common in contemporary America: "We live in self-imposed exile from communal conversation and action" (Borgmann 1992: 2–3).

Being in that class twice a week was an experience of "being nailed to the present moment." I had to keep talking myself into going, and I was doing a lot of similar talking outside class to several students who were upset about how disagreements often escalated into attacks. All the talking did not transform things, although I noticed small changes: students began to remind each other about not interrupting, respecting differences, and working to identify common ground. Still, I was relieved to see that semester end, and I braced myself before I read the course evaluations. What I read shocked me. Almost all of the students used the forms to write about how important the small group discussions were to the success of the class. They expressed gratitude for the opportunity to talk with their peers, for example, "Never have I been in a class where the expression of ideas was so encouraged and so vital to the class curriculum and learn-

ing.'' Another student wrote: ''I left class angry sometimes, frustrated sometimes, and occasionally hopeful. I was privileged to hear many people, male and
female, speak about things that are critically important to their lives.'' No one
wrote that the communal/collaborative format was too much trouble, should be
abandoned, or was a disaster. I was amazed, and I still am!

This class was my most difficult experience using collaborative learning methods; yet, in many important ways, it ''worked.'' We had to work together, to
co-labor. The classroom was clearly a public and therefore unsafe space, rather
than a haven. Abstract ideals about creating shared interpretations and cooper-
ating in the construction of knowledge were put to the test of sharp disagreements. Everyone was pushed to the brink, and no one was pleased to be there.
Dichotomies were flying around the room: ''That is absolutely wrong, irrational,
just your opinion!'' We were in a battle zone. I cannot say the course worked
because eventually everyone came on board, because we achieved a solid consensus, because we established a foundation of mutual trust, or any other
''good'' reason. Instead, I think it worked because *we* worked; that is, we stayed
with our anxieties and insecurities. We met our limit and did not shut down
completely. The most obvious meaning of collaborative learning is getting out
of the students' way: allowing them to struggle with themselves, each other,
and the course material. It is perhaps less obvious that a teacher needs to get
out of her own way by letting go of habitual patterns of reaction, by allowing
herself to feel awful and still stick with it.

THE PRESENT MOMENT

Our collaborative efforts that particular tumultuous semester were often com-
promised by intense conflict, and our failures in making these conflicts productive, rather than destructive, were numerous. My fretting about this continues
now—five years later—but has been somewhat lessened by reading courageous
admissions of similar ''failures'' and the self-doubting they produce (hooks
1994a: 8–9). Tompkins (1996: 180) reports an experience opposite to mine. She
thought that one of her courses went splendidly, but the student evaluations
were critical, and this devastated her: ''When you teach like this, you don't
know what failure is anyway, or success. What looks like victory could turn out
to be defeat, as well as the other way around.'' For me, the challenge is to get
unhooked from all this worrying and to keep going.

In my case, ''to keep going'' has meant more reading about various responses
of Black women to feminism (e.g., Lorde 1984a) and including an essay by bell
hooks (1994b) that analyzes the resistance of Black students to feminism on my
course syllabus. It has meant spending additional class time exploring students'
reactions to thinking of social science in political terms, figuring out how values
and emotions can be considered integral to research and theorizing, and considering why that integration seems troublesome. I continue to collaborate with
students after they have moved on, learning from, and applying, what they have

taught me but trying never to kid myself that now I have it all together. Next time, whatever I did wrong this time will be OK, but I will make a different mistake. I am grateful to the conflicts produced within this one semester of collaboration for showing me that I need to pay better attention to different forms of resistance to feminist scholarship and activism.

By "better attention," I mean listening and observing with minimal judgment and more compassion, as well as asking the students to do the same. It would have been better in that Introduction to Women's Studies class with the two highly vocal resisters if I had acknowledged right away that I was "on the edge" and scared. I should have admitted that I was searching in every direction for ways to counter the resistance or, even better, to *stop* it. I think if I had done this, I might have softened sooner. Softening would have allowed me to connect more fully with my feelings and with the students. Chodron (1991: 55) describes the journey of awakening as "realizing you've come up against your edge, that everything in you is saying no, and then at that point, softening." "Softening" does not mean withdrawing and giving up responsibility. It does not mean pretending that everything is OK or avoiding honest confrontation. It means recognizing what is going on, feeling instead of running, and then acting with clarity and decisiveness (Chodron 1994: 127–128). There is no guarantee that the actions taken by a softened heart will be the best ones, but mistakes can also be learning opportunities.

In my experience of this particular class, "the edge" was some combination of these things: the classroom environment is hostile, some students are challenging my basic assumptions, other students are waiting for me to assert my authority, we are not able to follow the syllabus because of too many interruptions, and I am afraid of making a mistake in how I handle this conflict. Sometimes, I overreacted; sometimes, I froze and did nothing. Eventually, I was able to regard my fears and strategies of escape with some humor. The handout I distributed and the discussion we had about the classroom dynamic were a small step toward bravery. It had the effect Chodron (1991: 55) predicts: "When somebody works with hardship in an openhearted humorous way, when somebody cultivates his or her bravery, everyone responds, because we know *we* can do that too." Enacting this kind of bravery, then, is not about becoming the admirable exception but serving as a reminder of what is possible for everyone. The student evaluations from that class indicate that many students valued the struggle and appreciated *their own* resilience, tenacity, and courage. At least some of the falling apart that happened during that semester was worthwhile.

The story I have told here is an especially dramatic one because the falling apart was very visible and immediate: vocal students with nothing good to say about the feminist scholarship they were expected to be reading and thinking about. More often, in my Introduction to Women's Studies classes, it is both less instantaneous and less public. The conflicts that students experience in their reading and talking with each other surface in their written assignments or in conversations with me during office hours, rather than at full throat in the class-room. Even in these more muted versions, I feel threatened and want to stop feeling that way. I am just like those students who are disturbed by words like "oppression" or by critiques of science.

Whereas I once tried to alleviate the discomfort, now I treat it as a necessary ingredient of what we are doing: "the point is still to lean toward the discomfort of life and see it clearly rather than to protect ourselves from it" (Chodron 1997: 17). Teaching and learning in Introduction to Women's Studies present me with a choice whether to wake up or not. I tell my students they have the same choice. "Waking up" is not acquiring a particular political or intellectual perspective, discarding our former confusions, and becoming perfect. It is dis-covering what is in us and in front of us; developing openness, wonder, humor, and kindness; and not giving up on ourselves or other people. I do not wish to be defensive when it is called to my attention that "some pretty intense stuff seems to be going on in that introductory women's studies class of yours, Jane, and some students are upset about it." I am more inclined to be pleased and to announce that pleasure up front, right from the beginning of the class: "We are here to feel the ground move out from under our feet; to ask basic questions about how society is organized, culture created and transmitted, and people's lives structured in terms of gender and sex. We will refuse easy answers; listen to our differences; and practice courage. For us, in this course, chaos is good news."

APPENDIX A: EXCERPT FROM THOUGHTS ABOUT "MALE BASHING" AND THE BEGINNING OF A DIALOGUE

When students first used the phrase "male bashing" and characterized it as a problem whenever feminist ideas are discussed, I did not realize that it would prove to be such a persistent concern. I guess I thought that it would be pretty easy to demonstrate that feminism is not identified with hatred of men and that feminist thinkers analyze sexism as a social and cultural force with negative effects on men as well as women. Feminist scholarship, I assumed, could speak for itself as an example of careful reflection and research that avoids blaming individuals for cultural beliefs and social practices. I also counted on the positive influence of a classroom environment self-consciously committed to mutuality, respect for differences in perspectives and experiences, and explicit rules for civil conversation. In other words, I thought I "had it covered."

Was I wrong! This thing called male bashing refuses to go away or be tamed by my hopes and strategies. This is not to say that I necessarily think there is actual male bashing taking place in the women's studies classes I teach; at this point, all I can say is that I am unsure about that. I know that I try to be aware of the possibility in my own presentations, and I encourage students to be sim-ilarly reflective about their comments in small group discussions or during lectures. I do not claim that this desire to avoid attacking men is perfectly attained—by me, by students, or by the authors we read. I am sure that lapses of kindness and carefulness do occur.

But I am not persuaded that these kinds of failures in speaking and writing are as significant as difficulties in listening and reading. I think that "male bashing" is often charged when a high level of defensiveness makes it difficult to assess what is actually being said and to respond with empathy or openness. The phrase "male bashing" can serve to protect us from having to think about things that are disturbing. Both women and men use this phrase against a speaker or writer who unsettles their assumptions about how things are or should be.

What do I mean? Let me try to explain by using an analogy from another kind of strained relationship: those between members of different "races." It seems to me that when I read or hear people of color describing how they have been oppressed by people of white European origins, I can feel defensive. I want to think about all the ways that I can separate myself from this problem. If I am face-to-face with a person of color who is honestly revealing the pain she or he suffers in a racist society (my society), I want to find a way to avoid taking it in fully. Taking in a critique of racism would mean having to face my own complicity in the forces that create it and accepting the anger directed my way. All of this feels threatening. An examination of my attitudes and actions in terms of race is troubling because I am often unhappy with what I learn about myself.

These fears and struggles and the choices we make about what to do with them are the individual side of what it means to live in a society that has institutionalized racism; that is, built negative images of groups of people into our organizations and daily practices. It is hard to live in such a society once you recognize it in this way. It is especially hard to acknowledge that perhaps you have benefited from racist assumptions and practices and are resistant to giving up those benefits. Racism is not a problem for nonwhites only; it is a problem for all of us. What we have made of skin color shapes our lives, and figuring out how to understand these effects and to change them takes courage and effort. Thinking about this helps me to understand the feelings that many women and men may have when confronted with some women's anger and pain about social injustice and personal mistreatment. I think I understand why it is so difficult to hear these things and why we often reach for a defense. Calling feminist analysis "male bashing" can be a way to avoid listening to things that challenge us to change.

APPENDIX B: GUIDELINES FOR CLASS PARTICIPATION

The three most important foundations for successful class participation are *preparation, reflection,* and *sensitivity.*

Preparation refers to doing the assigned reading and anything else suggested by the instructor to be ready for that day's work. Preparation expresses your commitment to the idea that everyone is responsible for the quality of the course and your willingness to do your share. Preparation allows you to participate honestly, rather than wasting time with superficial, time-filling talk.

Reflection is the act of paying deliberate attention to your own contributions to the class. It entails resisting the temptations to give away your own power or to blame others. The practice of reflection gives each of us a better understanding of our gifts and our "growing edges." It keeps us centered on something we can do something about: our own behaviors.

Sensitivity means being present in the situation. It means we care about what is going on and about the other people with us. The practice of sensitivity fosters skills of awareness, empathy, and tactfulness. One important manifestation of sensitivity is how you respond to the contributions of your classmates. At times, each of us may feel impatience or annoyance toward another member of the class. Each of us has the responsibility to control how we show those feelings; in other words, our negative feelings do not entitle us to be disrespectful or discourteous. We also need to remember that others in the class may have very different responses; in other words, what bothers you may be helping someone else in the class.

We are trying to become a learning community. In a community, we do not encounter only those people we might choose. We meet others with whom we do not agree, whom we might even dislike. Learning how to manage such responses, to use them creatively, is essential for our individual growth and for the vitality of social life. What we practice in the classroom is real—important skills for real life. If we regard other people as a bother or a distraction, we cannot build society and might as well stay home. Each of us has to "leave home" and all of its comforts in order to participate in the creation of our world. This is one place to do just that. Some suggestions for how to respond to the comments of classmates and the instructor are:

1. Be willing to risk making mistakes. Playing it safe means it is unlikely that the conversation will take us anywhere that we have not already been.

2. Try to be led more by a desire to understand more about the topic than by a desire to impress others with your wit, intelligence, and so on.

3. Be as specific as possible; for example, relate what you are saying to what has been said already, state reasons for your position, and avoid "grand generalizations."

4. Concentrate on sharing information and experiences, rather than giving advice, announcing judgments, or forcing agreement.

5. Conflict is not a bad thing, although it can be handled in good or bad ways. It is possible to affirm differences and allow these to be resources, rather than obstacles. Work on allowing differences and diversity to emerge in a context that is both respectful and challenging.

6. Sometimes you may be surprised at the intensity of your emotions. Instead of denying that you have feelings that influence your views, work at understanding their sources and effects.

7. Remember that class participation depends on the decisions of individuals. No one should be coerced into talking or pressed to the point of embarrassment. We are all facilitators and supporters of the conversation, not its directors or monitors.

APPENDIX C: NOTES TO THE CLASS AT MIDTERM

We are having our problems. I think it might help if I try to clarify a few things.

1. We are talking about things we care about personally. This means that we have to recognize that there is an emotional element in our conversations. We need to be careful and respectful of each other's feelings. We don't need to be afraid of feelings.

2. Attentive listening fosters such care and respect. This entails doing several things: endeavoring to be open to different points of view, being willing to rethink our positions, striving to hear others accurately, and being sensitive to the responses of other people to the ideas we express.

3. We want to have conversations in which it is possible to be moved and to change our minds. This cannot happen if we "hold on for dear life" to what we already know.

4. Conversation is promoted by questioning each other and is limited by repeated declarations of the same position. We need to show that we are hearing what others have to say and are willing to respond thoughtfully.

5. Individual members of the class have been willing to share their experiences. All of us need to affirm this and, at the same time, invite each other to enlarge our experience. Otherwise, we could learn by simply talking to ourselves.

6. There is a difference between disagreeing with people and dishonoring them. We each know what this difference feels like. It is intimidating to *tell* people to think differently. This means we do not respect them as people who are doing the best they can. We will have better conversations if we avoid telling people what they should think and instead concentrate on becoming clear about what they are saying and what we want to know about it.

7. We will fail. We will not be as reflective and patient as we want to be all of the time. Forgiveness is essential, including forgiving ourselves. If a learning community depended on perfection—of character, of communication—it would never happen. It depends on goodwill and trust.

8. Gender inequality can and often does produce feelings of victimization: hurt and anger. Sometimes we have these feelings for ourselves, sometimes on behalf of people we love. When we are feeling victimized, we are vulnerable. We need to be kind to each other and ourselves.

9. When positions on any topic become polarized, it often helps to assume that each side contains part of the truth. For example, Warshaw [1988] may be right that sexual violence happens frequently in our society and that this problem cannot be solved individually. Roiphe [1993] may be right that it is problematic for women to adopt the position of "victim" completely, that this gives away too much of our energy

and desire for change. What happens when we think that each side has something worthwhile to say?

10. Some advice: Look again at the "Guidelines for Class Participation" in your course packet.

NOTES

1. For examples of these critiques, see Bloom (1987), Denfeld (1995), D'Souza (1991), Lehrman (1993), Patai and Koertge (1994), and Sommers (1994).

2. As a founding director of my university's women's studies program, I have had numerous conversations with people "concerned" about what we are doing in women's studies. I have learned to ask the people at my university who raise concerns to get specific immediately: How does what you are saying apply to us? I let people know that I cannot answer for everything done in the name of feminism, women, or women's studies, but that I am happy to discuss the program at our institution. I endeavor to do this non-defensively; sometimes, I succeed.

3. For examples of defenses of women's studies, see Boxer (1982), McDermott (1995), Minnich (1990), O'Barr (1987, 1994), and Rhode (1997).

4. In my aspirations, I am following the model of Jane Tompkins (1996), who mentions meditation as something she tried as a treatment for migraines. Eventually, she realized it was changing her heart and soul and therefore also her professional orientation (117). Tompkins does not write about meditation but about how she did things differently in her classes.

5. I have read chilling descriptions of classroom rudeness that I cannot imagine occurring at Gonzaga. For several examples, see Trout (1997).

6. Elsewhere, I have described how I teach feminist theorizing as a conversation in a course called Feminist Thought (Rinehart 1998). This article provides more extensive discussion of why I regard conversation as central to theorizing and political action.

7. Since I wrote the first version of this handout, I have had the benefit of reading an article by Cataldi (1995) on "male bashing" that makes a similar point in a different kind of way. Cataldi makes a strong argument against the view that feminists and women's studies courses are engaging in male bashing. Her analysis is carefully reasoned and clearly stated. I am not sure, however, that it would draw my students into a conversation about male bashing, and that is my aim. I think it might evoke the defensiveness I am trying to steer us around.

SUGGESTED READINGS

Chodron, P. 1997. *When things fall apart: Heart advice for difficult times*. Boston: Shambhala.

hooks, b. 1994. *Teaching to transgress: Education as the practice of freedom*. New York: Routledge.

Palmer, P. 1998. *The courage to teach: Exploring the inner landscape of a teacher's life*. San Francisco: Jossey-Bass.

Tompkins, J. 1996. *A life in school: What the teacher learned*. Reading, MA: Addison-Wesley.

References

Editors' note: Every effort has been made to provide current Internet information. However, readers are advised that Internet and e-mail addresses are subject to change.

Adams, M., L. A. Bell, and P. Griffin, eds. 1997. *Teaching for diversity and social justice*. New York: Routledge.

Aisenberg, N. and M. Harrington. 1984. *Women of academe: Outsiders in the sacred grove*. Amherst: University of Massachusetts.

Allison, D. 1988. Mama. *Trash/stories by Dorothy Allison*, 33–47. Ithaca, NY: Firebrand.

Amott, T. and J. Matthaei. 1996. *Race, gender and work*. 2d ed. Boston: South End.

Andersen, M. and P. H. Collins. 1995. Preface. *Race, class and gender: An anthology*, 2d ed., ed. M. Andersen and P. H. Collins, xii–xx. Belmont, CA: Wadsworth.

Anderson, J. A. 1996. Keynote address presented at Annual Meeting of Professional and Organizational Development (POD) Network on Higher Education Conference, Snowbird, UT.

Anderson, J. D. 1994. School climate for gay and lesbian students and staff members. *Phi Delta Kappan*, October, 151–154.

Anzaldua, G. 1990. *Making face, making soul: Haciendo caras: Creative and critical perspectives by feminists of color*. San Francisco: Aunt Lute.

———. 1987. *Borderlands/La Frontera: The new mestiza*. San Francisco: Spinsters Ink/Aunt Lute.

Appleby, Y. 1993. Disability and compulsory heterosexuality. *Heterosexuality: A feminism and psychology reader*, ed. S. Wilkinson and C. Kitzinger, 266–269. London: Sage.

Asch, A. and M. Fine. 1988. Introduction: Beyond pedestals. *Women with disabilities*. Philadelphia: Temple University.

Atwood, M. 1985. *The handmaid's tale*. New York: Fawcett.

Bargard, A. and J. Hyde. 1991. A study of feminist identity development in women. *Psychology of Women Quarterly* 15: 181–201.

Bauer, D. 1990. The other ''f'' word. *College English* 52: 385–396.

Bauer, D. with K. Rhoades. 1996. The meaning and metaphors of student resistance. *Antifeminism in the academy*, ed. V. Clark, S. N. Garner, M. Higonnet, and K. H. Katrak, 95–113. New York and London: Routledge.

Belenky, M. F., B. M. Clinchy, N. R. Goldberger, and J. M. Tarule. 1986. *Women's ways of knowing: The development of self, voice, and mind*. New York: Basic Books.

Berger, John. [1972] 1977. *Ways of seeing*. London: British Broadcasting Company and Penguin.

Bethel, L. 1979. What chou mean *we*, white girl? *Conditions: Five* 11.2: 86–92.

Bion, W. 1961. *Experiences in groups and other papers*. New York: Basic Books.

Blinde, E. M. and D. E. Taub. 1992. Women athletes as falsely accused deviants: Managing the lesbian stigma. *The Sociological Quarterly* 33: 521–533.

Bloom, A. 1987. *The closing of the American mind: How higher education has failed democracy and impoverished the souls of today's students*. New York: Simon and Schuster.

Borgmann, A. 1992. *Crossing the postmodern divide*. Chicago: University of Chicago.

Boswell, A. and J. Z. Spade. 1996. Fraternities and collegiate rape culture: Why are some fraternities more dangerous places for women? *Gender & Society* 10: 133–147.

Bouton, C. and R. Y. Garth. 1983. Students in learning groups: Active learning through conversation. *Learning in groups, new directions for teaching and learning*, no. 14, ed. C. Bouton and R. Y. Garth, 73–81. San Francisco: Jossey-Bass.

Boxer, M. 1998. *When women ask the questions: Creating women's studies in America*. Baltimore: Johns Hopkins University.

———. 1982. For and about women: The theory and practice of women's studies in the United States. *Signs* 7: 661–695.

Boxer, S. 1997. One casualty of the women's movement: Feminism. *New York Times*, December 14, WK3.

Bray, R. 1992. How did I get here? *New York Times Magazine*, November 8, 35–42.

Brownmiller, S. 1984. *Femininity*. New York: Ballantine.

———. 1975. *Against our will*. New York: Simon and Schuster.

Bruffee, K. A. 1993. *Collaborative learning: Higher education, interdependence, and the authority of knowledge*. Baltimore: Johns Hopkins University.

———. 1984. Collaborative learning and the conversation of mankind. *College English* 46: 635–652.

Burack, C. 1988–1989. Bringing women's studies to political science: The handmaid in the classroom. *NWSA Journal* 1.2 (Winter): 274–283.

Butler, J., S. Coyner, M. Homans, M. Longenecker, and C. McTighe Musil. 1991. Women's studies. *Liberal learning and the arts and sciences major*. Vol. 2: *Reports from the fields*, 207–224. Washington, DC: Association of American Colleges.

Cannon, L. W. 1990. Fostering positive race, class, and gender dynamics in the classroom. *Women's Studies Quarterly* 18: 126–134.

Carby, H. 1986. White woman listen! Black feminism and the boundaries of sisterhood. *The empire strikes back: Race and racism in 70's Britain*, ed. Centre for Contemporary Cultural Studies. University of Birmingham. London: Hutchinson.

Carlip, H. 1995. *Girl power: Young women speak out*. New York: Warner Books.

Carvajal, D. 1996. For immigrant maids, not a job but servitude. *New York Times*, February 25, 11.

Cataldi, S. L. 1995. Reflections on male bashing. *NWSA Journal* 7 (Summer): 76–85.

Chambers, V. 1996. *Mama's girl*. New York: Riverhead.

Chan, S. [1989] 1998. You're short, besides! *Race, class and gender*, 3d ed., ed. M. L. Andersen and P. H. Collins, 421–427. Belmont, CA: Wadsworth.

———. 1990. You're short besides. *Making face, making soul: Haciendo caras: Creative and critical perspectives by feminists of color*, ed. G. Anzaldua, 162–168. San Francisco: Aunt Lute.

Cherny, L. and E. R. Weise, eds. 1996. *Wired women*. Seattle: Seal.

Chodron, P. 1997. *When things fall apart: Heart advice for difficult times*. Boston: Shambhala.

———. 1994. *Start where you are: A guide to compassionate living*. Boston: Shambhala.

———. 1991. *The wisdom of no escape and the path of loving-kindness*. Boston: Shambhala.

Christ, C. P. and J. Plaskow. 1979. *Womanspirit rising: A feminist reader in religion*. San Francisco: Harper and Row.

Cixous, H. 1976. Laugh of the medusa. *Signs* 1.4 (Summer) 1: 891.

Cofer, J. O. 1993. The myth of the Latin woman. *The Latin deli*, 148–154. Athens: University of Georgia.

Cole, C. L. 1995. Celebrity feminism: Nike style post-Fordism, transcendence, and consumer power. *Sociology of Sport Journal* 12.4: 347–369.

Collins, P. H. 1990. *Black feminist thought*. New York: Routledge.

Combahee River Collective. 1983. The Combahee River Collective statement. *Home girls: A Black feminist anthology*, ed. B. Smith, 272–282. New York: Kitchen Table: Women of Color.

Crumpacker, L. and E. M. Vander Haegen. 1993. Pedagogy and prejudice: Strategies for confronting homophobia in the classroom. *Women's Studies Quarterly* 21: 94–105.

Davis, A. 1981. *Women, race and class*. New York: Random House.

Davis, B. H. 1985. Teaching the feminist minority. *Gendered subjects: The dynamics of feminist teaching*, ed. M. Culley and C. Portuges, 245–252. Boston: Routledge, Kegan and Paul.

DeGroot, J. and M. Maynard. 1993. Facing the 1990s: Problems and possibilities for women's studies. *Women's studies in the 1990s: Doing things differently?*, ed. J. DeGroot and M. Maynard, 149–178. New York: St. Martin's.

Denfeld, R. 1995. *The new Victorians: A young woman's challenge to the old feminist order*. New York: Warner.

Devault, M. L. 1976. Images of women: A case study of consciousness-raising in an introductory women's studies course. Master's thesis, University of Wisconsin, Madison.

Dewey, J. 1916. *Democracy and education*. New York: Macmillan.

DiPalma, C. 1990–1991. Who counts as "we"? *Voices: The Hawai'i Women's Newsjournal* 4.2 (Winter): 33–35.

Disch, E. and B. Thompson. 1990. Teaching and learning from the heart. *NWSA Journal* 2: 68–78.

D'Souza, D. 1991. *Illiberal education: The politics of race and sex on campus.* New York: Free Press.

Duggan, L. 1995. Feminist historians and antipornography campaigns. *Sex wars*, ed. L. Duggan and N. Hunter, 68–73. New York: Routledge.

Dworkin, A. 1996. Dworkin on Dworkin. *Radically speaking: Feminism reclaimed*, ed. D. B. and R. Klein. Melbourne: Spinifex.

Ehrenreich, B. 1986. Feminism's phantoms. *New Republic* 194.11 (March 17): 33–35.

Eisen, V. and I. Hall. 1996. Introduction. *Harvard Educational Review* 66: v–ix.

Ellsworth, E. 1992. Why doesn't this feel empowering? Working through the repressive myths of critical pedagogy. *Feminisms and critical pedagogy*, ed. C. Luke and J. Gore, 90–119. New York: Rootledge.

Enloe, C. 1995. The globetrotting sneaker. *Ms.* (March–April): 10–15.

Faludi, S. 1991. *Backlash: The undeclared war against American women.* New York: Doubleday.

Feminist News. 1998. *Feminist Majority Foundation Online.* June 10. Published on the World Wide Web at *http://www/feminist.org/news/newsbyte/june98/html.*

Ferreira, L. 1995. Finding my Latina identity through women's studies. *Women, images and realities: A multicultural anthology*, ed. A. Kesselman, L. D. McNair, and N. Schniedewind, 22–24. Mountain View, CA: Mayfield.

Findlen, B., ed. 1995. *Listen up: Voices from the next feminist generation.* Seattle: Seal.

Finkel, D. and G. S. Monk. 1983. Teachers and learning groups: Dissolution of the atlas complex. *Learning in groups, new directions for teaching and learning*, ed. C. Bouton and R. Y. Garth, 83–97. San Francisco: Jossey-Bass.

Flax, J. 1990. *Thinking fragments: Psychoanalysis, feminism, and postmodernism in the contemporary West.* Berkeley: University of California.

Fonow, M. M. 1996. *Women, culture and society: A student workbook.* 2d ed. Dubuque, IA: Kendall/Hunt.

Fonow, M. M. and D. Marty. 1991. The shift from identity politics to the politics of identity: Lesbian panels in the women's studies classroom. *NWSA Journal* 3: 402–413.

Foucault, M. 1979. *Discipline and punish: The birth of the prison.* New York: Random House.

Fox O'Barr, J., et al. 1994. Just an experiment for my women's studies class: Female students and the culture of gender. *Feminism in action: Building institutions and community through women's studies.* Chapel Hill: University of North Carolina.

Freedman, R. 1986. *Beauty bound.* Lexington, MA: D. C. Heath.

Freeman, J., ed. 1995. *Women: A feminist perspective.* 5th ed. Mountain View, CA: Mayfield.

Freire, P. 1970. *Pedagogy of the oppressed.* New York: Continuum.

Friedan, B. 1963. *The feminine mystique.* New York: Norton.

Friskopp, A. and S. Silverstein. 1995. *Straight jobs, gay lives.* New York: Scribner.

Froula, C. 1984. When Eve reads Milton: Undoing the canonical economy. *Canons*, ed. R. von Hallberg. Chicago: University of Chicago.

Frye, M. 1992. Willful virgin or do you have to be a lesbian to be a feminist? *Willful virgin: Essays in feminism*, ed. M. Frye, 124–137. Freedom, CA: Crossing.

———. 1983. Oppression. *The politics of reality: Essays in feminist theory*, 1–16. Freedom, CA: Crossing.

Fuss, D. 1989. *Essentially speaking: Feminism, nature, and difference.* New York: Routledge.

Gaard, G. 1996. Anti-lesbian intellectual harassment in the academy. *Antifeminism in the academy*, ed. V. Clark, S. N. Garner, M. Higonnet, and K. H. Katrak, 115–140. New York and London: Routledge.

Gabelnick, F., J. MacGregor, R. S. Matthews, and B. L. Smith. 1990. *Learning communities: Creating connections among students, faculty, and disciplines, new directions for teaching and learning.* San Francisco: Jossey-Bass.

Garfinkel, H. 1967. Studies of the routine grounds of everyday activities. *Studies in ethnomethodology.* Englewood Cliffs, NJ: Prentice-Hall.

Geiger, S. and J. N. Zita. 1985. White traders: The caveat emptor of women's studies. *Journal of Thought* 20: 106–121.

George, D. H. 1992. Bridges over the gender gap: Male students in women's studies. *Radical Teacher* 42: 28–31.

Gerver, E. 1997. Computers and gender. *Literacy, technology and society: Confronting the issues*, ed. G. Hawisher and C. Selfe, 361–383. Upper Saddle River, NJ: Prentice-Hall.

Gilbert, L. and C. Kile. 1996. *SurferGrrrls.* Seattle: Seal.

Gilligan, C. 1982. *In a different voice.* Cambridge: Harvard University.

Giroux, H. A. 1988. *Teachers as intellectuals: Toward a critical pedagogy of learning.* Granby, MA: Bergin and Garvey.

Gordon, L. 1994. *Pitied, but not entitled: Single mothers and the history of welfare.* New York: Free Press.

Graff, G. 1992. *Beyond the culture wars: How teaching the conflicts can revitalize American education.* New York: Norton.

Green, C. 1995. One resilient baby. *Listen up: Voices from the next feminist generation*, ed. B. Findlen, 138–148. Seattle: Seal.

Greene, G. 1986. Choice of evils. *Women's Review of Books* 3 (October): 14.

Grella, C. E. 1990. Irreconcilable differences: Women defining class after divorce and downward mobility. *Gender & Society* 4 (March): 41–55.

Grosz, E. 1989. *Sexual subversions: Three French feminists.* Sydney: Allen and Unwin.

Grumet, M. 1988. *Bitter milk: Women and teaching.* Amherst: University of Massachusetts.

Hancock, K. A. 1986. Homophobia. (Part of the Lesbian and Gay Issue in Psychology Series of the Committee on Lesbian and Gay Concerns.) Washington, D.C.: American Psychological Association.

Haraway, D. 1991. The actors are cyborg, nature is coyote, and the geography is elsewhere: Postscript to "cyborgs at large." *Technoculture*, ed. C. Penley and A. Ross, 21–26. Minneapolis: University of Minnesota.

Hardin, E. 1998. Designing information technology to support feminist pedagogy. Master's thesis, Department of English, North Carolina State University.

Hardy, M. A. and L. E. Hazelrigg. 1995. Gender, race/ethnicity, and poverty in later life. *Journal of Aging Studies* 9 (Spring): 43–63.

Hekman, S. J. 1990. *Gender and knowledge: Elements of a postmodern feminism.* Boston: Northeastern University.

Hernandez, A. 1997. *Pedagogy, democracy, and feminism: Rethinking the public sphere.* Albany, NY: SUNY.

Herring, S. 1994. Gender differences in computer-mediated communication: Bringing familiar baggage to the new frontier. Keynote talk at panel entitled: Making the Net*Work*: Is there a Z39.50 in gender communication? at the annual convention of the American Library Association, Miami, June 27. Published on the World Wide Web at *http://cpsr.org/cpsr/gender/herring.txt.*

Hesse-Biber, S. and M. K. Gilbert. 1994. Closing the technological gender gap: Feminist pedagogy in the computer-assisted classroom. *Teaching Sociology* 22.1: 19–31.

Hill, S. and N. Silver. 1993. Civil rights antipornography legislation. *Transforming a rape culture*, ed. E. Buchwald, P. R. Fletcher and M. Roth, 283–300. Minneapolis: Milkweed.

Hirsch, M. and E. F. Keller. 1990. Conclusion: Practicing conflict in feminist theory. *Conflicts in Feminism*, ed. M. Hirsch and E. F. Keller, 370–385. New York: Routledge.

Hochschild, A. 1989. *The second shift.* New York: Viking

Hogeland, L. M. 1994. Fear of feminism: Why young women get the willies. *Ms.* (November/December): 18–21.

hooks, b. 1997. The wisdom of hopelessness: My conversation with Pema Chodron. *Utne Reader* (May-June): 61–63, 96–98.

———. 1994a. *Teaching to transgress: Education as the practice of freedom.* New York: Routledge.

———. 1994b. Black students who reject feminism. *The Chronicle of Higher Education* (July 13): A44.

———. 1993. *Sisters of the yam.* Boston: South End.

———. 1990. *Yearning: Race, gender, and cultural politics.* Boston: South End.

———. 1989. *Talking back: Thinking feminist, thinking black.* Boston: South End.

———. 1981. *Ain't I a woman?* Boston: South End.

Hopkins, P. 1992. Contemporary Hawaiian culture workshop notes. [unpublished notes]

Hunter College Women's Studies Collective. 1995. *Women's realities, women's choices: An introduction to women's studies.* 2d ed. New York: Oxford University.

Hurston, Z. N. [1926] 1995. Sweat. *Sweat*, ed. C. A. Wall, 25–40. Reprint, New Brunswick, NJ: Rutgers University.

Hutchins, L., and L. Kaahumanu, eds. 1991. *Bi any other name: Bisexual people speak out.* Boston: Alyson.

Igra, A. 1998. E-mail communication to A. Mussey, May 24.

Inness, S. A. 1997. "They're here, they're flouncy, don't worry about them": Depicting lesbians in popular women's magazines, 1965–1995. *The lesbian menace: Ideology, identity, and the representation of lesbian life*, 52–76. Amherst: University of Massachusetts.

Jamison, K. 1995. *Beyond the double bind: Women and leadership.* New York: Oxford University.

Jessup, E. 1997. Feminism and computers in composition instruction. *Literacy, technology and society: Confronting the issues*, ed. G. Hawisher and C. Selfe, 199–211. Upper Saddle River, N.J.: Prentice-Hall.

Joycechild, L. D. 1988. Presenting feminism: Toward a reflexive pedagogy in the introductory women's studies course. Master's thesis, Mankato State University.

Kamen, P. 1991. *Feminist fatale*. New York: Donald Fine.

Kane, K., ed. 1992. In celebration of students: Reflections on learning at the University of Hawai'i at Mānoa. Honolulu: University of Hawai'i at Mānoa, Center for Teaching Excellence.

Kaplan, J. 1988. *The accused*. 35 mm, 110 min. Los Angeles: Paramount Pictures.

Kesselman, A., L. D. McNair, and N. Schniedewind, eds. 1995. *Women, images and realities: A multicultural anthology*. Mountain View, CA: Mayfield.

Kimmel, M. S. 1993. Clarence, William, Iron Mike, Tailhook, Senator Packwood, Spur Posse, Magic and us . . . *Transforming a rape culture*, ed. E. Buchwald, P. R. Fletcher, and M. Roth, 119–138. Minneapolis: Milkweed.

Kimmel, M. S. and M. A. Messner. 1992. *Men's lives*. 2d ed. New York: Macmillan.

King, J. E. 1994. Dysconscious racism: Ideology, identity, and the miseducation of teachers. *The education feminism reader*, ed. L. Stone with the assistance of G. M. Boldt, 336–348. New York and London: Routledge.

King, Y. 1997. The other body: Reflections on difference, disability, and identity politics. *Women, culture, and society: An introduction to women's studies*, ed. M. M. Fonow, E. Allan, and L. Bailey, 47–53. Needham Heights, MA: Simon & Schuster Custom.

———. 1993. The other body. *Ms.* (March-April): 72–75.

Klein, R. D. 1989. The "men-problem" in women's studies: The expert, the ignoramus, and the poor dear. *Radical voices: A decade of feminist resistance from Women's Studies International Forum*, ed. R. D. Klein and D. L. Steinberg. Oxford: Pergamon.

Krane, V. 1996. Lesbians in sport: Toward acknowledgment, understanding, and theory. *Journal of Sport and Exercise Psychology* 18: 237–246.

Lakoff, R. T. 1989. Review essay: Women and disability. *Feminist Studies* 15 (Summer): 365–375.

Langston, D. 1988. Tired of playing Monopoly? *Race, class, and gender: An anthology*, 2d ed., ed. M. L. Andersen and P. H. Collins, 100–110. Belmont, CA: Wadsworth.

Lather, P. 1991a. *Getting smart: Feminist research and pedagogy with/in the postmodern*. New York: Routledge.

———. 1991b. Staying dumb? Student resistance to liberatory curriculum. *Getting smart: Feminist research and pedagogy with/in the postmodern*, 123–152. New York: Routledge.

LeBihan, J. 1991. *The Handmaid's Tale, Cat's Eye* and *Interlunar*: Margaret Atwood's feminist(?) futures (?). *Narrative strategies in Canadian literature: Feminism and postcolonialism*, ed. C. A. Howells and L. Hunter, 93–107. New York: Open University.

Lehrman, K. 1993. Off course. *Mother Jones* (September/October): 45–51, 65–68.

Lensink, J. N. 1991. Strategies for integrating international material into the introductory women's studies course. *Women's Studies International Forum* 14: 277–283.

Lenskyj, H. 1990. Power and play: Gender and sexuality issues in sport and physical activity. *International Review for Sociology of Sport* 25: 235–243.

Levine, M. P. and R. Leonard. 1984. Discrimination against lesbians in the work force. *Signs* 9 (Summer): 700–710.

Lindsey, L. L. 1990. *Gender roles*. 2d ed. Englewood Cliffs, NJ: Prentice-Hall.

Lorde, A. 1984a. *Sister outsider*. Freedom, CA: Crossing.

———. 1984b. Age, race, class, and sex: Women redefining difference. *Sister outsider*, 114–123. Freedom, CA: Crossing.

———. 1981. The master's tools will never dismantle the master's house, and An open letter to Mary Daly. *This bridge called my back: Writings of radical women of color*, ed. C. Moraga and G. Anzaldua. Watertown, MA: Persephone.

Lu, J. 1998. Orientalizing the Oriental in paradise. Master's thesis in theatre, University of Hawai'i at Mānoa.

Luft, R. E. 1997. Challenging second wave narratives in order to tell a different future: Anti-racist pedagogy in the feminist classroom. Manuscript.

Lugones, M. 1991. On the logic of pluralist feminism. *Feminist ethics*, ed. C. Card. Lawrence: University of Kansas.

———. 1990. Playfulness, ''world'' travelling, and loving perception. *Making face, making soul/Haciendo caras: Creative and critical perspectives by women of color*, ed. G. Anzaldua, 390–402. San Francisco: Aunt Lute.

Luke, C., ed. 1996. *Feminisms and pedagogies of everyday life*. New York: State University of New York.

Luke, C. and J. Gore, eds. 1992. *Feminisms and critical pedagogy*. New York: Routledge.

MacGregor, J. 1990. Collaborative learning: Shared inquiry as a process of reform. *The changing face of college teaching, new directions for teaching and learning*, no. 42, ed. M. Svinicki, 19–30. San Francisco: Jossey-Bass.

Maher, F. A. and M. K. T. Tetreault. 1994. *The feminist classroom: An inside look at how professors and students are transforming higher education for a diverse society*. New York: Basic Books.

Marshall, C. 1997. *Gender equity and schooling: Policy and practice*. New York: Garland.

Martin, B. and C. T. Mohanty. 1986. Feminist politics: What's home got to do with it? *Feminist studies/Critical studies*, ed. T. de Lauretis, 191–212. Bloomington, IN: Indiana University.

Martin, P. Y. and R. A. Hummer. 1989. Fraternities and rape on campus. *Gender & Society* 3: 457–473.

McCarthy, M. 1986. Breeders, wives and unwomen. *New York Times Book Review*, February 9, 1.

McCulley, L. and P. Patterson. 1996. Feminist empowerment through the Internet. *Feminist Collections* 17, 2: 5–6.

McDermott, P. 1995. On cultural authority: Women's studies, feminist politics, and the popular press. *Signs* 20: 668–684.

McIntosh, P. [1988] 1998. White privilege and male privilege: A personal account of coming to see correspondences through work in women's studies. *Race, class and gender: An anthology*, 3d ed., ed. M. L. Andersen and P. H. Collins, 94–105. Belmont, CA: Wadsworth.

———. 1995. White privilege: Unpacking the invisible backpack. *Women images and realities: A multicultural anthology*, ed. A. Kesselman, L. D. McNair, and N. Schniedewind, 264–266. Mountain View, CA: Mayfield.

———. 1989. White privilege and male privilege: A personal account of coming to see correspondences through work in women's studies. *Race, class, and gender: An anthology*, 2d ed., ed. M. L. Andersen and P. H. Collins, 76–87. Belmont, CA: Wadsworth.

McMahon, J. 1997. Ideas in motion: A teaching artist uses dance to confront stereotypes. Southern Poverty Law Center Home Page *http://www.splcenter.org/ teachingtolerance/tt-1b.html*, December 10.

Merleau-Ponty, M. 1962. *Phenomenology of perception*, trans. Colin Wilson. New York: Humanities.

Meyerhoff, B. 1978. *Number our days*. New York: E. P. Dutton.

Miner, M. 1991. "Trust me": Reading the romance plot in Margaret Atwood's *The handmaid's tale*. *Twentieth Century Literature* 37. 2 (Summer): 148–168.

Miner, M. M. 1994. "You're going to be the only guy in there": Men's minority experience in introduction to women's studies. *NWSA Journal* 6. 3: 452–467.

Minnich, E. K. 1990. *Transforming knowledge*. Philadelphia: Temple University.

Misciagno, P. S. 1996. De-facto feminism and praxis. *Women & Politics* 16: 1–17.

Moore, C. W. 1986. The mediation process: Practical strategies for resolving conflict. San Francisco: Jossey-Bass.

Moraga, C. and G. Anzaldua. 1983. *This bridge called my back*. New York: Kitchen Table.

Musil, C. M. 1992. *The courage to question: Women's studies and student learning*. Washington, DC: Association of American Colleges and National Women's Studies Association.

Myers, L. J. 1988. *Understanding an Afrocentric world view: Introduction to an optimal psychology*. 2d ed. Dubuque, IA: Kendall/Hunt.

Neitz, M. J. 1985. Resistances to feminist analysis. *Teaching Sociology*, 12: 339–353.

Nelson, E. S. and S. L. Krieger. 1997. Changes in attitudes toward homosexuality in college students: Implementation of a gay men and lesbian peer panel. *Journal of Homosexuality* 33: 63–81.

Nobles, W. W. 1972. African philosophy: Foundations for black psychology. *Black psychology*, ed. R. L. Jones. New York: Harper and Row.

Nochlin, L. 1988. *Women, art, and power and other essays*. New York: Harper and Row.

O'Barr, J. F. 1994. *Feminism in action: Building institutions and community through women's studies*. Chapel Hill: University of North Carolina.

———. 1987. Reconstructing the academy. *Signs* 12 (Winter).

O'Barr, J., M. LaRocque, and M. Peskowitz. 1994. "Just an experiment for my women's studies class": Female students and the culture of gender. *Feminism in action*, ed. J. O'Barr, 119–132. Chapel Hill: University of North Carolina.

Orner, M. 1992. Interrupting the calls for student voice in "liberatory" education: A feminist poststructuralist perspective. *Feminisms and critical pedagogy*, ed. C. Luke and J. Gore, 74–89. New York: Routledge.

Orr, C. 1998. Quoted in women's studies twenty-five years later. *On campus with women*, 4–5. Washington, DC: Association of American Colleges and Universities.

Pagano, J. A. 1994. Teaching women. *The education feminism reader*, ed. L. Stone with the assistance of G. M. Boldt, 252–275. New York and London: Routledge.

Palmer, P. 1991. *The company of strangers: Christians and the renewal of America's public life*. New York: Crossroad.

———. 1987. Community, conflict, and ways of knowing: Ways to deepen our educational agenda. *Change: The Magazine of Higher Learning* 19 (September/October): 20–25.

Parker, P. 1978. *Movement in black*. Ithaca, NY: Firebrand.

Patai, D. 1992. The struggle for feminist purity threatens the goals of feminism. *The Chronicle of Higher Education*, February 5, B1.

Patai, D. and N. Koertge. 1994. *Professing feminism: Cautionary tales from the strange world of women's studies*. New York: Basic Books.

Paxton, J. T. 1996. Webucation: Using the Web as a classroom tool. *Association for Computing Machinery* (February): 285–289.

Pershing, L. 1991. There's a joker in the menstrual hut: A performance analysis of comedian Kate Clinton. *Women's comic visions*, ed. June Sochen, 193–230. Detroit: Wayne State University.

Pharr, S. 1988. *Homophobia: A weapon of sexism*. Inverness, CA: Chardon.

Piercy, M. 1991. *He, she and it*. New York: Ballantine.

Plaskow, J. and C. P. Christ, 1989. *Weaving the visions: New patterns in feminist spirituality*. San Francisco: Harper and Row.

Pratt, M. B. 1984. Identity: Skin, blood, heart. *Yours in struggle*, ed. E. Bulkin, M. B. Pratt, and B. Smith, 11–63. Brooklyn, NY: Long Haul.

Ramsay, H. 1994. Lesbians and the health care system. *Canadian Woman Studies* 14.3: 22–27.

Ramsden, P. 1992. *Learning to teach in higher education*. London: Routledge.

Rau, W. and B. S. Heyl. 1990. Humanizing the college classroom: Collaborative learning and social organization among students. *Teaching Sociology* 18: 141–155.

Reagon, B. J. 1983. Coalition politics: Turning the century. *Home girls: A Black feminist anthology*, ed. B. Smith, 356–368. New York: Kitchen Table: Women of Color.

Reesman, J. C. 1991. Dark knowledge in *The Handmaid's Tale*. *CEA Critic*, no. 53.3 (Spring/Summer): 6–22.

Rensenbrink, C. W. 1996. What difference does it make? The story of a lesbian teacher. *Harvard Educational Review* 66: 257–270.

Rhoades, K. 1996. Women's studies students and the politics of empowerment. Ph.D. dissertation, University of Wisconsin, Madison.

Rhode, D. L. 1997. *Speaking of sex: The denial of gender inequality*. Cambridge: Harvard University.

Rich, A. 1980. Compulsory heterosexuality and lesbian existence. *Signs* 5: 631–660.

———. 1979. *On lies, secrets, silence: Selected prose 1966–1978*. New York: Norton.

Richardson, L. and V. Taylor, eds. 1993. *Feminist frontiers III*. New York: McGraw-Hill.

Rinehart, J. A. 1998. Feminist theorizing as a conversation: The connections between thinking, teaching, and political action. *Women and Politics* 19: 59–89.

Robinson, L. 1970. The sexual order. *Female Studies II*, ed. F. Howe, 41–43. Pittsburgh: Know.

Roiphe, K. 1993. *The morning after: Sex, fear, and feminism on campus*. Boston: Little, Brown.

Romero, M. 1992. *Maid in the U.S.A.* New York: Routledge.

Rosaldo, R. 1989. *Culture and truth: The remaking of social analysis*. Boston: Beacon.

Rosenberg, D., M. Miller, and J. Leland. 1994. Homophobia. *Newsweek* 123: 42–45.

Rosenberg, P. M. 1997. Underground discourses: Exploring whiteness in teacher education. *Off white: Readings on race, power, and society*, ed. M. Fine, L. Weis, L. C. Powell, and L. M. Wong, 79–89. New York: Routledge.

Ruddick, S. 1992. From maternal thinking to peace politics. *Explorations of feminist ethics and practice*, ed. E. B. Cole and S. C. McQuin. Bloomington: University of Indiana.

Russell, M. 1982. Black-eyed blues connections: Teaching black women. *All the women are white, all the men are black, but some of us are brave*, ed. G. T. Hull, P. Bell-Scott, and B. Smith, 196–207. New York: Feminist.

Rutgers, J. 1998. E-mail communication to Sandra D. Shattuck, May 14.

Ruth, S. 1998. *Issues in feminism: An introduction to women's studies.* 4th ed. Mountain View, CA: Mayfield.

Sanday, P. R. 1990. *Fraternity gang rape: Sex, brotherhood, and privilege on campus.* New York: New York University.

Sandoval, C. 1991. U.S. Third World feminism: The theory and method of oppositional consciousness in the postmodern world. *Genders* 10 (Spring): 1–24.

Sartre, J. P. 1966. *Being and nothingness*, trans. Hazel E. Barnes. New York: Washington Square.

Schieder, E. 1993. Integrating lesbian content. *Women's Studies Quarterly* 21: 46–56.

Schneider, A. 1998. Insubordination and intimidation signal the end of decorum in many classrooms. *Chronicle of Higher Education* (March 27).

Schniedewind, N. 1993. Teaching feminist process in the 1990s. *Women's Studies Quarterly* 21: 17–30.

Schoem, D., L. Frankel, X. Zuniga, and E. A. Lewis. 1993. *Multicultural teaching in the university*. Westport, CT: Praeger.

Scott, P. B. 1994. Life notes: Black women's personal writings as autoethnography. Keynote address presented at the Research on Women and Education Conference, St. Paul, MN, October.

Shah, S. 1998. *Dragon ladies: Asian American feminists breathe fire*. Boston: South End.

Showalter, E. 1997. Up front—is it possible to live the life of the mind while minding the length of your skirt? *Vogue* (December): 80+.

Smith, B. 1983. Home. *Home girls: A Black feminist anthology*, ed. B. Smith, 64–69. New York: Kitchen Table: Women of Color.

Smith-Rosenberg, C. 1975. The female world of love and ritual: Relations between women in nineteenth-century America. *Signs* 1: 1–29.

Sommers, C. H. 1994. *Who stole feminism? How women have betrayed women.* New York: Simon and Schuster.

Spelman, E. V. 1997. Gender and race: The ampersand problem in feminist thought. *Issues in feminism: An introduction to women's studies*, ed. S. Ruth, 22–34. Mountain View, CA: Mayfield.

Spender, Dale. 1995. *Nattering on the net*. Melbourne, Australia: Spinifex.

Spivak, G. 1988. *In other worlds: Essays in cultural politics*. New York and London: Routledge.

Spivak, G. C. and E. Rooney. 1993. In a word: Interview. *Outside in the teaching machine*, ed. G. C. Spivak, 1–23. New York: Routledge.

Spivak, G. with E. Rooney. 1989. Interview. *differences* 1.2: 124–156.

Steinem, G. 1983. *Outrageous acts and everyday rebellions*. New York: Holt, Rinehart, and Winston.

Stetz, M. 1998. Women's studies, still on the defensive. Paper presented at the National Association for Women in Catholic Higher Education plenary session, Trinity College, Washington, DC.

Stone, L. 1994. Toward a transformational theory of teaching. *The education feminism reader*, ed. L. Stone with the assistance of G. M. Boldt, 221–228. New York and London: Routledge.

Swearingen, J. A. 1996. Promoting tolerance in preservice teachers. *Social Education* 60: 152–154.

Szikla, C. 1996. Lesbianism: Dispelling the myths. *Women's Issues and Social Empowerment*, (Melbourne, Australia) Home Page. *http://www.infoxchange.net.au/wise/HEALTH/LesO.htm*: December 10, 1997.

Tarule, J. M. 1996. Voices in dialogue: Collaborative ways of knowing. *Knowledge, difference, and power: Essays inspired by "Women's Ways of Knowing,"* ed. N. Goldberger, J. Tarule, B. Clinchy, and M. Belenky, 274–304. New York: Basic Books.

Tavris, C. 1992. *Mismeasure of woman*. New York: Simon and Schuster.

Taylor, V. and L. J. Rupp. 1996. Lesbian existence and the women's movement: Researching the "lavender herring." *Feminism and social change: Bridging theory and practice*, ed. H. Gottfried, 143–159. Urbana: University of Illinois.

Terry, J. and Melodie C. 1997. Introduction. *Processed lives: Gender and technology in everyday life*, ed. J. Terry and M. Calvert, 1–19. London: Routledge.

Thompson, B. 1996. A way outa no way. *Race, class and gender*, ed. E. N. Chow, D. Wilkinson, and M. B. Zinn, 52–69. Thousand Oaks, CA: Sage.

Thompson, M. E. 1981. Comment on Rich's "Compulsory heterosexuality and lesbian existence." *Signs* 6: 790–794.

Tokarczyk, M. and E. Fay. 1993. *Working-class women in the academy: Laborers in the knowledge factory*. Amherst: University of Massachusetts.

Tompkins, J. 1996. *A life in school: What the teacher learned*. Reading, MA: Addison-Wesley.

Trinh, T. M. 1989. *Woman native other: Writing postcoloniality and feminism*. Bloomington: Indiana University.

Trout, P. 1997. Conflict in the college classroom. *The Cresset: A Review of Literature, Arts, and Public Affairs* 60: 28–36.

Tsing, A. L. 1993. *In the realm of the diamond queen: Marginality in an out-of-the-way place*. Princeton: Princeton University.

University of Hawai'i at Mānoa. 1993–1995. Equal Employment Opportunity and Affirmative Action Office (UH EEOAA). Unpublished data.

U.S. Department of Justice Web site: *http://www.usdoj.gov/bjs/abstract/vbl.htm*.

Van Zoonen, L. 1992. Feminist theory and information technology. *Media Culture and Society* 4: 9–29.

Villarosa, L. 1994. Introduction. *Body and Soul*, xiv–xviii. New York: Harper Perennial.

Wakeford, N. 1997. Networking women and girls with information/communication technology: Surfing tales of the World Wide Web. *Processed lives: Gender and technology in everyday life*, ed. J. Terry and M. Calvert, 51–64. London: Routledge.

Walker, A. 1993. *Warrior marks: Female genital mutilation and the sexual blinding of women*. London: Jonathan Cape.

———. 1983. *In search of our mother's gardens: Womanist prose*. San Diego: Harcourt Brace Jovanovich.

Walker, R., ed. 1995. *To be real: Telling the truth and changing the face of feminism.* New York: Doubleday/Anchor.

Walkerdine, V. 1994. Femininity as performance. *The education feminism reader,* ed. L. Stone with the assistance of G. M. Boldt, 57–69. New York and London: Routledge.

Walters, S. D. 1995. *Material girls: Making sense of feminist cultural theory.* Berkeley: University of California.

Warshaw, R. 1988. *I never called it rape: The Ms. report on recognizing, fighting, and surviving date and acquaintance rape.* New York: Harper and Row.

Waxman, B. F. and E. Byington. 1997. Teaching Paul Monette's memoir/manifesto to resistant readers. *College Literature* 24: 156–170.

Weiss, D. E. 1991. *The great divide.* New York: Poseidon.

Weitzman, L. 1985. *The divorce revolution.* New York: Free Press.

Whipple, W. R. 1987. Collaborative learning: Recognizing it when we see it. *AAHE Bulletin* 40: 3–5.

Whittaker, E. 1986. *The mainland haole: The white experience in Hawaii.* New York: Columbia University.

Williams, P. 1995. The unbearable autonomy of being. *The rooster's egg: On the persistence of prejudice,* 169–181. Cambridge: Harvard University.

Williamson, J. 1980. *Consuming passions: The dynamics of popular culture.* London: Marion Boyars.

Wilson, S. R., T. B. Friedman, and S. Hengen, eds. 1996. *Approaches to teaching Atwood's "The Handmaids Tale" and other works.* New York: Modern Language Association.

Winkler, B. S. 1997. Raising c-r: Another look at consciousness-raising in the women's studies classroom. *Transformations: A Resource for Curriculum Transformation and Scholarship* 8: 66–85.

———. 1996. Straight teacher/queer classroom: Teaching as an ally. *Teaching what you're not: Identity politics in higher education,* ed. K. J. Mayberry, 47–69. New York: New York University.

———. 1992. A comparative history of four women's studies programs, 1970 to 1985. Ph.D. dissertation, University of Michigan.

WMST-L (Women's Studies List). 1995. Lesbi in_ws. WMST-L at *listserv@umdd.umd.edu.*

———. 1993. Feminist label. WMST-L at *listserv@umdd.umd.edu.*

Wolf, N. 1993. *Fire with fire.* New York: Random House.

———. 1992. Radical heterosexuality . . . or how to love a man and save your feminist soul. *Ms.* (July/August): 28–31.

———. 1991. *The beauty myth: How images of beauty are used against women.* New York: Doubleday.

The Women's Guild. 1997. *The guide: A little beige book for today's Miss G.* Washington, DC: Independent Women's Forum.

Women's Support Group of the Waianae Coast. 1982. *A time for sharing: Women's stories from the Waianae Coast.* Wai'anae, Hawai'i: Women's Support Group of the Waianae Coast.

Woodbridge, L. 1994. The centrifugal classroom. *Gender and academe: Feminist pedagogy and politics,* ed. S. M. Deats and L. T. Lenker, 133–151. Lanham, MD: Rowman and Littlefield.

Zinn, M. B. and B. T. Dill. 1996. Theorizing difference from multiracial feminism. *Feminist Studies* 22.2: 321–331.

Zúñiga, X. and P. Myers. 1993. Multiple roles and multiple choice exercise. *Multicultural teaching in the university*, ed. D. Schoem, L. Frankel, X. Zúñiga, E. A. Lewis, 316–318. Westport, CT: Praeger.

Index

231; misconceptions about, 154; *The Handmaid's Tale* course and, 191–92, 193–94, 197–98; negative attitudes toward, 66, 102, 228, 231–32; power of, 42, 73; radical, 90–91, 93; relevance of, 62; Second Wave, 8, 40, 42, 213; stereotypes of, 99, 175; Third Wave, 8, 42; Third World, 74, 78, 79; University of Hawai'i course and, 144; victim, 42

Feminist action project, 202, 207

Feminist Classroom: An Inside Look at How Professors and Students Are Transforming Higher Education for a Diverse Society, 9

Feminist continuum, 193

Feminist Frontiers III, 108 n.6

Feminist identity: conceptions about, 91; current enrollment and, 7; early introductory courses and, 5–6; Internet course and, 154; lesbianism and, 99, 100, 101; love interests and, 103; outrageous act assignment and, 209; qualitative research study and, 67–68; radical feminism and, 91; University of Wisconsin course and, 176

Feminist Majority, 154

Feminist pedagogy. *See* Teacher/teaching

Feminist Research Methods, 99

Feminist space, 78, 80, 83, 84

Feminist Studies, 55

Ferreira, L., 114

"Finding My Latina Identity through Women's Studies," 114

Findlen, Barbara, 42

Finkel, D., 229

Fire with Fire: The New Female Power and How It Will Change the 21st Century, 42

First Amendment, 169

Florida Atlantic University (FAU), 184, 186, 188, 189

Fonow, Mary Margaret, 10, 51, 52, 105, 106–7

Foster, Joanna, 207

Fourth World Conference on Women, 56–57

Freed-Fagan, Elise, 37, 47

Freeman, Jo, 192

Friedan, Betty, 40–41

"From Maternal Thinking to Peace Politics," 46–47

Frye, Marilyn, 100, 105

Fuji, Louise, 139, 142

Fund for the Improvement of Postsecondary Education (FIPSE), 8

Gaard, G., 102

Garfinkel, Harold, 210 n.2

Gay men, 56, 100, 101, 112, 113, 206. *See also* Homosexuality

Gearhart, Sally, 5

Gender discrimination: all-female classes and, 6; class (socioeconomic) and, 185; emphasis on, 5; First Wave feminism and, 40; Internet course and, 155; interracial teaching team course and, 124; moral decisions and, 41; North Carolina State University course and, 165–67; race and, 185–86; religion and, 190, 195; workplace and, 44–45. *See also specific subject matter*

General Education (GED), 7

Georgetown University, 111–13. *See also* Course on diversity

Gilbert, Laurel, 166

Gilligan, Carol, 41

Girls Industrial College of Texas, 21

Glamour magazine, 13. *See also* Course on *Glamour* magazine

"The Globetrotting Sneaker," 52

Gonzaga University. *See* Course at Gonzaga University

"Ground Rules for Discussion," 133

Group development. *See* Course on group development

Group dynamics theory, 88, 89, 90

Guerrilla Girls, 57

The Guide: A Little Beige Book for Today's Miss G, 113

"Guidelines for Class Participation," 232

Haitians, 189

Hall, I., 100

Handedness, 188

The Handmaid's Tale. See Course on *The Handmaid's Tale*

Haraway, Donna, 163

About the Contributors

LUCY BAILEY is the managing editor of *Reading Women's Lives* at The Ohio State University. Her areas of interest are history, diversity, and pedagogy. She has written about the narrative and coding strategies of Julia MacNair Wright, a nineteenth-century domestic novelist, and has taught the introductory women's studies course for three years.

HELEN M. BANNAN is Director and Associate Professor of women's studies at the University of Wisconsin, Oshkosh, where she teaches a wide range of women's studies courses. Her research focuses on the histories of intercultural (American Indian/Anglo) and intergenerational (grandmother/mother/daughter) relationships among women. She has taught introductory women's studies courses since 1983 at the University of New Mexico, Florida Atlantic University, and West Virginia University.

KAREN BOJAR is Professor of English at Community College of Philadephia, where she teaches Introduction to Women's Studies, codeveloped with Elise Freed-Fagan in 1995. She also teaches a service learning course, Community Involvement: Theory and Practice. Her major research interest is the role of women in voluntary organizations. Her article "Volunteerism and Women's Lives: A Lens for Exploring Conflicts in Contemporary Feminist Thought" was included in *Women's Studies in Transition: The Pursuit of Interdisciplinarity*, 1998. She has a long history of involvement in feminist organizations and in grassroots community and political organizations. She has taught the introductory women's studies course since 1995.

LISA BOWLEG is Assistant Professor in the Department of Psychology, University of Rhode Island, where she teaches the Psychology of Women. Her research interests include psychosocial predictors of women's HIV/AIDS protective practices; coping and resilience among populations such as racial/ethnic minority gay, lesbian, bisexual, and transgender people; and psychosocial implications of Black women's images of beauty. She taught Introduction to Women's Studies as an adjunct at Georgetown University during the fall 1997 semester.

AUDRE JEAN BROKES is Assistant Professor of philosophy at Saint Joseph's University in Philadelphia, where she teaches philosophy and gender studies. Her current research focuses on the epistemology of perception and feminist issues in the philosophy of science. She has been teaching introductory women's studies courses since 1994.

CAROL J. BURGER is Assistant Professor of immunology and of women's studies and coordinator of the Science and Gender Equity Program at Virginia Tech. She has published over forty-five immunology research papers and, recently, *A Guide to Gender Fair Education in Science and Mathematics*. She currently supervises two National Science Foundation (NSF)-funded projects that focus on the recruitment of girls into science careers, teaches courses in women in science, biology, and microbiology, and has been teaching Introduction to Women's Studies since 1997.

CAROLYN DiPALMA is Assistant Professor in the Department of Women's Studies at the University of South Florida. She teaches Introduction to Women's Studies as well as courses in feminist theory, political theory, body politics, women's health, and human sexual behavior. Currently, she is working on a manuscript that addresses the production of sex and race and the challenge for feminist theory to discuss sex and race at the same time. She has been teaching introductory women's studies courses since 1991.

MARGARET DUNCOMBE is Professor of sociology and women's studies at Colorado College, where she teaches courses in research methods and statistics, gender, and deviant behavior. In addition to the Introduction to Women's Studies course, she teaches Feminist Research Methods for the Women's Studies Program. Her research examines the feminist critique of quantitative sociology and the use of the lesbian label to enforce traditional enactments of femininity. She has taught the introductory women's studies course since 1990.

MARY MARGARET FONOW is Assistant Professor of women's studies at The Ohio State University and editor of *Reading Women's Lives*. Her areas of interests are feminist methodology and pedagogy, theories of difference, and working-class feminism. She is currently working on a book about women's activism in the United Steelworkers of America. She has taught the introductory women's studies course and has supervised and trained graduate teaching associates who teach the course since 1985.

BETH HARDIN is Performance Support Developer at SAS Institute. She owns Online Design, a small Web publishing business, and has a special interest in helping women get on-line. She has written about how to design information technology so that it works in support of feminist pedagogy.

GLYN HUGHES teaches Masculinity and Mass Media, the Sociology of AIDS, and Writing at the University of California, Santa Barbara. His research analyzes the athletic shoe as a nexus of discourses about fitness, sports, race, gender, and the corporate. He has taught courses and trained teachers since 1994 and is currently a coordinator of the Teaching Assistant Training Committee in women's studies.

KATHLEEN O. KANE is Faculty Specialist at the Center for Teaching Excellence and Affiliate Faculty in the Women's Studies Program at the University of Hawai'i at Mānoa, where she teaches courses on feminist theory and pedagogy, women and film, and media and politics. Her professional and research interests in pedagogy and culture bridge the work she does in women's studies and faculty development. She began teaching introductory women's studies courses in 1987.

AMY KESSELMAN is Professor of women's studies at the State University of New York, (SUNY), New Paltz. She is the author of *Fleeting Opportunities: Women Shipyard Workers in Portland and Vancouver During World War II and Reconversion* (1990) and, with Lily McNair and Nancy Schniedewind, *Women: Images and Realities, A Multicultural Anthology* (1995). She taught a women's studies course in a Chicago high school in 1968 and has been teaching women's studies at the college level since 1974.

TONI C. KING, is Associate Professor of Black women's studies, holding appointments in Black studies and women's studies at Denison University. She teaches Issues in Feminism, Cultural and Social Methods, Introduction to Black Studies, and Black Women and Organizational Leadership. Her research explores the role of within- and across-race bonding relationships in women's development and recovery from race, class, and gender oppression. She has been teaching introductory women's studies courses since 1997.

LISA M. LOGAN is Assistant Professor of English at the University of Central Florida, where she teaches courses in American literature and women's studies. Her research interest is North American women's popular narrative before 1865, especially early captivity narratives and domestic fiction. She has been teaching introductory women's studies courses since 1994.

FRANCES MAHER is Professor and Chair of the Education Department at Wheaton College. She teaches feminist theory and taught "Introduction to Women's Studies" for many years. She is the co-author, with Mary Kay Tetreault, of *The Feminist Classroom* (1994).

VIVIAN M. MAY is Assistant Professor of women's studies at Texas Woman's University, where she teaches introductory women's studies courses and graduate women's studies seminars in feminist epistemology, feminist theories, and special topics courses such as feminist geographies. Her research analyzes the intersections between theory and literature, especially contemporary American and Canadian multiethnic literatures, and feminist theories of embodiment, disability, race, space/geography, and sexuality. She has been teaching introductory women's studies courses since 1995.

MARTHA MCCAUGHEY is Assistant Professor of women's studies in the Center for Interdisciplinary Studies at Virginia Tech. She is the author of *Real Knockouts: The Physical Feminism of Women's Self-Defense* (1997) and teaches courses in women's studies, sociology, and science and technology studies. She has been teaching introductory women's studies courses since 1996.

JUDITH MCDANIEL is Adjunct Professor in the Women's Studies Department of the University of Arizona, where she teaches Women's Activisms and Organizations, a graduate class designed to use activism to create theory and to use theory as an aid to action. She is a poet and fiction writer and is also writing the biography of feminist activist and writer Barbara Deming. She has been teaching women's studies courses since 1972.

ANN MUSSEY has been teaching women's history and lesbian history at Portland State University and is currently working on the development of curriculum in queer studies. She first taught the women's studies introductory course at Portland State as an undergraduate teaching assistant in 1985 and has since taught the course at Rutgers and SUNY, New Paltz.

MARIA PRAMAGGIORE is Assistant Professor in the English Department at North Carolina State University, where she teaches film and women's studies. She has published articles on women and film and on Irish cinema in *Screen, Cinema Journal*, and *College Literature* and is coeditor of *RePresenting Bisexualities: Subject and Cultures of Fluid Desire* (1996). She has been teaching women's studies courses since 1993.

KATHERINE ANN RHOADES is Assistant Professor in the School of Education at the University of Wisconsin, Eau Claire, where she teaches courses in diversity and the foundations of education as well as women's studies courses, including Women and Poverty and Women's Leadership for Social Action. Her research interests focus on the effects of educational efforts forged with the will to "empower" students. She has been teaching introductory women's studies courses since 1991.

JANE A. RINEHART is Associate Professor of sociology and women's studies at Gonzaga University, where she teaches courses on the sociology of gender and on feminist social theory. She has published articles in *Feminist Teacher, Frontiers*, and *Women and Politics*. She has been teaching the introductory course in women's studies since 1974 as a sociology course and since 1991 as a sociology/women's studies course.

SANDRA D. SHATTUCK is Adjunct Faculty in various departments at the University of Arizona, where she has taught intercultural perspectives, women and Western culture, and writing. Shattuck writes young adult novels as well as nonfiction. She has been teaching introductory women's studies courses since 1996.

JUDY NOLTE TEMPLE is Associate Professor of women's studies/English at the University of Arizona, where she teaches courses on women's journals and women's narratives of the West. She has published a diary study (under the surname Lensink) and edited two volumes on Southwestern literature. She is currently at work on the manuscript diary fragments of Colorado's legendary Silver Queen, "Baby Doe" Tabor, and has been teaching women's studies courses since 1990.

FRANCE WINDDANCE TWINE is Associate Professor at the University of Washington, Seattle, where she teaches critical race feminisms and international studies. Her recent publications include *Racism in a Racial Democracy: The Maintenance of White Supremacy in Brazil*, and she is coeditor of "Feminisms and Youth Cultures," a special issue of *Signs: Journal of Women in Culture and Society* (Spring 1998). She has been teaching introductory women's studies courses since 1994.

BARBARA SCOTT WINKLER is Visiting Assistant Professor at the Center for Women's Studies at West Virginia University. She supervises and teaches Introduction to Women's Studies and seminars on the women's movement and feminist theories, the history of sexuality in the United States, women and popular culture, and women, race, and class. Her research interests include the relationship of feminist pedagogy to feminist theory, the institutionalization of women's studies, and the history of socialist-feminism and the contemporary women's movement. She has been teaching introductory courses in women's studies since 1990.

STACY WOLF is Assistant Professor in the Departments of English and Theatre and Dance at George Washington University, where she teaches theatre history, dramatic literature, and performance theory. Her current research analyzes American musicals from a queer and feminist perspective. She taught Introduction to Women's Studies at the University of Wisconsin, Madison, in 1992–1994.

ISBN 0-89789-590-8

HARDCOVER BAR CODE